SCIENCE FICTION
AN ILLUSTRATED HISTORY

SCIENCE FICTION
AN ILLUSTRATED HISTORY
SAM J. LUNDWALL

GROSSET & DUNLAP
A FILMWAYS COMPANY
PUBLISHERS NEW YORK

Previous pages: Scene from 'Japan Sinks' (1973)

For Don and Elsie

Designed by Rick Fawcett and produced by
London Editions Limited, 30 Uxbridge Road,
London W12 8ND, England.

Grateful acknowledgements are given for permission to reproduce
the illustrations appearing on the following pages: 126 (20th
Century Fox); 24-5, 28 (left), 29 (right), 134, 135-6, 148-9 (Kobal
Collection, London). All other illustrations apart from Hans
Arnold's illustration on the front of the jacket are reproduced from
the author's own collection.

Library of Congress catalog card number: 77-75997

ISBN (hardcover edition) : 0-448-14413-1
ISBN (paperback edition) : 0-448-14414-X

Printed in the United States of America

Published in the United States of America by Grosset & Dunlap Inc.,
51 Madison Avenue, New York, New York 10010
First American edition 1978

CONTENTS

ORIGINS

The fantastic tale, which in this technological age is known as science fiction, has roots in the earliest fairy tales and tall tales, in its desire to entertain, romance and satirize by means of stories with a more or less factual basis. The hero making incredible travels through known and unknown lands, encountering the unusual and the bizarre on his way, appears throughout all literary history, from the Gilgamesh epic on. All such tales were the offspring of their own day and age, and it is hardly surprising that the age of industrialization should give birth to a literature based upon science and its possible uses.

I do not intend to work my way through the hundreds and thousands of stories and novels dealing with fantastic journeys, utopias, satires and plain fairy tales that make up the bulk of popular fiction from early Greece, but it should be remarked that the Greeks certainly enjoyed the genre, as attested by Lucian of Samosata (born circa AD 125) who wrote several fantastic tales for the amusement of his contemporaries, the best known today being *A True History*. In more modern times, the French soldier and man of letters, Savinien Cyrano de Bergerac (a commoner with the real name of Savinien Cyrano, who upclassed himself), is known for his classic space travel fantasies *Histoires comiques des états et empires de la lune* (1648–50) and *Histoires comiques des états et empires du soleil* (1662), venomous satires on Cyrano's contemporaries and interesting from a science fiction point of view because he also introduced rocket travel and modern amenities like phonographs. The Age of Enlightenment saw the first trickle of the coming flood of science fiction with classic satires like Voltaire's *Micromégas* (1752), Ludvig Holberg's *Nicolai Klimii Iter Subterraneum* (Niels Klim's Subterranean Journey, 1741) and Jonathan Swift's *Gulliver's Travels* (1726). Thomas More's *Utopia* (1516) had earlier described the perfect state, and François Rabelais had made fun of it in *Les livres des faictz et dicts héroiques du noble Pantagruel* (1532–64). The first literary travel to Mars was made in 1744 by the German astronomer Eberhard Christian Kindermann in his novel *Die geschwinde Reise auf dem Luft-Schiff nach der obern Welt, welche jügsthin fünf Personen angestellet*, and the first time-travel story appeared in 1781, a play by the Norwegian playwright Johan Herman Wessel, *Anno 7603*. That same year also saw the publication of the first pornographic science fiction novel, *La découverte australe par un homme volant, ou le Dédale français*, by Nicolas Restif de la Bretonne, the famous author of *Monsieur Nicolas* and other fruits of this permissive age.

Modern science fiction in a sense appeared with the German romanticists of the late eighteenth century—Clemens Brentano, Achim von Arnim, Adalbert von Chamisso, E. T. A. Hoffmann and others. These romantic *Märchen* writers wrote what in effect were fairy tales for adults, including all the various paraphernalia common in modern sf, such as robots, monsters, strange machines etc, set against a curious Gothic background. They demanded an almost boundless credulity from their readers, for they described life, not as a reality, but as a dream of sorts—not as it is, but as it might be. When some critics argue that the English author Mary Shelley invented modern science fiction with the novel *Frankenstein* (1818), they forget that she was drawing upon more than fifty years of German *Märchen* literature, most of it infinitely better and more modern than *Frankenstein* was.

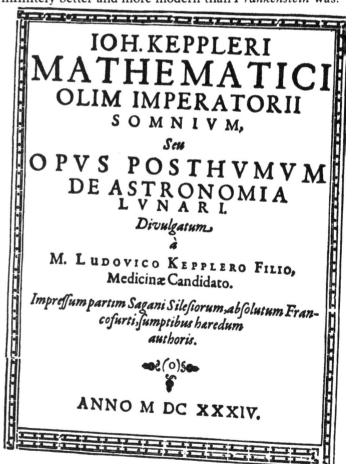

Above: Title page of first edition of Johannes Kepler's 'Somnium'
Right: The flying boy, Icarus, who flew too near the sun, falls as the wax in his wings melts. Drawing, 1646

Mary Shelley was certainly a *Märchen* writer—and the novel was conceived in German-speaking Switzerland where *Märchen* literature was enormously popular—but she was only one among many, and not even one of the best. What Kurd Lasswitz, Jules Verne and others later did, was to modernize this *Märchen* literature, putting more emphasis on mechanical gimmicks and less on the Gothic setting (although Verne later wrote a straight *Märchen* novel, *Le Château des Carpathes* (1829), which almost reads like an early Achim von Arnim tale with its Gothic setting in which a mad inventor spends his nights gazing at a sort of video tape recording of his late beloved, scaring the pants off the local peasants in the process). *Märchen* literature was dead by then, of course; industrialization had changed it beyond recognition. Instead of *Märchen* romances, we got scientific romances, with the Gothic aspect exchanged for the scientific or pseudo-scientific one—a completely natural and inevitable process. The last *Märchen* novel was probably the British author William Hope Hodgson's strange *The Night Land* (1912), describing a world of total darkness millions of years into the future, inhabited by monstrous beasts vaguely described, more hinted at than

Left: The flying man, from Nicolas Restif de la Bretonne's novel 'La découverte australe' (1781)
Above: The space traveller sets out for the kingdom of the sun, from 'Les estats et empires du soleil' (1662)

seen—wise choice by the author. At this time the Irish author, playwright, big game hunter et cetera, Lord Dunsany, also revived the *Märchen* tale and created modern Fantasy literature, today known mostly through numerous sword-toting heroes cutting and slashing their bloody way through a neo-*Märchen* world which has to be read about to be believed.

The term 'science fiction' was first coined in 1851 by the British essayist William Wilson, in *A Little Earnest Book Upon A Great Old Subject.* Wilson wrote:
Campbell says that 'Fiction in Poetry is not the reverse of truth, but her soft and enchanting resemblance.' Now this applies especially to Science Fiction, in which the revealed truths of Science may be given, interwoven with a pleasing story which may itself be poetical and true—thus circulating the knowledge of the Poetry of Science, clothed in a garb of the Poetry of Life.

This is as good a definition of science fiction as any, and typical of the dawning scientific age. Up to then, the genre had usually been known as Imaginary Voyages, which certainly was and is a much better term, and the first big collection of science fiction novels, a 36-volume set published in Paris from 1787 to 1789 under the editorship of Charles-Georges-Thomas Garnier, used the time-honoured term Voyages Imaginaires for this literature. The French were apparently not impressed by the British term, and when Jules Verne's works began to appear in 1863 they were labelled Voyages Extraordinaires. The British term did not really gain any wider usage until the American editor and publisher Hugo Gernsback revived it in the 1920s, although a Swedish science fiction magazine, *Hugin,* had used Wilson's term from 1916, offering to bring the reader into the 'Fairyland of Science' through 'The Scientific Fiction, the Technical Causerie, the Idea-stimulating Sketch, the Adventure Story and the Scientific Fairy Tale.' The first book about science fiction and the standard work on the genre up to the early nineteenth century, the French author and astronomer Camille Flammarion's excellent *Les mondes imaginaires et les mondes réels* (Imagined and Real Worlds) (1864), used the French term Voyages Imaginaires. Flammarion had probably never heard about Wilson's name for the genre; and if he had, he was too good a Frenchman to acknowledge a term coined by an Englishman.

Now, the definition as to what constitutes this literary genre, Science Fiction or Voyages Imaginaires or Nauchnaya fantastika or Fantascienza or Phantastik der Technik or Bilim-Kurgu or Tieteiskirjallisuus or Fineolaiocht or Naturvetenskaplig Roman or whatever is not one but thousands, and really appears to rest with the good safe definition that 'Science Fiction is what I consider to be Science Fiction.' One of the better definitions was made at the Second Consultative SF Writers Congess in Poznan, Poland, in 1973, where the Bulgarian sf writer Elka Konstantinova said:
Even though the origins of science fiction go back to the mid-19th century, nonetheless as a new literary genre, charged with special social functions, science fiction is the undoubted product of the nuclear age. The more meaningful the scientific and technological breakthroughs and their impact on modern life, the greater the role of science fiction, stimulating our vision of new things to come, especially in the aspect of changes wrought in Man's mentality by the scientific and technological revolution. Science fic-

tion brings home the awareness that the future will continue to bring radical changes in all areas of Man's life; science fiction is there to prepare him for this eventuality.

Does science fiction, then, predict the future? I would say not. It never did, and it never will, for the simple and obvious reason that science fiction is not a crystal ball wherein we search and find hidden secrets about tomorrow; it is a literary tool, pure and simple. As a tool, it is a marvellously multifarious and deep cutting instrument, at least in the hands of one who knows to handle it well. But seeing into the future? I am sorry, sir or madam, but this I cannot offer you.

Of course, we all have our favourites in the nice, friendly parlour-game of science fiction come true, best played at a friendly neighbourhood bar with a few like-minded souls. One of my personal favourites is a Utopian novel by the Brazilian author Monteiro Lobato, *O presidente negro ou O choque das racas* (1926), now mercifully forgotten except for the memorable fact that it describes a Brazilian Utopia from 1988 where the capital of Brazil is aptly named Brasilia. Jolly good, since Brasilia it is as I write this, and presumably also in the glorious Utopian year of 1988. But is it really prediction? And should we

Above: Storm Pedersen's (1922) illustration in 'Nicolai Klimii Iter Subterraneum', by Ludvig Holberg (1741)
Right: Frank R. Paul's cover for the November 1929 issue of 'Science Wonder Stories' had a powerful impact. 'True' stories of flying saucers are still being written

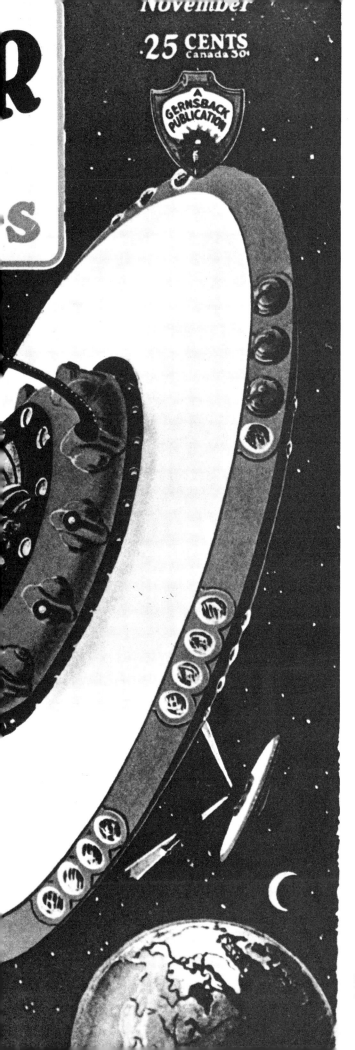

care if it is? Opening the Sunday paper on a day with less murders, arson and shootings than usual, we may be confronted with an article describing in enthusiastic terms the marvellous predictions made by Jules Verne or some similar Victorian writer. Television and submarines are mentioned in awed tones. True, Jules Verne described television in his short story *La journée d'un journaliste américain en 2889* (The Day of an American Journalist in 2889) (1889), although he called it a telephot. This is very good, but the telephot, or television, already existed when Verne wrote his prophetic work, and the French inventor Dussaud actually achieved a form of television in 1898. Verne did not invent it; he was an avid reader of patent applications, and got the idea from there. Even better is the submarine *Nautilus,* famous from Verne's novel *Vingt mille lieues sous les mers* (20,000 Leagues Under the Sea—1867). We all love *Nautilus,* but tend to forget that the *real Nautilus* was invented and built by Robert Fulton in 1801. He demonstrated it for the Parisians upon the Seine in May that year. Later that year he successfully torpedoed a pontoon and also proved he could stay submerged for more than five hours. We know from where Jules Verne got this brilliant idea. This does not make Verne a lesser man in any way; he did not invent anything, but then he never purported to have done so, just as later science fiction authors haven't. He realized the great value of the submarine as an instrument of war—which, luckily, the original financier of the project, consul Bonaparte, did not—and the ability to realize the potentials of an invention is just as great as that of having invented it in the first place. This also goes for television, or telephots. A number of television systems, all of them eminently functionable, were devised from the 1880s and on, but the device was considered to be little more than an amusing toy. Verne, and many other writers of science fiction, realized at least vaguely the revolution this communications device would bring to modern civilization. That piece of hardware, be it a submarine or a TV set or a rocket ship is just a mechanism—metal, and so on to be used or misused as people may see fit. The machine is unimportant—the uses it will be put to, *that* is important.

So, science fiction does not predict the future, except accidentally. It extrapolates, it amplifies, it magnifies. It deals with changes, the inventions of a scientific, social or political nature that inevitably must change our world, whether we like it or not. How we will react to those changes, and how they will affect our lives, *that* is the rub. This is not prediction, even though some Utopian and particularly Dystopian works purport to do just that. Science fiction is a way of bringing out the hopes and fears of a society in rapid change; the hardware is there only because we live in a machine-orientated culture which means that machines have to be brought into the story. Once magic sufficed just as well, since magic seemed to be good enough for the reader; today, hardware is used to suspend the reader's disbelief. That is all. If that piece of machinery is then invented, good. But it has absolutely nothing to do with science fiction as such or even with that particular story. How could science fiction ever predict anything, when it really is about here and now?

John W. Campbell, the editor of one of the most influential American science fiction magazines and a leading personality in the American science fiction

11

world, has given a definition of sorts of the genre, which recognizes the true roots of modern science fiction as the German *Märchen* tales of the late eighteenth century. 'Fiction is simply dreams written out,' he said. 'Science fiction consists of the hopes and fears and dreams (for some dreams are nightmares) of a technically based society.' This, I think, is what science fiction really is about, and the history of the genre proves it, as we soon shall see.

I think it would be best for all of us to point to what we see as science fiction and term it as such. This is certainly what I mean to do in this book, to the best of my ability, and this is what we all are doing when we select a particular book in a book store, a library or our own bookshelf, knowing that this book probably or surely will give us what we want in the way of imagination, adventure, satire or just plain good entertainment. The very best way would be, I think, to follow Brian W. Aldiss's sensible suggestion at the Third European Science Fiction Congress in Poznan, Poland, 1976: That critics and readers alike remind themselves three times before breakfast every morning that science fiction does not exist, there are only individual authors. And that should be enough for all of us.

Just a little more before concluding this chapter: English-language books about science fiction tend to give readers the impression that science fiction is mainly an English or American phenomenon, acknowledging of course pioneers like Jules Verne, Kurd Lasswitz and a few other authors too well-known to be ignored. This is certainly not true, as I shall try to show; on the contrary, science fiction appeared very late in English-speaking countries and appeared later in America than almost anywhere else. Still, many avid readers of science fiction firmly believe that science fiction was and is a typically Anglo-American phenomenon. A leading expert on science fiction, the Romanian scholar Ion Hobana, has pointed out:

It is a paradox of the modern theory and history of literature that, when dealing, however nonchalantly, with science fiction writers, and Kingsley Amis above all, see this literary genre as a typical product of the Anglo-Saxon civilization, disregarding other literatures and their eminent representatives, such as Alfred Robida, Rosny aîné, Gustav le Rouge and Maurice Renard in France, the Italians Luigi Motta and Emilio Salgari, the Poles Jerzy Zulawski and Antoni Slonimski, the Czechs Karel Capek and Ian Weiss, the Germans Kurd Lasswitz and Hans Dominik and the Russians Alexander Belayev and Vladimir Obruchev. These are the names of authors whose science fiction works were published before World War II.

One reason for this may be the simple problem of languages. Several hundred million people speak English, and several countries in different parts of the world, including England, the United States and India, have English as their official language (or one of their official languages). In Europe, schoolchildren learn English as one of several foreign languages. English-speaking people often cannot speak or read any language but their own. Thus, we Continental Europeans, Latin Americans, Japanese and so on can read the literature of our own country as well as that of France, Germany, England and the United States, while most in England and the United States cannot read anything but the literature written in, or translated into, their native language. This leads to

ignorance, of course, a literary and cultural parochialism, and eventually the belief that English-language science fiction must be the only one existing in the world.

This situation has, however, changed somewhat during the past few years, mainly through the internationalizing of the writers of science fiction. This has led to quite a number of international conventions and congresses, such as the International Science Fiction Symposium in Rio de Janeiro, 1969; the World Symposium of SF Writers in Tokyo, 1971; the First Consultative Conference of SF Writers in Budapest, 1971; the three European Conferences in Trieste, Grenoble and Poznan in 1972, 1974 and 1976 respectively; and the First World SF Writers Conference in Dublin, 1976. (The annual 'World SF Conventions' do not fall into this category. They are not international in any sense of the word, just local meetings for American fans.)

A reader not previously acquainted with particularly European science fiction will probably find quite a number of unfamiliar names and works in this book. Some of you might even think I am making it all up, that science fiction really began with a man called Hugo Gernsback and a magazine called *Amazing Stories,* and that the Europeans, Latin Americans and Japanese are merely newcomers to a field invented by the United States pulp magazine industry in New York. I can assure you it is not so. What I am trying to achieve is to present not the final word on the themes and development of science fiction—that would need a book at least ten times the size of the present work—but a brief survey of the themes and the history of this genre, giving individual writers and countries the space and the attention they deserve within the limits of this single book. I have had to ignore much good and important science fiction, par-

Above: The panel of the Third European SF Conference, Poznan, 1976, with representatives from 18 countries seated behind the chairman
Top right: An issue of 'Newsweek' airs its views on science fiction
Right: Russian cosmonaut Aleksandr Leonov speaking at the 1976 Poznan Conference

ticularly from Japan, Latin America and certain European countries, again because of the limitations imposed upon me by the need to cram everything into a single volume. Sacrificing hundreds of eminent writers and works from dozens of countries, I have paid more attention to science fiction in America and the Soviet Union than these countries perhaps deserve, and for this I must take the blame. Since I obviously had to restrict myself to a small number of writers and countries, I have done so as honestly and carefully as I could. The history of science fiction is a multi-faceted one, with roots in all countries of the world and a development that, at one point or another, has encompassed all countries where books ever have been published. It is not a genre of one country or one language or one time, it is the legacy of all who have ever dreamt of worlds and times beyond this one and of changes that someday will confront us all. This book is about some of these dreams.

TALES FROM THE CRYPT

The Gothic novel is distinguished by a number of peculiar traits; high literary qualities in the traditional meaning are not among them. There are, however, high passions and powerful effects in ample measure. The genre as such is less concerned with literary form than contents, which makes grading it according to the usual scale of literary values difficult. Examples of finer literature within the Gothic novel are few, and only one of its writers has been recognized as a 'real' author—Edgar Allan Poe who, significantly, does not belong to the proper body of Gothic writers but is more a later worker in the Gothic fields, using psychology where the others contented themselves with ghosts, castles and living dead on a wholesale scale.

It is, nevertheless, a fascinating genre, offering effects strong enough to tickle even the most jaded palate. Its strong connections with the Medieval *chansons de geste* and other tales of chivalry with their unbearable noble heroes, incredible, constantly swooning ladies and unbelievable villains, gives the genre life and gusto and guarantees new, staggering thrills on every page. It is very dramatic, alternating between the pathetic and the grotesque and characterized by mighty heroics, swords, blood and hideous slithering things in the darkness of convenient crypts. The scene is usually an old robber baron's castle of exceedingly bad repute or a monastery of even worse repute where brooding knights or fallen monks go to blasphemous excesses in the pale, flickering light of the full moon. Monsters are abundant, usually in the form of vampires, werewolves, living dead or the Devil himself. The plots are so complicated that no one can ever hope to untangle them, and to make it even more interesting, most of the participants are usually closely related to each other, which opens the way for intriguing incestuous situations. All this and even more can be found in the culmination of the Gothic tale, Matthew Gregory Lewis's novel *The Monk* (1796), in which the evil monk Ambrosio not only sells his soul to the Devil and shacks up with a female devil, but also in the magnificent finale rapes his poor sister, the noble nun Antonia, in the monastery crypt among the coffins. This is Gothic horror on a high level and the novel became an enormous success, never out of print since its first scandalous edition.

THE MONK:

A

ROMANCE.

Somnia, terrores magicos, miracula, sagas,
Nocturnos lemures, portentaque.   HORAT.

Dreams, magic terrors, spells of mighty power,
Witches, and ghosts who rove at midnight hour.

IN THREE VOLUMES.
VOL. I.

LONDON:
PRINTED FOR J. BELL, OXFORD-STREET.
M.DCC.XCVI.

Above: Title page of first edition of 'The Monk' (1796)
Right: A tender scene between the monk and an emissary of the Devil, from the film 'Le moine' (1971), loosely based on Lewis's novel. Inset is the cover of a recent Belgian edition

LE MOINE

Le chef-d'œuvre du Roman noir

This, however, belongs to the climax of the Gothic horror at the end of the eighteenth century, and the first true Gothic novel, Horace Walpole's *The Castle of Otranto* (1765), as decidedly more fit for innocent readers. It had form but no substance, its horrors all lay on the surface as it were, and while *The Monk* actually managed to convey some of the profound horrors of the monk Ambrosio as he slid deeper and deeper towards degradation and death, and greater authors like the marquis de Sade described the real horrors of the time in works like *Justine, ou les Malheurs de la Vertu* and *Les 120 Journées de Sodom*, the seminal *The Castle of Otranto* succeeded only in building up baroque façades without much content. In many ways this was the forerunner to the Penny Dreadfuls and the pulp magazines—lots of form, no content.

The action of *Otranto*, written by Horace Walpole, author, politician and a man as eccentric as any of his literary creations, the builder and proud owner of a Gothic castle which had to be seen to be believed, takes place in the castle of Otranto, where the terrible sovereign Manfred reigns in the place of the rightful owner, who went out to participate in the Holy War and never returned. A frightening ancient prophecy haunts the background, and one day a giant helmet crashes down in the courtyard, smashing in the empty head of Manfred's son and heir Conrad, who quickly passes away, leaving Manfred with Conrad's bride-to-be, the beautiful Isabella. Manfred starts making unpleasant advances, and before you know it the circus is going full blast with bleeding statues, groaning ghosts, talking pictures and other merry goings-on calculated to raise the spirit of the thrill-seeking reader. Heroines and villains spend much time running around in the labyrinthine subterranean vaults of the castle while the evil Manfred plots to murder a suddenly appearing rightful heir. Virtue triumphs in the end, as it should, and everyone lives happily ever after. Except perhaps Manfred.

This celebrated work was followed by a veritable flood of more or less terrifying Gothic tales—Clara Reeve's *The Old English Baron* (1777), William Beckford's *Vathek, An Arabian Tale* (1786), Ann Radcliffe's *The Mysteries of Udolpho* (1794) and so on and so forth, up to the masterpiece of the genre, Matthew Gregory Lewis's outstanding *The Monk* (1796), in which we finally begin to find something behind all these mouldering castle walls and echoing crypts, in this case an alarming description of the gradual moral destruction of the monk, Ambrosio. This novel is not very much better written than any of the already mentioned works, but its probings of psychological terrors, however clumsily done, shocks more than groaning ghosts and black magic, with which, indeed, this novel is also amply endowed.

The enormous popularity of the Gothic tale in Britain during this period is attested by the appearance of the first weird magazine in the world, the British *Marvellous Magazine*, published in London 1802–1803 in four volumes offering the reader all sorts of ghastly thrills, mostly in the form of uncredited and drastically reduced and rewritten versions of Gothic novels. *Marvellous Magazine* was way before its time, preceding the German *Der Orchideengarten* by 117 years and the American *Weird Tales* by 121 years, and does not appear to have been quite the success its publisher had been hoping for. As a matter of interest, *Marvellous Magazine* was one of

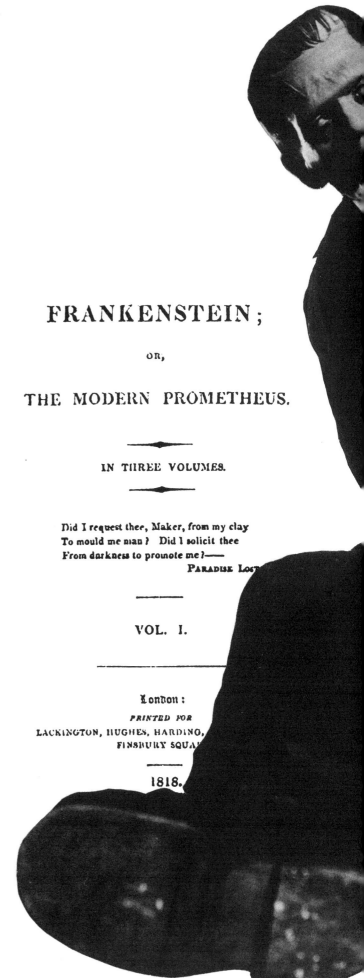

FRANKENSTEIN;

OR,

THE MODERN PROMETHEUS.

IN THREE VOLUMES.

Did I request thee, Maker, from my clay
To mould me man? Did I solicit thee
From darkness to promote me?——
PARADISE LOST

VOL. I.

London:
PRINTED FOR
LACKINGTON, HUGHES, HARDING,
FINSBURY SQUARE

1818.

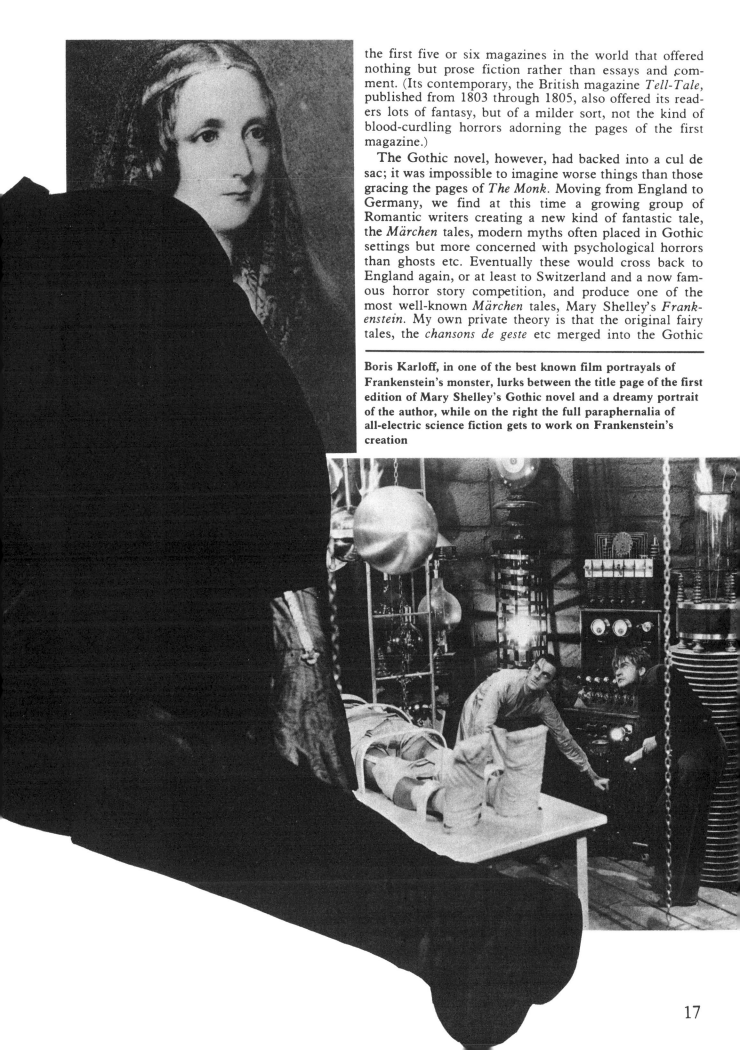

the first five or six magazines in the world that offered nothing but prose fiction rather than essays and comment. (Its contemporary, the British magazine *Tell-Tale*, published from 1803 through 1805, also offered its readers lots of fantasy, but of a milder sort, not the kind of blood-curdling horrors adorning the pages of the first magazine.)

The Gothic novel, however, had backed into a cul de sac; it was impossible to imagine worse things than those gracing the pages of *The Monk*. Moving from England to Germany, we find at this time a growing group of Romantic writers creating a new kind of fantastic tale, the *Märchen* tales, modern myths often placed in Gothic settings but more concerned with psychological horrors than ghosts etc. Eventually these would cross back to England again, or at least to Switzerland and a now famous horror story competition, and produce one of the most well-known *Märchen* tales, Mary Shelley's *Frankenstein*. My own private theory is that the original fairy tales, the *chansons de geste* etc merged into the Gothic

Boris Karloff, in one of the best known film portrayals of Frankenstein's monster, lurks between the title page of the first edition of Mary Shelley's Gothic novel and a dreamy portrait of the author, while on the right the full paraphernalia of all-electric science fiction gets to work on Frankenstein's creation

Above: Cover of a recent Swedish edition of E. T. A. Hoffmann's 'Die Elixire des Teufels'
Right: Lon Chaney as the werewolf in the 1941 US version of 'The Wolf Man'

tale, which then, having spent itself in a frenzy of castles, ghosts, murder, necrophilia, incest and other top-selling subjects, itself merged into the *Märchen* tale, which was already what we might call science fiction. The man who first made the modern *Märchen* tale acceptable to a wider reading public was the German Ludwig Tiech, one of the pioneers of Romantic fiction. Filled with nostalgia for the Middle Ages, and in many ways a Gothic writer, he nevertheless managed to escape the bony clutches of the Gothic tale in his best works, notably *Der blonde Eckbert* (1797) in which the protagonist simultaneously views his dreams from the outside and experiences them from the inside—spectator and protagonist at the same time. When Eckbert's dream-like delusion disintegrates, and he wakes up to reality, the impact is too violent: he

VARNEY, THE VAMPYRE;

OR,

THE FEAST OF BLOOD

A Romance.

CHAPTER I.

——" How graves give up their dead;
And how the night air hideous grows
With shrieks !"

MIDNIGHT. — THE HAIL-STORM. — THE
DREADFUL VISITOR.—THE VAMPYRE.

THE solemn tones of an old cathedral
clock have announced midnight—the air is
thick and heavy—a strange, death-like
stillness pervades all nature. Like the
ominous calm which precedes some more
than usually terrific outbreak of the elements, they seem to have paused even in
their ordinary fluctuations, to gather a terrific strength for the great effort. A faint
peal of thunder now comes from far off.
Like a signal gun for the battle of the winds
to begin, it appeared to awaken them from
their lethargy, and one awful, warring hurricane swept over a whole city, producing
more devastation in the four or five minutes
it lasted, than would a half century of ordinary phenomena.

It was as if some giant had blown upon
some toy town, and scattered many of the
buildings before the hot blast of his terrific

Left: Opening of Prest's 'Varney, the Vampyre' (1847)
Above: Vlad Tepesch Drakula in a 15th-century woodcut as the Impaler and (top right) as the noble count
Overleaf: Bela Lugosi about to sup—a touching scene from the 1930 US film version of 'Dracula'

goes mad and dies, unable to endure the disillusionment, after his long sojourn in his own dream world of deception. Achim von Arnim's *Isabella von Ägypten* (1812), Clemens Brentano's *Das Märchen von den Märchen* (1812) and Friedrich Baron de la Motte Fouqué's *Undine, Eine Erzählung* (1811), and particularly Adalbert von Chamisso's *Peter Schlemihls wundersame Geschichte* (1814), are fantastic *Märchen* acting as bridges between the old Gothic tales and modern science fiction, discarding much of the Gothic paraphernalia and instead concentrating on human beings set in fearsome or unusual situations—like Peter Schlemihl who sells his shadow, or the beautiful water nymph Undine who turns out to be somewhat less than perfect when married.

The greatest writer of horror stories and fantastic *Märchen* was, of course, E. T. A. Hoffman (1776–1822), writer, musician, artist and the leading and most fascinating writer in the genre during this period. His novels and short stories are famous, for good reason, and he actually led much of the development of the fantastic *Märchen* away from the fairy tale to the truly modern tale of psychological terror. A good example of this is the novel *Der Goldne Topf, Ein Märchen aus der neuen Zeit* (The Golden Pot, 1814), in which the somewhat romantic poet Anselmus is imprisoned in a magic glass bottle, finally released and flees into another imprisonment which he

Three more typical scenes, with Gothic crypts, cobwebs and sweetly sleeping maiden, and Bela Lugosi as Dracula

regards as freedom. More powerful is the novel *Die Elixire des Teufels* (The Devil's Elixirs, 1815), introducing the *Doppelgänger* theme with great force in an almost Gothic setting as the monk Medardus drinks the Devil's elixirs and is transformed into the mad adventurer Count Victorin. The mechanical doll Olympia in *Der Sandmann* (1816) is of course a classic, and most probably the prototype for many literary robots and androids, from Mary Shelley's *Frankenstein* and Villiers de l'Isle Adam's android Hadaly, to the robot Maria in Thea von Harbou's *Metropolis*.

Mary Shelley's celebrated novel, more a *Märchen* tale than a true Gothic one, is discussed elsewhere in this book. It is sufficient here to say that it is certainly the

most widely known of all these tales; and I suspect it is less because of supreme literary or psychological qualities than from the fact that this was the first of the true *Märchen* tales written in the English language, and also the one that most easily lent itself to film adaptation. Three of Hoffman's *Märchen* tales were adapted for an opera by Jacques Offenbach, *Les Contes d'Hoffman* (Tales from Hoffman) (1881), and this opera is now a classic of its kind, but while at least Hoffman, Chamisso and Kleist are still widely read and indeed have never

been out of print, they had the misfortune not to write in the language of a successful colonial nation. This is of course not the entire reason, but I believe it is a large part of it.

The *Märchen* tale, however, blended into the Gothic tale in the early nineteenth century, something that was easy enough since both these genres were quite preoccupied with black magic, wizards, strange science and a love of the Medieval. One of the best known offsprings of this merger was Charles Maturin's *Melmoth the Wanderer* (1820), a variation on the legend of the Wandering Jew. Melmoth had sold his soul to the Devil, in return for eternal life. Somewhat illogical, he spends the long, rambling novel searching for ways of escaping from Hell. The theme became quite popular, with the most famous example being the French author Eugène Sue's novel *Le juif errant* (The Wandering Jew, 1844), a fat ten-volume work based upon the legend of Ahasuerus, the man who taunted Christ as he carried his cross to Calvary. This was something for which Christ could never forgive him,

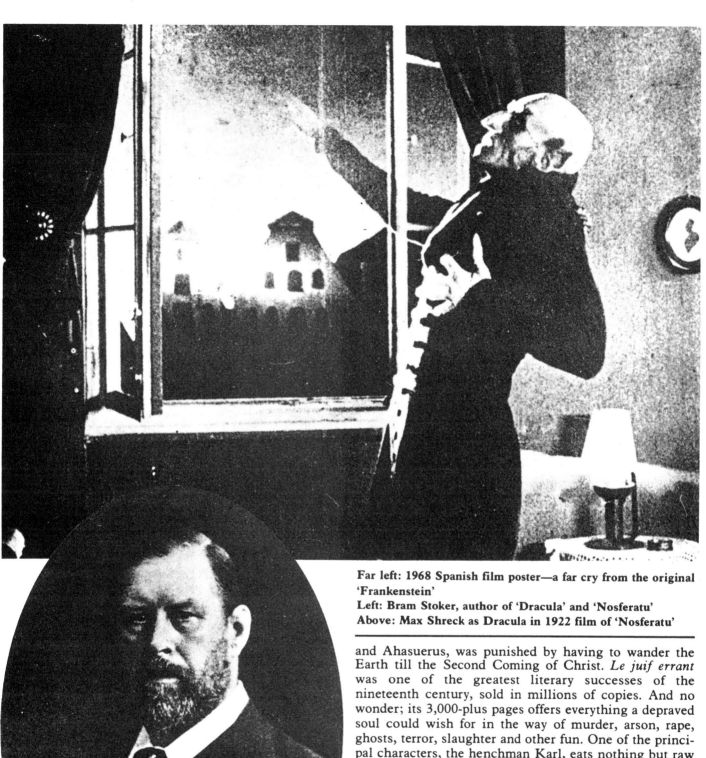

Far left: 1968 Spanish film poster—a far cry from the original 'Frankenstein'
Left: Bram Stoker, author of 'Dracula' and 'Nosferatu'
Above: Max Shreck as Dracula in 1922 film of 'Nosferatu'

and Ahasuerus, was punished by having to wander the Earth till the Second Coming of Christ. *Le juif errant* was one of the greatest literary successes of the nineteenth century, sold in millions of copies. And no wonder; its 3,000-plus pages offers everything a depraved soul could wish for in the way of murder, arson, rape, ghosts, terror, slaughter and other fun. One of the principal characters, the henchman Karl, eats nothing but raw meat and murders with his bare hands anyone who comes too close to his beloved master, the black magician Morok. The opening chapter of the novel is magnificent, with the Wandering Jew crossing Siberia on his way to Bering's Strait in a blizzard of more than usual violence, while on the American side of the Strait a female friend of his approaches. The storm howls and aurora borealis flames over their heads, until they reach their arms towards each other over the gulf, but to no avail. They have to turn back, presumably for another rendezvous at the South Pole. They do not write opening chapters like that any more. But nor do they sell 3,000-page novels in 16-page instalments either.

The latest version of this legend is by no means a *Märchen* or Gothic tale—Swedish Nobel laureate Pär

Lagerkvist's novel *Ahasverus död* (The Death of Ahasuerus) (1960) certainly starts in a way that would have made Sue proud, with Ahasuerus staggering into a cheap inn amid drunken wanderers, whores and suchlike but soon widens into a grandiose story about Man and God. Sue would not have appreciated that quite so much. Nor would, I imagine, Sue's readers.

Not content with wandering Jews, screaming ghosts and living dead, *Märchen* writers ransacked the accumulated filth of aboriginal faiths, coming up with, among others, the vampire. A widespread and ancient myth which can be found everywhere in the world, it turned up in popular fiction relatively late and the first example I have been able to locate is a beautifully grisly ballad by one John Stagg, called *The Vampyre* (1810), in which the vampire, the dead Sigismund, drinks the blood of men and women alike, but evidently prefers the blood of his dear old friend Herman. The description of Sigismund is worthy of Matthew Gregory Lewis at his best:

His jaws cadaverous were besmear'd
With clotted carnage o'er and o'er,
And all his horrid whole appear'd
Distent, and fill'd with human gore!

Sigismund ends up, as all well-behaved vampires do, with a stake through his black heart.

More well-known is John William Polidori's short story *The Vampyre* (1819), one of the results of the horror story competition that eventually produced *Frankenstein*. Polidori's vampire also sports certain homosexual, or rather bisexual, traits, as he sucks the blood of both young women and a dear male friend. The story was later dramatized for the stage and became a great success, inspiring a veritable flood of vampire stories, the most

One of the best films of 'Dr Jekyll and Mr Hyde' was this 1941 version, starring Spencer Tracy, Ingrid Bergman (seen far left) and Lana Turner

notable one being Thomas Preskett Prest's enormous 900-page penny dreadful novel *Varney, the Vampyre, or, The Feast of Blood* (1847). Prest had already produced scores of neo-Gothic penny dreadfuls with promising titles like *The Maniac Father, or the Victim of Seduction; The Death Grasp, or a Father's Curse; The Skeleton Clutch, or the Goblet of Gore; The Black Monk, or the Secret of the Grey Turret;* and *Ranger of the Tomb, or the Gypsy's Prophecy.* I do not think I need go into details regarding the outstanding merits of Prest's vampire novel; sufficient to say that it is by far the longest, bloodiest and most spectacular of all the vampire novels that have survived to our days, a treasure for anyone who loves vampires and (or) penny dreadfuls. (It is now available in an unexpurgated facsimile edition from Arno Press (USA) in case you would want to spend a few weeks in the delightful company of Sir Francis Varney, vampire par excellence.) One interesting point is that Sir Varney is a strangely complex person, hardly the kind of vampire villain one expects to meet in a penny dreadful, and some parts of this incredible (but lovable) novel actually are reminiscent of the *Weltschmertz* found in Matthew Gregory Lewis's *The Monk.* One has to search for these parts amid the legions of blood-chilling murders, rapes, mutilations and terrors, but they are there and they give the novel an added value for the aficionado of the genre. I personally find this novel the most fascinating of all the penny dreadful-type *Märchen* tales. When Sir Varney after 120 blood-dripping chapters finally throws himself into Vesuvius, one almost feels an acute sense of loss, as if a dear friend has departed.

The most famous of the current vampires, though—again, mostly thanks to Hollywood misinterpretation—is of course Bram Stoker's celebrated *Dracula* (1897), published in the same year as another classic dealing with Man being attacked by the unknown, H. G. Wells's *The War of the Worlds.* England and the world successfully managed to fight off the brutal Martians, but Count Dracula was made of harder stuff, as attested by scores of increasingly sillier Dracula films during the past forty years. Count Dracula is the refined, pale and demonic gentleman, a Jack the Ripper in evening dress, the last of a family which traces its history back to the beginnings of time. His castle is ancient and dilapidated, situated in the wild Transylvanian mountains, the very prototype of a Gothic castle. We expect to see Horace

Walpole's Manfred appear any minute and to behold the giant helmet crash down upon its poor victim again. Not so; instead, we are confronted with Count Dracula, who welcomes the narrator to his castle, thereby starting the modern classic in this field.

Count Dracula plans to move coffin and household gear to England, and the narrator, the British lawyer Jonathan Harker, has been sent to the castle in order to handle some of the details. The novel describes in diary form the horrors our hero is subjected to in the castle, and how the Count later on lands in England. He gets himself a helper, a mentally sick person, at a nearby hospital, alternatively pursues Jonathan Harker's fiancée and her best friend, and towers throughout the novel as an avenging demon above all the others, right up to his final destruction not far from his old castle in Transylvania.

Dracula bears too many resemblances to Prest's *Varney* to be considered totally original, but it is also based upon a once living person, Voivod Tepesch Drakula (1430–1476) in Transylvania, now part of Romania, in contemporary sources described as a tyrant of monstrous cruelty. He was known for many things, and indeed also accused of vampirism, but his speciality was impaling his victims on long wooden stakes (a favourite pastime of soldiers at the time and, later on, of Swedish soldiers in Germany during the Thirty Years' War.) Thus it is as Vlad Tepesch (The Impaler) that he is now known in Romania, where, by the way, he is considered, again for good reasons, to be one of the great national heroes, a liberation fighter who for many years kept the Ottoman Turks away from Wallachia. His castle can still be seen and is a popular tourist object. A French tourist bureau is these days offering a special journey 'Au pays de Dracula', including the castle Bran of Dracula repute.

Personally, I find the stories about the real Vlad Tepesch Drakula much more interesting than Bram Stoker's somewhat boring vampire novel. It is not interesting enough from a literary point of view to make it good reading (like, for example, Sheridan Le Fanu's excellent vampire novel *Carmilla*, 1872), and it is certainly not exaggerated enough to be unconsciously funny (like Prest's *Varney, the Vampyre*). It is just one of those horror tales that happened to be written in the right language at the right time, by an author who had excellent contacts with the stage and soon got it dramatized, soon to be filmed.

I am convinced that the most terrifying horrors must be the unseen ones, those without shape or form or substance, those only hinted at, those only imagined. The real terrors are those lurking in the darkness just outside our field of vision. The best example of this, I think, and surely the most frightening of all these horror stories, is Guy de Maupassant's short story *Le Horla* (The Horla, 1886), drawn from somewhere in his private world of hallucinations and madness, written as his final madness overtook him. The theme, an invisible being which sways the minds of others, was not entirely an original one, but what we have here is less a literary creation to entertain and horrify the reader than a glimpse into a disintegrating mind. The Horla is the final horror, unseen,

Gaston Leroux's moving horror tale of an appallingly disfigured man haunting the Paris Opéra has been filmed five times. Here Lon Chaney takes the role in the 1925 US version of 'The Phantom of the Opera'

31

unknown to everyone but the narrator, the horror from which there is no escape. (The American writer H.P. Lovecraft was to use this particular idea many times in his short stories, but to much less effect than de Maupassant's poignant and truly terrifying story.) The Horla is the archetype of all nightmares, described in clear, lucid prose, a masterpiece of a short story and without peer in this particular literary genre. It is not merely written; it is experienced. The narrator of the tale finally sets his house on fire, in the vain hope of trapping the invisible being in flames. His servants die, but the Horla escapes, as all nightmares do, since fear lives not outside you but inside your own skull. The real horror must be de Maupassant's Horla, the feeling Coleridge expresses in *The Rime of the Ancient Mariner* (1798):

Like one, that on a lonesome road
Doth walk in fear and dread,
And having once turned round walks on,
And turns no more his head;
Because he knows, a frightful fiend
Doth close behind him tread.

But this would, alas, be too subtle for the Gothic tale. There, we would surely be confronted with everything at close sight, destroying all vestiges of real terror.

This is what happened to one of the oldest and best of the old nightly terrors, the werewolf, which, once a terrifying beast lurking in the South European woods, now has been degraded to the leading parts in films like *I Was a Teenage Werewolf* and *Werewolf in a Girl's Dormitory* (with the theme song 'The Ghoul in School').

The werewolf was long one of the most common nightly terrors, and one of the first literary werewolves appears, in *The Feast of Trimalchios* by the Roman satirist Petronius, in which a Roman soldier turns into a werewolf and does what we expect from him. A traditional werewolf also appears in Prest's *Varney, the Vampyre*. The most well-known werewolf novel, however, is Alexandre Dumas's *Le Meneur de loups* (The Wolf Leader, 1857), a Gothic novel in the grand tradition in which the French shoemaker Thibault sells his soul to the Devil in return for eternal life and worldly riches. An interesting parallel is Honoré de Balzac's *La peau de chagrin* (The Fatal Skin, 1832), in which every wish shortens the protagonist's life; in Dumas's novel a strand of the shoemaker's raven black hair turns red as blood with every wish. The shoemaker plans to restrict his wishes, but avarice causes him to employ them faster and faster. When his hair becomes one mass of flame, he is turned into a werewolf for good and is ultimately taken by the Devil. Good, gruesome Gothics, and the novel has never been out of print. A more recent variation on the theme is the American writer Jack Williamson's novel *Darker Than You Think* (1948), in which we learn that there is actually a race of werewolves, known as Homo Lycanthropus, and the hero of the novel soon realizes that he is not only one of the chosen few but actually their chronicled leader—The Child of the Night.

More interesting from a *Märchen*, or Gothic, point of view, is Robert Louis Stevenson's novel *The Strange Case of Dr Jekyll and Mr Hyde* (1888), in which the werewolf theme is used as the basis for an analysis of the nature of evil. Once again, it is a tale about externalization of evil into a figure outside ourselves; but whereas the werewolf of traditional folklore turns into an animal with the aid of black magic, or simply the full moon, the

AMERICAN INTERNATIONAL presents

EDGAR ALLAN POE'S

classic tale of THE EVIL...

HOUSE OF USHER

in CINEMASCOPE and COLOR

STARRING VINCENT PRICE

evil beast lurking inside Dr Jekyll breaks loose with the aid of the chemicals of modern science. The result is a human being, liberated from all the conventions that usually makes Man a civilized animal. I would trace an obvious heritage from the Marquis de Sade in this very convincing description of Man as wolf, the human animal in total freedom. For what is Mr Hyde, if not the original, inmost Man, liberated from the tyranny of the super-ego, mocking the frozen and imprisoned Dr Jekyll, who terror-stricken regards the total, uninhibited freedom of his own subconsciousness?

The theme is a recurrent one, witness the *Doppelgänger* themes in tales like E. T. A. Hoffmann's *Die Elixire des Teufels*, Edgar Allan Poe's *William Wilson* and Oscar Wilde's *The Picture of Dorian Gray*, all dealing with personalities split into good and evil. What makes Stevenson's novel particularly interesting, apart from obvious literary qualities, is his almost maniacal digging in Man's evil subconscious in the tradition of the best of the German *Märchen* writers. Stevenson uses the werewolf and *Doppelgänger* theme to good effect, but only as the basis for a discussion about Man's hidden animal nature, and the novel can actually be read as a wry commentary on the promise of the new science to liberate Man from the burden laid upon him by the aesthetic values of older days. When Dr Jekyll drinks the drug furnished by modern science, he becomes truly liberated, becomes Mr Hyde who cares for nothing but himself and who lives for the fulfilment of his lusts alone. H. G. Wells went on with this discussion in the novel *The Time Machine*, originally published as *The Chronic Argonauts* in 1888, the same year as Stevenson's novel. Wells goes one step further: he proposes a world in which industrialization has divided Mankind into two different races, the Morlocks and the Eloi. The Morlocks are ape-like, evil and cannibal—the Eloi are almost etheric in their innocent purity. As in Stevenson's novel, there is no doubt as to which of them will ultimately triumph: it is the Morlocks, Mr Hyde, Man as wolf, the true, liberated Man.

Edgar Allan Poe (1809–1849) was surely the best of the post-Gothic authors, infusing in many of his best stories, notably *The Fall Of the House Of Usher* (1839), a strange, dreamlike quality comparable to the best of the German *Märchen* writers. His psychological insight and almost tender handling of his themes made him stand out above everyone else within the field (with the possible exception of E. T. A. Hoffmann), obsessed with pain and death, but using the obvious horror elements only as a means to convey a deeper significance. He used the Gothic setting for most of his famous stories, but the emphasis was on psychological terror, not on the Gothic surfaces, which makes him less a Gothic writer and indeed more a *Märchen* one. I will not attempt to discuss him here, since he is too well known to be introduced in full in a brief survey like this one; it is sufficient to point out that Poe managed to break free from the dim dungeons of Gothic literature and widen *Märchen* literature into something universal, a profound discussion of Man's relation to his own hidden self, again perhaps best exemplified in *The Fall of the House of Usher*, where a brother, his twin sister and their ancient home all share a single soul and meet one common dissolution at the same moment.

A compatriot of Poe, H. P. Lovecraft (1890–1937), has

Left: Advertisement for 1960 US film version of Edgar Allan Poe's short story 'The Fall of the House of Usher'
Above: Poe, commemorated on a stamp—fame indeed

during the past decade or so grown into something of a cult, particularly in the United States and France, with a number of truly Gothic tales offering a profusion of terrors, monsters and crawling, clawing, slithery horrors in the Grand Guignol style.

Sad to say, these are not much more than Gothic surfaces once again, with Lovecraft assuring us all the time that these horrors really are unspeakably evil, loathsome and revolting, but never proving why. Heavily influenced both by the Irish fantasy author Lord Dunsany (perhaps the last real *Märchen* writer) and Edgar Allan Poe, he paints all the appropriate pictures of decay, degradation and corruption, but it all ends up as mere sounds, terrors without substance. The glimpses he gives of his own tormented and alienated soul are far more interesting than the somewhat pathetic horrors he offers. In a way, Lovecraft is a throwback to the Horace Walpole and Ann Radcliffe school of Gothic tales, without the power of Matthew Gregory Lewis or E. T. A. Hoffmann, and his enormous popularity is a constant surprise to me.

Much of Lovecraft's appeal may lie in his successful externalization of unspeakable evil, a characteristic trait for all successful Gothic tales. Here we are confronted with pure, unadulterated Evil; it can be identified and fought, just as the pure-hearted Hobbits in J. R. R. Tolkien's *The Lord of the Rings* trilogy fight the sub-human Orcs. An unbearable complicated reality is dissolved into simple parts of black and white, of good and evil. Werewolves, witches and vampires of popular folklore were evil, period, and a good silver bullet was an effective way of stopping them. This was an age of straight, uncomplicated emotions, and witches were burned at the stake all over Europe as the good peasants successfully liberated themselves from these spawn of the Devil.

This is the basis of the Gothic tale and its philosophy, faithfully built upon the Christian faith and its rituals,

Above: Boris Karloff in the film 'Die, Monster, Die!', based on H. P. Lovecraft's story 'Colour out of Space'
Right: Lovecraft's 'Pickman's Model', art by Hannes Bok
Far right: Lovecraft's first collected stories (1939)

and this may be the main reason for its popularity in our complicated age when nothing is purely black or white any longer. In the Gothic tale, evil is easily recognizable, just as grotesque and deformed, loathsome and corrupted as it ought to be, but never is. It is no coincidence that the number of Black Masses is growing and the belief in the Devil as an actual fire-and-brimstone person is returning. The fallen Monk Ambrosio and Lucifer are so much more agreeable than Song My. Only the improbable is enjoyable in this context; when the horrors become too real, they become unpleasant.

So much for Lovecraft and his colleagues in the damp dungeons of Gothic terror. As for pure, untrammelled horror, I can think of no better example than a small vignette in the American writer Robert W. Chamber's collection *The King in Yellow* (1895). I believe that this is not only the shortest of all Gothic tales, but also the best one, refreshingly free from all the usual pompous superstructures of the genre:

CAMILLA: *You, sir, should unmask.*
STRANGER: *Indeed?*
CASSILDA: *Indeed it's time. We all have laid aside disguise but you.*
STRANGER: *I wear no mask.*
CAMILLA: (Terrified, aside to Cassilda.) *No mask? No mask!*

THE OUTSIDER AND OTHERS

BY H.P. LOVECRAFT

36

SCIENCE FICTION AT THE CROSSROADS

The turn of the century saw an unparalleled boom of science fiction everywhere in the world. There were many reasons for this—industrialization and urbanization being only two of many concurrent factors. The foundations had been laid much earlier by the German *Märchen* writers and the British Gothic writers as well as by satirists and natural scientists of a former age, but it now flowered as never before as the industrialized nations prospered—particularly France, Germany, England and the United States. In my own view of science fiction, the genre takes on its modern form at this time, and also disperses in four different directions. For me, these four directions of modern science fiction are embodied in four writers, two French and two British, who were active in the year 1900. Three of them had already written their main works, three were to die within seven years (1905, 1906 and 1907, respectively). Two are acknowledged as 'fathers' of modern science fiction. One is virtually unknown today. One is not considered to be a science fiction writer at all by many readers. Yet all of them contributed in his own, personal way to the development of present-day science fiction. The four writers were Jules Verne, H. G. Wells, George Griffith and Alfred Jarry.

Jules Verne (1828–1905) was, of course, the foremost of the Victorian science fiction writers and the man who, in the mind of most readers, embodies the origins of modern science fiction. As much the nightingale of Victorian optimism as Rudyard Kipling was the nightingale of imperialism, his was the voice that promised unlimited and unending scientific evolution and Utopia on Earth within the foreseeable future. In an age when the steam engine and the new power of electricity carried progress onward to new wonders, displayed to awed crowds at the World Exhibitions, he was the mouthpiece for the unbounded optimism of the new age. The universe was a finite, comprehensible piece of clockwork. Intrepid English, French and German explorers fought their way into unexplored parts of the world, civilizing and killing without discrimination but with great enthusiasm. Some ignorant aborigines fought back, but justice, that is,

The 47-volume Hetzel 'Polychrome' edition of novels by Jules Verne (Left), published 1867-1919, was something of a work of art. It is now a rarity.

Above: Jules Verne's birth certificate and a stamp commemorating the 50th anniversary of his death. Note the extraordinary error in his date of birth
Right: The Victorian way of flying, from Verne's 'From the Earth to the Moon'

Europe, always triumphed. The machine propagated itself over the world and Jules Verne sang its praise in many books. After the debut with *Cinq semaines en ballon* (Five Weeks in a Balloon, 1863) he wrote a seemingly endless stream of enthusiastic stories dealing with the scientific revolution—novels like *Vingt mille lieues sous les mers* (20,000 Leagues Under the Sea, 1870), *De la Terre à la Lune* and *Autour de la Lune* (From the Earth to the Moon *and* Around the Moon, 1865, 1870), *Le Tour du monde en quatre-vingt jours* (Around the World in Eighty Days, 1873) and *Michel Strogoff* (1876) are now classics. Electricity, the new wonderful cheap energy, powered Captain Nemo's submarine and Engineer Robur's aircraft; modern engineering changed a barren island into a Victorian paradise complete with a well-behaved ape servant; one could even blast away to the Moon if one had enough gunpowder, money and engineers. The future was wonderful, at least for a gentleman. This was before *Titanic* and the World War I.

But Verne was not only the naive popularizer of science. His later works give ample evidence of a deepening pessimism, particularly in sequels to earlier optimistic works, like *Sans dessus dessous* (The Purchase of the North Pole, 1889) in which the gentlemen of the Gun Club in Baltimore (who successfully did shoot their columbiad at the Moon in *De la terre à la lune*) now turn out to be little more than gangsters, willing to sacrific millions of people in order to make a profit. The great engineer Robur from *Robur le Conquérant* (Robur the Conqueror, 1886) later turns out to be little more than a

power-mad criminal in the sequel *Maître du monde* (Master of the World, 1904). Also, of course, Jules Verne's Victorian dream world had not exactly been perfect even in the days of his most unbridled optimism. It is significant that almost all Verne's heroes have serious mental defects: Captain Nemo harbours a maniacal lust for revenge; William Storitz, the great inventor who succeeds in making himself invisible, in *Le Secret de Wilhelm Storitz* (published posthumously in 1910) is mentally sick; the scientist Thomas Roch invents in *Face au drapeau* (For the Flag, 1896) both the guided missile and something resembling the atomic bomb, but he has certain difficulties in using them since he, for good reasons, is confined to a mental institution. The list could be made much longer.

And what happens when these wonderful machines are built and put to use? The engineer Robur uses his fantastic flying machines, *Albatross* and *Terror*, to spread terror over the world, as does Captain Nemo with his submarine, *Nautilus*. The wonderful future city in *L' étonnante adventure de la mission Barsac* (posthumously published in 1920) is built and run by gangsters, the incredible floating island in *L'île à hélice* (Propeller Island, 1895), built and inhabited by the super rich, is destroyed because of the rivalry of its inhabitants. And so on. Jules Verne believed in the Machine, but he does not appear to have had much faith in Man, its creator and master.

Jules Verne was certainly an important writer in his time, even from a literary point of view (something not easily recognizable from translations of his novels, usually made for the juvenile market and excluding all puns and finer literary points). His great importance, however, for a literary historian, was that of an example. Verne was translated everywhere, from Uruguay to China; he was even during his lifetime probably the most widely read author in the world, and this as much as anything else created the upswing for modern science fiction. In Italy, modern science fiction was largely the result of Verne translations and the works of a local Verne imitator, Emilio Salgari, who became very popular with novels like *Il Re dell' aria* (The King Of the Air, 1906) and *Le meravigle del duemile* (The Wonders of the Year 2000) (1908). The pioneer of Russian rocketry and modern science fiction, Konstantin Tsiolkovskiy, admitted that his first enthusiasm for space and science fiction came from reading Jules Verne, and he then wrote classics of Russian science fiction like *Na lune* (On the Moon, 1893), *Grezy o zemle i nebe* (Fantasies about Heaven And Earth, 1895), and the novel that later became the favourite of generations of Russian science fiction readers, including the cosmonaut Gagarin, *Vne zemli* (Beyond the Earth, 1896). Tsiolkovskiy was also the pioneer of rocket flight, first proposing space travel with rocket propulsion in 1883. Another avid Russian reader of Jules Verne, Aleksey Tolstoy, later wrote the most enduring of the Russian science fiction classics, *Ayelita* (1922). In Germany, Kurd Lasswitz even surpassed the master with *Auf zwei Planeten* (Two Planets, 1897), a bestseller incorporating a number of modern science fiction devices and inventions, which almost single-handedly launched German science fiction and sold a record 70,000 copies in two years. The Hungarian writer Maurus Jokai (1825–1904) was as important for Eastern Europe as Jules Verne was for the West, but curiously enough is still virtually

unknown outside his native Hungary (or perhaps not so curiously. French is an international language, but who reads Hungarian—except the Hungarians?). With a background amazingly similar to that of Jules Verne, he launched his literary career before Verne and wrote a number of classics which, together with the omnipresent Verne works, created Hungarian science fiction. His best known novel, *Jovo szazad regenye* (The Novel Of the Next Century, 1872), an Utopian adventure novel, with lots of cliffhanging intrigue as good as the best US pulp fiction, is still popular in Hungary. He was also just as honoured as Verne—his fiftieth anniversary as a writer was celebrated throughout Hungary in 1894, and his collected works, most of it science fiction, were published in a 100-volume set. In 1900 he was received officially by the French government and the French writers, including Jules Verne, at the Paris World Exhibition.

In Japan, where Verne was immensely popular, a science fiction boom appeared in the 1890s, spawning a number of local writers in the Verne tradition, like Ryukei Yano, who wrote, among other books *Ukishiro Monogatari* (A Castle on the Sea, 1890) and the leading Japanese science fiction author of the period, Shunru Oshikawa, a sort of Japanese Otto Witt or Hugo Gernsback, who after his debut with the novel *Kaitei Gunkan* (Undersea Battleship, 1900) launched several magazines and publishing companies. In the United States, Verne earned himself a number of imitators, including Luis Senarens, who plagiarized several of his novels in the Frank Reade Jr pulp series.

Verne appeared everywhere, and like rings on the water science fiction writers appeared in his path. Much of the credit for the incomparable science fiction boom of the 1890s throughout the world must go to Verne. He was a

40

Top left: A scene from a 1954 US remake of '20,000 Leagues Under the Sea'
Left: Cover of Hungarian fan magazine bearing portrait of Maurus Jokai
Above: Konstantin Tsiolkovskiy (left) and Gustav le Rouge

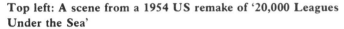

splendid example of the right man at the right time, attracting not only numerous imitators but also science fiction writers who attacked him and his views, the Wellses and the Jarrys of the science fiction world. He was also to a large degree responsible for the science fiction ghetto, though not through any fault of his own. When Hugo Gernsback decided to launch the first North American science fiction magazine, *Amazing Stories*, he realized that he would have to publish mainly European science fiction, since nothing of comparable quality was available in America. So Jules Verne and H. G. Wells were often reprinted during the first years of that magazine—the very first issue of *Amazing Stories* (April 1926) actually had as lead story Jules Verne's *Hector Servadac* (1877). That novel was by then fifty years old and science fiction had moved a long, long way since Verne wrote it. But it suited Gernsback's mind and somewhat limited imagination to perfection, as did subsequent Verne novels. Between 1926 and 1933 *Amazing Stories* reprinted eleven of Jules Verne's novels, and these novels, which fifty years earlier had launched hundreds of literary careers that were to regenerate European, South American and Japanese science fiction, now in effect set American science fiction in a mould that was to hold it for years to come.

If the emphasis had been on Wellsian attitudes instead of Vernian ones in this magazine while Gernsback was consciously manipulating American science fiction

authors for his use, things might have turned out different. But Wells was an intellectual writer, a complex writer, and also a political writer whom Gernsback never could understand. Those of Wells's stories that were reprinted in *Amazing Stories* (no less than twenty-six between 1926 and 1930) were those that could serve as prototypes for the sort of 'scientific' wild west tales Gernsback wanted. And, of course, Wells had been writing and was still writing for a much more sophisticated readership than the one which devoured *Amazing Stories*. All that came through were the simplest and crudest of his ideas—and these were frequently misunderstood. His attack on British imperialism in *The War of the Worlds* (1897) became only the prototype for thousands upon thousands of silly monster stories after *Amazing Stories* reprinted the novel (with a suitably garish pulp cover depicting, in glorious four-colour printing, Martian war machines trampling people to death). 'The Martian fighting machines with their heat rays were a unique contribution by Wells to the adventure of sf,' writes David Kyle in a recent history of American science fiction. This is what stayed in the minds of pulp magazine readers: robots and heat rays.

Herbert George Wells (1866–1946) revolutionized the entire science fiction genre, with the obvious exception of the pulp jungle, and he is indeed one of the few science fiction authors who was respected also as a serious author. (Jules Verne was respected mainly as a playwright and the author of quite a number of immensely popular novels and serious non-fiction books; George Griffith was respected because he made much money; Alfred Jarry was not respected until he was dead.) Wells's greatest achievements, however, were not within the field of science fiction but in politics. His 'classic' works, *The*

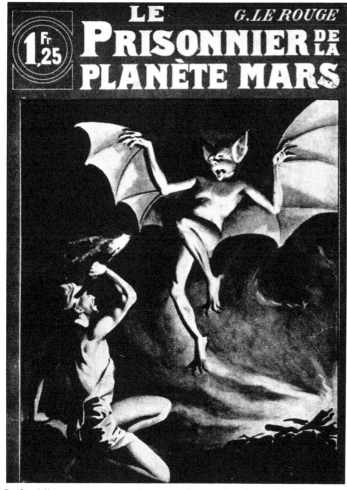

LE PRISONNIER DE LA PLANÈTE MARS

G. LE ROUGE

1 Fr. 25

Left: Alien monsters, pulp magazine style. Cover by Frank R. Paul for August 1927 'Amazing Stories'
Above: 1908 Gustav le Rouge novel, when SF paperbacks were immensely popular in France

Time Machine, The Invisible Man, The Island of Dr Moreau, The First Men in the Moon, When the Sleeper Wakes, The Food of the Gods etc, appeared within a comparatively short period between 1895 and 1903. These novels, and quite a number of excellent short stories, were the ones that really formed science fiction at this time and made 'scientific romances' respectable. Wells had something that Verne and Griffith and even Jarry lacked, a political conscience. All his novels are political in nature, a fact recognized by his contemporary readers, although those most popular in this day and age are usually considered to be little more than extremely well-written and intelligent science fiction. Much of his enormous impact in his day can be attributed to the political content: the anti-imperialism of The War of the Worlds, the Darwinist anti-Utopianism of The Time Machine, the terrible dissection of the nature of man and beast in The Island of Dr Moreau, the uncomfortable discussion of man versus insect civilization in The First Men in the Moon sometimes shocked his readers, but also started debates and discussions that went far beyond the purely literary impact of his works. Still, he was unsatisfied with being regarded mainly as an author of science fiction; he had greater goals. 'I am doomed to write "scientific romances" and short stories for you creatures of

the mob,' he lamented to Arnold Bennett, 'and my novels must be my private dissipation.' He later turned to other fields of debate literature, with novels like Anne Veronica (1909), the shocking discussion of free love in Victorian England, and to thinly disguised social pamphlets like The Shape of Things to Come (1933), Men Like Gods (1923) and The World Set Free (1914). He was at heart a Utopian, trying to create Utopia, or his version of Utopia, through politics, and his ultimate failure made him disillusioned and bitter. The lasting monument to his endeavours was to be his outline of Man's evolution towards the perfect Utopia, Outline of History (1920), and the two following volumes of this magnificent trilogy, The Science of Life (1931) and The Work, Wealth and Happiness of Mankind (1932).

Most of his political works are forgotten now, largely for good reasons. An idealist pursuing the impossible, he finally had to content himself with the, for him, unsatisfying fame of being the leading science fiction author of his time. His main contribution towards Utopia was the Declaration of Human Rights, originally drafted by Wells and dropped in over occupied Europe during World War II. The Declaration of Human Rights is an impressive document but, alas, we do not have to look very far to find that this, too, was a Utopian dream.

Wells was at heart an educator, just like Jules Verne, but with the great difference that Verne used the educational method of writing, while Wells had the education of Mankind as an ultimate goal. Indeed, as Wells's fiction with time turned more and more into thinly disguised pamphlets advocating political views, so they became less and less interesting as literature. Wells fell into the trap of turning preacher, which proved fatal. Most of his novels of ideas, after 1910, are of little literary or political merit, inviting perhaps the heretical thought that his political ideas cannot bear too close a scrutiny.

Still, Wells was and is an extremely important writer, and a grossly underrated one. Vladimir Nabokov has hailed his marriage novel The Passionate Friends (1913) as the century's most 'unjustly ignored masterpiece', and novels like Ann Veronica (1909) and Tono-Bungay (1909) are certainly masterpieces unjustly ignored today. Comparing Wells to current superstars of pop literature, Wells stands out like a beacon in a sea of mediocrity. A cult writer like Kurt Vonnegut Jr may be amusing and witty, but he lacks substance. Wells has it all in ample measure, as I am sure time will prove.

Wells, like Verne, set an example for science fiction, which in this survey is the most interesting aspect of his literary legacy. He differed from the Vernian school of science fiction not only in his political slant, but also, with his a much better scientific education and understanding than Verne, he did not want to be a slave to scientific accuracy. Fantastic fiction, he said, 'has to hold the reader to the end by art and illusion and not by proof and argument.' In his novel The Wonderful Visit (1895), he went even further, saying that 'Explanations are the fallacy of a scientific age.'

This could not fail to fascinate Alfred Jarry, who held an identical view but expressed it even more freely than Wells. Jarry later extrapolated several of Wells's ideas in a particularly Jarryesque way and he appears to have been especially fascinated by Wells's time machine, one of the earliest and best of the surrealistic Bachelor Machines (about which more later). An avid cyclist, Jarry found the

Above: Aerial battle, art by F. T. Jane, from George Griffith's novel 'The Angel of the Revolution' (1894)
Right: As future-war tales became more popular, they became increasingly improbable. This example is from 1917

idea of travelling through time on a machine resembling a cycle irresistible and wrote a brilliant essay, *Commentaire pour servir à la construction pratique de la machine à explorer le temps* (How to Construct and Use a Time Machine) in 1899.

I believe the French 'pataphysicists owe Wells a greater debt than any of them realize; but Wells's greatest contribution to science fiction lies of course in another direction, that of forming what is now known as the Wellsian, as opposed to the Vernian, attitude towards the world, to Man, and to the future. In the United States this attitude is best exemplified by the sf magazine *Galaxy,* which first appeared in 1950 and finally brought the Wellsian attitude to the fore in American science fiction with satirists like Frederik Pohl, Cyril M. Kornbluth and Robert Sheckley. The sort of corporativistic future envisaged in modern sf classics such as Pohl/Kornbluth's *The Space Merchants* (1952) and *Gladiator-at-Law* (1954), both originally published in *Galaxy,* would be unthinkable without the influence of H. G. Wells. When the Vernian monopoly of American science fiction—and through that, of a large part of post-war science fiction from other countries—finally ended (thanks to such editors and authors as Ilya Varshavskiy, Robert Sheckley and Donald A. Wollheim), it was the influence of Wells being felt at last. It was fifty years later, as had been the case with Jules Verne's influence over American sf magazines, but it came. The evolution proceeded along similar lines in the other super power, the Soviet Union, where the official Party 'theory of limits' regarding science fiction finally disappeared together with the Stalin Cult. The leading authors and editors in the Soviet

Union are now as much Wellsian as their colleagues in other countries—Arkadiy and Boris Strugatskiy, Anatoliy Dneprov, Ilya Varshavskiy and others. When commenting with all due modesty upon the fact that science fiction now, by and large, is respected as much as any other form of literature, I think we should remember that a very large part of the credit must go to H. G. Wells.

When I say that Jules Verne held a virtual monopoly of the attitudes of pulp magazines in the United States, this is not strictly true. His influence was certainly there, the mad search for pseudoscientific accuracy where there could be no accuracy of this sort, the belief that science fiction should be educational, this was purely Vernian. But Verne was not only filtered, as it were, through the strange personality of Hugo Gernsback, but also through an Englishman whose space opera stories set the tone for pulp fiction for decades to come. His name was George Griffith.

George Griffith (1857–1906) was probably the most popular science fiction author in England until the phenomenal success of H. G. Wells's *The War of the Worlds* in 1897. Forming a link between Jules Verne, who influenced him in his youth, and H. G. Wells, whom he certainly influenced and for whose greatest success, *The War of the Worlds,* he paved the way, his importance from a literary historical point of view is great, although the quality of his works is low by most standards. Briefly,

his success in British magazines, particularly *Pearson's Weekly* which published most of his novels and short stories, was a result of the future war novels craze in England following the publication of George Tomkyns Chesney's novel *The Battle of Dorking* (1871), which vividly described a successful German invasion of England. Up to the turn of the century, British readers appear to have enjoyed a masochistic pleasure from a flood of detailed descriptions of England being invaded by all sorts of enemies, and many of the novels catering for this need were written by Griffith, starting with the phenomenally successful *The Angel of the Revolution* (1893), a sort of modernized penny dreadful about a future world war in which everyone except Germany is ganging up on England, using submarines, air ships and conventional troops to defeat proud Albion. Luckily, the hero and the heroine have their own fleet of airships which eventually defeat the aggressors and impose a world government upon them, creating, in effect, a true modern Utopia. The novel was later that year also published in book form, and turned out to be one of the greatest bestsellers of the time. Griffith immediately wrote a sequel, *Olga Romanoff, or The Syren of the Skies*, which was serialized in *Pearson's Weekly* from 30 December, 1893 to 4 August, 1894. Taking place in 2030, 125 years after the formation of the World Government, it tells of the anarchist Olga Romanoff, a woman as ruthless as she is beautiful, who is totally devoted to the Russian Tzar. She builds a secret fleet of air ships with Russian money and attacks the air fleet of Aeria, the world police of the future. World war breaks out again, the world reverts to barbarism and anarchy, the plague kills most of the people of Aeria, chaos reigns until the Aerians finally locate Olga Romanoff in her secret Antarctic abode, and she dies a tragic death.

Griffith wrote a number of wars-to-come novels, with alluring titles like *The Outlaws of the Air* (1894), *The Great Pirate Syndicate* (1898) and *The Great Weather Syndicate* (1906), but he also spent more and more time travelling round the world as a roving journalist for the Pearson magazines while other talents attempted to satisfy the reading public's insatiable thirst for more and more stupendous wars. One of the new writers who attempted to fill his place as a purveyor of bloodier and bloodier future-wars tales was H. G. Wells. Wells had for years been writing short stories for *Pearson's Magazine* as well as for one of its competitors, *Strand Magazine*, and he had made his reputation with the publication of *The Time Machine*, as a serial in *New Review*, in 1895. With Griffith perhaps getting tired of repeating the same old future war formula, Cyril Arthur Pearson, the owner of *Pearson's Magazine* and *Pearson's Weekly*, commissioned Wells to write the future war story to end all future war stories. This Wells did with *The War of the Worlds* (1897), to the delight of English readers who now could

taste the exquisite pleasure of being raped not by the usual Huns but by real extraterrestrial monsters.

Soon after, Europe and America realized that Japan was a greater threat than the usual enemies; Kaiser Wilhelm II was scared into coining the phrase 'Die gelbe Gefahr' (The Yellow Peril), loosing yet another avalanche of future war stories upon the public, featuring brutal Chinamen and Japanese intent upon world domination. The celebrated American author Jack London outdid them all, and all future war stories ever written, with his short story *The Unparalleled Invasion* (1910), in which China becomes a world power with one billion inhabitants seeking *lebensraum*. Europe and America solve the Yellow Peril problem by wholesale mass murder of one billion Asians with biological warfare, thus once again making the world fit for WASP gentlemen. A later, and particularly obnoxious, variation on this theme is a novel by Robert A. Heinlein, *Sixth Column* (1941), in which noble American scientists invent a weapon that kills Asiatics but not true WASPs and proceed to exterminate the Yellow Peril once and for all. Such weapons are, incidentally, now being developed. Talk about applied science fiction!

Griffith turned more and more to the subject of anarchists versus capitalists, the latter baddies usually in the form of the United States, a country which he deeply resented. Griffith's world was one of constant wars on a large or small scale, between nations, gangs or individuals, with the poor for ever fighting the rich, and the rich forever trying to strangle the poor. It was also a world of female emancipation, which was unusual for the time. Griffith had led an adventurous life, bumming, starving, struggling for life in a world which did not appear to want him or even to endure him, and this must have coloured his views on life as a continuous struggle. Wells regarded the world and mankind with different eyes, as did Verne and Jarry. At bottom, Griffith's novels related the basic struggle to survive at all costs, no more, no less. New scientific wonders were only means enabling one person or group of persons to get ahead of another, and the number of unusual weapons employed in Griffith's future war stories it quite staggering. He believed in an inevitable change in mankind, but all his stories dealing with the subject point out that the change must be a violent one, that probably terrorists and anarchists will be the ones ultimately to bring it about. Bakunin and Kropotkin, the anarchist apologists, would have applauded parts of *The Angel of the Revolution* and *The Syren of the Skies*, in which the new World Government, composed of former anarchists, appears to live strictly according to Pierre Proudhon's anarchistic slogan that 'property is theft'.

Griffith's repeated, vitriolic attacks against the United States in practically all his novels made him somewhat less than popular there, and the first of his novels to be published in America was his celebrated interplanetary novel, *Honeymoon in Space*, serialized in 1900 in the British and American editions of *Pearson's Magazine*. The story of an interplanetary sightseeing tour by a British nobleman of exalted ancestry, his American bride and a faithful servant, it was the real precursor of thousands of space opera stories, filled to bursting point with the wonders of the universe, evil Martians, etheric Venusians and everything else a pulp magazine reader ever could ask for. As I show elsewhere, the difference

One of the strangest British artists at the turn of the century was Sidney Sime, certainly a 'pataphysicist if ever there was one. The text to this drawing reads: 'No one has gazed upon the MEKON in his real shape, for he never appears in it. Any one of his appearances, and they are legion, will shed a blight upon silly wandering ghosts. Seeing that the crabs were getting out of the way before he awoke, I seized my double's arm—for there were two of me—and retired. Take warning when you wander in dreams to avoid the MEKON.'

Robert Sheckley

Docteur Faustroll, 'pataphysicien (1898) as 'The science of imaginary solutions, which symbolically ascribe to objects the qualities they evince by their effects.' This sounds like a definition of science fiction; anyone who has read, for example, E. E. Smith's *The Skylark of Space*, realizes that many science fiction authors have entertained Jarryesque methods without being aware of it. Jarry was, to be sure, what we might call an avid science fiction fan, an admirer of Jules Verne and H. G. Wells, and the author of a number of science fiction stories, including the brilliant novel *Le Surmâle* (1902). 'Pataphysics is a metaphysical approach to the riddles of reality, which, again, is another definition of science fiction with its imaginary solutions to problems that might, or might not, confront us. 'All people are 'pataphysicists,' said Jarry: 'although only a few are aware of it.' How true.

Jarry's sardonic humour and wry comments on the present and the future, particularly in plays like *Ubu Roi* (1896), *Ubu Enchaîné* (1900) and *Ubu sur la Butte* (1906), made him a focus for the French surrealist writers Alphonse Allais, Marcel Schwob, Raymond Roussel, Jacques Rigaut and others. All these were science fiction authors as we see it, not in the Vernian tradition but rather in the Wellsian, as examplified by present-day writers like Jorge Louis Borges, Robert Sheckley, Philip K. Dick and the Strugatskiy brothers. In 1949, a Collège de 'Pataphysique was founded in Paris to study 'pataphysics, treating life and the universe with the same lack of respect as Jarry did. 'Pataphysicists of this later era included René Daumal, Raymond Queneau, Jacques Prévert, Jean Ferry, René Clair, Eugène Ionesco and Boris Vian, all of them representatives of the kind of fantastic literature and drama that had emerged in France,

between Griffith's interplanetary novel and the first American space opera classic, E. E. Smith's *The Skylark of Space* (1928), is mostly one of scale, and the numerous space opera tales following this novel are certainly much in debt to Griffith, even though another important part of the true space opera, that of the abducted princesses, empires to be won and dynasties to be founded, came to a large degree from the Edgar Rice Burroughs space adventures starting with *Thuvia, Maid of Mars* (1916). Griffith offered future space opera writers plenty of material to work from, including battles with alien airships and Martians foolishly resisting the noble Earthmen.

George Griffith is now largely forgotten, even though his two most popular future war novels now are available in recent American editions and *A Honeymoon in Space* has been reprinted a number of times during the past seventy-five years. The reasons for this are many; one is certainly, to quote Sam Moskowitz's excellent essay on Griffith prefacing a recent collection of some of his stories (*The Raid of Le Vengeur*, London, 1974), that 'his literary output was for the most part a reflection, not a shaper, of the feelings of the period. He danced to the beat of the nearest drummer.' As a writer, Griffith cannot be compared to Verne or Wells or Jarry; but the space opera tradition is still with us, and although Griffith was not the first to write about interplanetary sightseeing tours, his version of the theme, and his almost maniacal concentration upon warfare in the seas, the air and in space, gave inspiration for other and greater talents in that particular branch of science fiction.

The French author and playwright Alfred Jarry (1873–1907) is by far the most complex and fascinating of the four fathers of modern science fiction. For many years a cult figure among intellectuals, he was the first of the 'pataphysicists. He introduced and defined 'pataphysics in his celebrated novel *Gestes et opinions du*

A. E. Van Vogt

EUROCON 1
12-16 luglio TRIESTE '72

Aldo BRESSANUTTI - MUGGIA (Trieste)   NEMESI   Olio su legno - 40x50 - 1972

1° CONGRESSO EUROPEO DI S. F.
I° MOSTRA INTERNAZIONALE D'ARTE FANTASCIENTIFICA 11-21 LUGLIO
STAZIONE MARITTIMA

COLLABORAZIONE:

Poster for First European SF Convention 1972

Above: Japanese SF magazine

Right: Cover of British SF magazine

SPECIAL ANNIVERSARY ISSUE

VISION

OF TOMORROW   AUGUST   5/-

AST VIGIL

Michael Moorcock

EDDIE JONES

KOSMOPLOV

ZELENI SF DODATAK

ket lomer

KOSMIČKA ODISEJA

BROJ 1
MART
Cena:
1.50 d.

DUGA

Cover of Yugoslav SF magazine

beginning with Jarry. The Collège de 'Pataphysique still exists, larger and more active than ever, still publishing its magazine *Viridis Candela*.

A Russian version of 'pataphysic surrealism also appeared in 1910, known as Futurism, and probably much more influenced by Italian Futurists such as Filippo Tommaso Marinetti than by Jarry. Led by the poets Vladimir Mayakovskiy, Velimir Shchlebnikov and Aleksey Krutenych, they caused quite a stir until the regime became progressively displeased and the movement finally died around 1919. Indeed, Futurism in the Soviet Union and Italy influenced science fiction more than most science fiction scholars realize. It was not only Futurist writers such as Mayakovskiy, but also architects such as Lissitskiy and Leonidov who created fantastic cities of the future that later were incorporated into pulp magazine illustrations of the twenties and the thirties. One example of this is the Italian Futurist architect Antonio Sant'Elia, who in 1914 made detailed plans for 'Città Nuova', 'The New City'—which suddenly appeared in a sort of cheap Buck Rogers form but with all the original details there as the super city in an American B-movie, *Just Imagine*, in 1930—without any credits to the creator of the city.

Jules Verne was, of course, the father of modern science fiction, but Verne idolized the machine, while Jarry and other 'pataphysicists had a more complex love-hate relationship with it and spent much time poking fun at it, using absurdity when Verne persisted in cloaking his imaginary solutions in a veil of scientific respectability. A good example of the fundamental difference between these two schools appears in Jules Verne's critical comments to H. G. Wells's *The First Men in the Moon* (1901). Verne could not understand Wells's space ship, based upon the imaginary gravity-nullifying metal Cavorite (which was not in fact invented by Messrs Wells and Cavor, but by an Italian science fiction author, Ulisse Grifoni, whose novel *Dalla Terra alle Stelle* [From the Earth to the Moon, 1887] incorporated this ingenious metal and all its characteristics). 'I make use of physics,' Verne lamented. 'He invents. I go to the Moon in a cannon ball, discharged from a cannon. Here there is no invention. He goes to Mars in an airship, which he constructs of a metal which does away with the law of gravitation. . . . Show me this metal. Let him produce it.'

Verne shot his Moon travellers to the Moon with a cannon that never could have worked but which was constructed according to the scientific knowledge of the time and which appeared to work. Wells, who in this case acted in true 'pataphysic manner, did not give a damn about scientific credibility. His imaginary solution worked in his novel, as did Verne's in Verne's novel, and that was all that counted. It is a difference of attitude, not of method. Later 'pataphysic writers did away with scientific or pseudoscientific explanations altogether, introducing 'black boxes' of unparalleled power into their stories. When Jacques Rigaut wrote the famous time travel story *Un brillant sujet* (1920), he described his time machine even more briefly than H. G. Wells had done; why bother with that particular imaginary machine? Instead he went right on to the real point of the story, that of time travel paradoxes and of changing past history. Similarly, when more recent authors of the genre introduce strange artifacts or events, they very seldom explained in the way Verne or Gernsback would have pre-

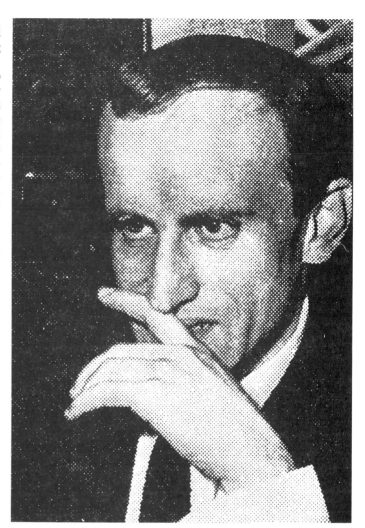

The French writer Boris Vian

ferred. We know they are imaginary solutions, symbolically ascribing to objects the qualities they evince by their effects, to quote Jarry's definition again. The brilliant Italian writer Italo Calvino has mastered this technique and put it into ingenious use in several 'pataphysic novels, notably *Il cavaliere inesistente* (The Non-existent Knight, 1956), *Il visconte dimezzato* (The Cloven Viscount (1957) and *Il barone rampante* (The Baron in the Trees, 1957), three allegorical novels quite unlike anything else in fantastic fiction. Two collections of short stories, *Le cosmicomiche* (Cosmicomics, 1965) and *Ti con zero* (t zero, 1967) describe the improbable adventures of one Qfwfq in a universe getting more and more Jarryesque. Calvino's description of a journey to the land of the birds, in *Ti con zero*, is a beautiful example of the imaginary solution brought to perfection:

There's no use my telling you in detail the cunning I used to succeed in returning to the Continent of the Birds. In the strips it would be told with one of those tricks that work well only in drawings. (The frame is empty. I arrive. I spread paste on the upper right-hand corner. I sit down in the lower left-hand corner. A bird enters, flying, from the left, at the top. As he leaves the frame, his tail becomes stuck. He keeps flying and pulls after him the whole frame stuck to his tail, with me sitting at the bottom, allowing myself to be carried along. Thus I arrive at the land of the Birds. If you don't like this story you can think up another one: the important thing is to have me arrive there.)

William Burroughs has used this ingenious science fiction tool in several novels, notably *Nova Express* (1964), while the modern master of the genre, Robert Scheckley, has produced dazzling examples in a number of increasingly 'pataphysical novels. *Options* (1975) is one of the latest, loaded with images from a technically oriented civilization.

The difference between the Jarryesque method and the traditional Vernian method is to a large degree a matter of form. Eugène Ionesco describes vividly, in his well-known play *Rhinocéros* (Rhinoceros, 1959), how everyone turns into rhinoceroses except one man, and satirizes modern mechanization in *La salon de l'automobile* (The Motor Show, 1953), in which a young man drives away a new car that turns out to be a girl. In an American magazine version we would very probably have the Mad Professor turning his Green Ray upon the people, turning everyone into rhinoceroses except one able-bodied WASP who finally defeats the villain. The young man of *Le salon de l'automobile* would probably appear as a terrible extraterrestrial monster using nubile women for transportation until the WASP hero enters and. . . . They are all imaginary solutions, so why bother with them? French, Italian and South American science fiction authors have known this for a long, long time. Now even a growing number of writers in English-speaking countries are beginning to realize this. J. G. Ballard introduces a world, including men and animals, turning into glittering crystals (without the aid of the Mad Scientist and his Green Ray) in *The Crystal World* (1964); Michael Moorcock and others break up the imaginary reality of time and space in the Jerry Cornelius stories; A. E. Van Vogt builds peculiar absurd worlds in which the basic assumptions constantly change, for example in *The World of Null-A* (1945)—the protagonist dies in one chapter and is alive in the next, he develops superhuman powers, he loses them, his personality changes and so on. Robert Sheckley lets people exchange bodies at will, in *Mindswap* (1966), and Philip K. Dick lets time runs backward in *Counter-Clock World* (1967). Boris Vian describes a world in which emotions turn into tangible form in the novel *L'écume des jours* (1947). Philip José Farmer has also gone quite far in breaking down the rigid barriers between reality and imagination with his biographies of literary creations, *Tarzan Alive* (1972) and *Doc Savage, His Apocalyptic Life* (1973), creating as it were his own world within the world of meta-sf wherein all literary creations really lived (and live!). This is an eminently 'pataphysic way of approaching 'reality', reminiscent of Jarry's 'pataphysicist friend, Marcel Schwob, who in 1896 published his *Vies imaginaires* (Imaginary Lives), giving imaginary and amazing details from the lives of historical persons. Some literary creations are so well-known that they have become historically established (many people really believe that Sherlock Holmes and Tarzan existed), while many historical characters are mere myths. So where is the difference between man-turned-myth and myth-turned-man? None. (The American sf author Norman Spinrad used this amusing fact in 1973, publishing the novel *The Iron Dream* which purports to be a science fiction novel by Adolf Hitler called *Lord of the Swastika*, with Michael Moorcock commenting tongue-in-cheek on the back cover that 'This exciting and tense fantasy adventure . . . is bound to earn Hitler the credit he so richly deserves.')

These are all 'pataphysicist ideas, executed in a style, sometimes better than the first 'pataphysicists managed. They are also a part of science fiction, of course, a result of the 'pataphysical revolt against the stern scientific, or pseudo-scientific, attitudes of fantastic literature in the Victorian age. Jarry regarded the laws of physics as a collection of unexceptional exceptions which thus are uninteresting, since only the exceptional exception is interesting. It is important, Jarry assures us, to remember that the only true danger lies in taking anything, including 'pataphysics, too seriously, and that 'natural laws' only exist in the mind of the unimaginative. Verne could never understand this.

English-language science fiction was cut off from this invigorating aspect of science fiction when Hugo Gernsback, an avid Vernian with as much true imagination as an empty bucket, created the English-speaking science fiction ghetto with his magazine *Amazing Stories*. Soviet and East European science fiction suffered a similar fate during the years of the Stalin Cult and the Stalinist attitude towards science fiction, known as 'the theory of limits'. In his excellent anthology of science fiction from socialist countries, *Other Worlds, Other Seas* (1970), the Yugoslavian science fiction scholar Darko Suvin quotes the Soviet science fiction critic Ryurikov as remarking: 'Its acolytes . . . began trussing up the wings of imagination. They said that literary anticipation had to solve only technological problems of the nearest future, and that it should not attempt to go beyond such limits.' In fact, only Vernian science fiction was published in the Soviet Union from Vladimir Mayakovskiy's downfall to well into the fifties. Pulp magazine standards did the same thing to science fiction in English-speaking countries. The walls of the science fiction ghetto rose everywhere apart from French and Spanish-speaking countries, with a few notable exceptions such as the American author A. E. Van Vogt, who managed to act out his absurdism within the rigid framework of the pulp formula. The 'pataphysic tradition of science fiction remained strong in Italy, France, Spain and Latin America, however (the Argentine authors Jorge Louis Borges and Julio Cortazar are particularly well-known examples of this), and was also quite respectable, since the genre did not have the hack writers and insensitive editors of the Anglo-American pulp magazine industry to be ashamed of.

A. E. Van Vogt's novels have been heavily criticized in the United States for not being logical (i.e. Vernian) enough, and of course they would appear absurd and incomprehensible for a reader reared on American pulp magazines. The more sophisticated French science fiction readers knew better, recognizing that America had finally produced a science fiction author in the 'pataphysicist tradition. *The World of Null-A* was translated and introduced for French readers by the leading 'pataphysicist Boris Vian in 1953, and the novel became an enormous success, ultimately selling some 150,000 copies in France alone. Van Vogt is still more popular in France than anywhere else, including his homeland, because he was the first American science fiction writer to return to the original modern science fiction which had been ruthlessly murdered by Hugo Gernsback and

One of the late US artist Vaughn Bodé's unusual comic strips. With Dadaistic texts, they are unique

55

new
worlds
Speculative Fiction
August · 3s. 6d.

But the advance of the human intellect has not lain solely in the realm of natural science and what things I have seen there, excuse me, not many can do because of their bulk and because of their lack of retention of breath

Paolozzi:
Language Mechanisms
Disch · Aldiss · Sallis · Tate · and others

Above: The British SF magazine 'New Worlds', for a time the voice of neo-Dadaistic fiction. The fad is amply illustrated on this 1967 cover

Right: Applied science fiction. Lissitskiy's project for a twin building in Nikitskiy Square, Moscow. A number of futurist marvels were built—not this one!

his followers. Today, Robert Sheckley, J. G. Ballard and Philip K. Dick have a much larger following in France than in their native countries; again, because they are part of a literary tradition older and more sophisticated than the slam-bam space operas of American literature.

As might be gathered from the examples given here, 'pataphysic science fiction is not equivalent to 'New Wave' science fiction. 'Pataphysics is a way of looking at reality, different from the Vernian way of doing it. 'New Wave' is a matter of form alone, the juxtaposition of fleeting images, invented words, an updated Dadaism as it were. It can be powerful and exciting in the hands of a master, and James Joyce indeed created a masterpiece with *Finnegan's Wake*. The trouble is that science fiction so far has not produced a James Joyce, alas, but it has authors who do their best to emulate him before an awed crowd of readers who do not know what Dadaism was and have never read Joyce and think these great science fiction authors have created the so-called 'New Wave' all by themselves. Brian Aldiss may be the only science fiction author who has managed to make a pass at New

Wave Dadaism without making an ass of himself, because he is a sensible and intelligent author who knows his limitations and those of the media. His novel *Report on Probability A* (1968) is a good example of this. But Aldiss is also an *intellectual* writer, writing with his brains and with all the symbols neatly thought out. A more typical 'pataphysic science fiction writer, Robert Sheckley, writes with his guts, permitting the subconscious to handle the show. Aldiss, whom I cannot call a 'pataphysic writer, uses words, language, images, plot, the way a chemist would use strange chemicals in his laboratory; mixing, changing properties and values, searching for the perfect mixture for the perfect occasion.

Lesser talents have to resort to pastiches of former greats, like J. G. Ballard who had some success in the United States with the short story *The Assassination of*

56

JFK Seen as a Downhill Motor Race (1965), recently hailed by the American critic and author Barry Malzberg as one of 'the two most important short stories of the decade.' Actually, Ballard was 'influenced', to put it mildly, by a famous short story by Alfred Jarry, *La Passion considérée comme course de côte* (1903), which was published in English translation as *The Passion Considered as an Uphill Bicycle Race*, shortly before Ballard wrote his 'important' story. Pressed on this point, Barry Malzberg told me he was impressed partly because of 'the utter audacity of Ballard's gesture.' I am most decidedly not.

J. G. Ballard was for a number of years the Great White Hope of Anglo-Saxon science fiction and the real power behind the great British science fiction experiment, the new version of the British magazine *New Worlds*, edited by Michael Moorcock from 1964 for a few years. He turned out to be the promise that failed, though, sinking deeper and deeper into pointless and repetitive avant-garde fiction which was as crude as literature as it was unreadable as science fiction. His was the most powerful voice behind the 'New Wave', but it soon turned out that 'New Wave' was merely a science fiction term for Dadaism, an avant-garde movement which appeared in 1916 in Zürich and disappeared within a few years. Ballard's collection of 'condensed novels', *The Atrocity Exhibition* (1970), was the last sigh of British neo-Dadaism disguised as science fiction. In an interview with the Danish science fiction critic Jannick Storm shortly after the publication of *The Atrocity Exhibition*, Ballard said, speaking about his avant-garde literary methods: 'It is a big mistake to write about the life of 1970, using a technique of 1870. We do not use horse-

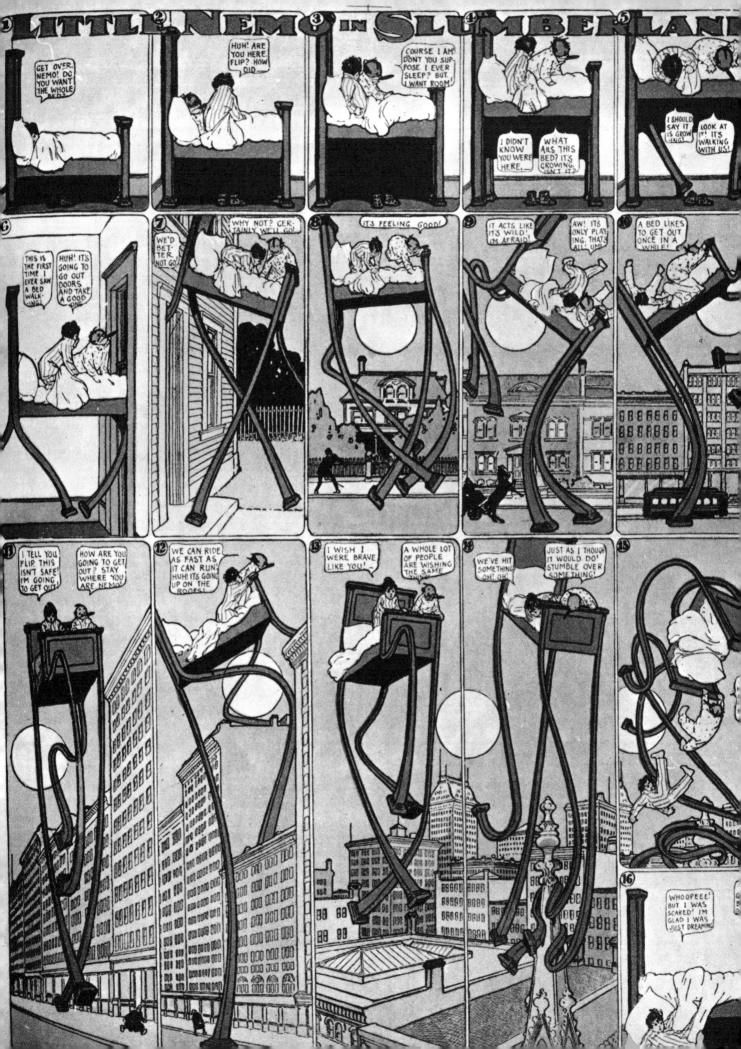

drawn vehicles, and we use modern science, tape recorders, computers and so on, and we need literary methods like them.' How true. But why then use literary methods that were dead fifty years ago, and rewrite stories more than seventy years old?

Ballard was not the saviour of neo-Dadaism. Brian Aldiss did some pushing for a more gifted surrealist writer, the late Helen Edmonds, who wrote catastrophe tales under the name of Anna Kavan, but that too failed, for the simple reason that Kavan, too, floundered and sank when trying to navigate the stormy waters of metaphysics and surrealism. Her Dadaistic novel *Ice* (1967) caused a brief stir, then sank without a trace.

Dadaism has had some influence on the 'pataphysic aspect of science fiction, though, and even on science fiction as such, particularly in its way of regarding machinery and technological artifacts. Science fiction of the pulp tradition (and I am including here all 'hard' science fiction, particularly as it was encouraged and developed from the forties on, in the United States primarily by the editor John W. Campbell, and in the Soviet Union by the official Party 'theory of limits') was and is preoccupied with and dependent upon the hardware of science and the wonders of outer space, always described in awed tones. The 'pataphysic tradition regards technological artifacts with totally different eyes. The surrealistic and metaphysical approach to the machines is a mixture of wonder and dread, in surrealism examplified by the *Machines célibataires,* the Bachelor Machines. The time machine of H. G. Wells's novel is certainly a Bachelor Machine, taking off from hard reality through surrealism, as are the love-making machines in Alfred Jarry's *Le Surmâle* and Jean-Claude Forest's *Barbarella.* The planetoid-sized machine in John W. Campbell's pulp magazine novel *The Mightiest Machine* (1935) could probably be regarded as the ultimate Bachelor Machine, if seen from a more surrealistic point of view. Many Bachelor Machines, however, are scarcely recognizable as machines by someone used to the sort of mechanical wonders usual in American pulp science fiction—the artifacts that fade from view when not remembered, for example, as described in Jorge Louis Borges's *Tlön, Uqbar, Orbis Tertius* (1940). The greatest and best-known of all the Bachelor Machines, Marcel Duchamp's *La mariée mise à nu par ses célibataires, méme* (The Bride Stripped Bare by Her Bachelors, Even, 1915–23), one of the most significant pieces of modern avant-garde art, would give any pulp science fiction fan ulcers. Still, Duchamp's curious machine belongs to the same group of non-existent machines as most science fiction inventions (including magnificent science fiction Bachelor Machines like the Space Warp, Parallel Worlds, the Time Paradox and the sort of fifth dimensional artifacts exemplified in Robert A. Heinlein's short story . . . *And He Built a Crooked House,* 1941). The difference is mostly that science fiction authors usually endeavour to give plausible explanations to the workings of their Bachelor Machines. Surrealists never bother. And why should they? We live in an age where the greater part of civilization is incomprehensible for most people. Modern science fiction still fights with its own conscience, inventing 'space warps' to get away from the light barrier, and 'time machines' to get away from the insurmountable obstacles of Time. These machines could never work, and we know it, but the impressive pseudo-scientific jargon surrounding them

Left: The US artist Winsor McCay (1871-1934) created an odd comic strip with 'Little Nemo in Slumberland'. This walking bed adventure is a classic.

Above: A typically fantastic illustration by Grandeville for La Fontaine's 'Fables'

gives us a feeling of security. But the Universe is really no secure place, the 'natural laws' are the ever-changing products of our own imagination and, really, *anything* could happen. This is the lesson I learn from Jarry and the 'pataphysicists, and this is the lesson learned by a growing number of science fiction authors. Change is upon us, gentlemen, and this time not even the powerful spells of science and technology will help you!

THE ETERNAL BLISS MACHINE

An old Chinese fairy tale tells of a fisherman who gets lost in a peach wood where he finds a spring and a narrow cave opening which he manages to crawl into with some difficulty. Inside the cave he finds a beautiful plain dotted with well-kept farm houses. The farmers tell the fisherman that they fled into this hidden place several hundred years ago and never intended to return to the outer world again. The fisherman gets food and drink, but must promise never to reveal their secret to anyone.

Returning back to the poverty of his own life, he tells the mayor of his town about the fairy land inside the mountain, and he is sent back with other men to find the place. They never succeed. Once lost, Utopia can never be rediscovered.

This theme is a recurrent one in Chinese fairy tales and, indeed, in fairy tales in many other parts of the world. H. G. Wells has written a beautiful version of this tale, the short story *The Door in the Wall* (1906), in which a man finds a door in a wall, leading into a long-lost childhood. In a sense, Wells's story may capture all the bitter-sweet feelings of the true Utopia, the unattainable one, the one that caters not only for the body, as all the classic Utopias do, but for the mind as well. Unfortunately, almost all Utopian tales are more simple than that, hardly more than catalogues of the wonders awaiting us all as soon as we get cheap energy and the world dictatorship necessary for this kind of wish-fulfilment. Exceptions exist, but they are few and far between. If your idea of happiness is living in an army camp for the rest of your life, or playing the harp for eternity on a cloud with nothing whatsoever else to do, then the traditional Utopia, nineteenth-century style, or the traditional Western Paradise, old, old style, would suit you to perfection. The rest of us would probably find it somewhat less than perfect. The best comment on this sort of Utopia is probably Mark Twain's short story *Captain Stormfield's Visit to Heaven* (1908), in which the rough, hard-drinking, hard-living Captain dies and comes to Heaven where he is given a harp and a couple of wings and is told to sing and play the harp and behave like a good, solid angel. Heaven soon bores him out of his mind. He throws away wings and harp, hating the whole place, realizing at last that Utopia might be fine for a fairy tale, but only a fool would want to stay in it for more than five minutes.

The dream of the perfect society, the ideal commonwealth, Utopia, Schlaraffenland, is as old as mankind—for obvious reasons. Man has never ceased to hope for a better world for his descendants, and this recurrent dream is, in fact, the basis for nearly all fantastic fiction, be it Utopian tales of descriptions of the horrors awaiting us all, should we not do exactly what the writer wants us to do.

All these dreams of mastery over Nature, of unlimited power, the key to this eternal bliss machine as it were, are associated with one single literary work, whose title neatly sums up everything in the genre—*Utopia* by Sir Thomas More. Few social polemical works have had such a profound significance as this book—and few have been so profoundly misunderstood. The Utopian state in this book is described as a totalitarian and puritanical dictatorship where everything is based upon utilitarian aspects—and yet the word 'Utopian' now signifies something visionary and unpractical, a paradise on Earth that

Above: Edward Bellamy, author of 'Looking Backward'
Right: More's 'Utopia', first edition, 1516

can never be attained.

For *Utopia* (which was written 1515–16 by a man who had seen more than enough of the worst sides of his society) is a polemical pamphlet advocating Socialism and Communism, and visionary only in that it looks forward to an ideal commonwealth that might appear when Man is governed not by money but by justice. It is not the dream of Schlaraffenland—personally I have always considered More's Utopia a good place to stay away from—but of the ultimate utilitarian society, created by the dream of freedom from want and governed by an absolute altruism. For those who had experienced the plight of the common man in fourteenth-century England, a totalitarian government seemed to be a small price to pay for this welfare.

More's Utopia, this gigantic prison where everything was regulated, from what clothes to wear to furnishing one's home, to one's political opinions, was and is certainly better than starving, but it still falls somewhat short of being the ideal commonwealth. Also, More in his enthusiasm for his beautiful new creation, forgot that you don't have mindless cattle in a society, but human beings. This is the trap into which all Utopian writers have fallen. Utopian societies are invariably boring, and I think the worst punishment one could mete out to a Utopian writer would be to put him into his own creation as a common labourer. For in creating these marvellous complicated social systems, these Utopians have forgotten the one thing, perhaps the only thing, that really matters when creating a new state. If everything is tops, what is there to live for?

'*I don't want comfort,*' *cries Aldous Huxley's John Savage to the World Controller in* Brave New World.

'*I want God, I want poetry, I want real danger, I want freedom, I want goodness, I want sin.*'

'*In fact,*' *said Mustapha Mond, '*you're claiming the right to be unhappy.*'

Mr Savage does, heartily. And through Mr Savage's reactions toward the apparent Utopia, a Utopia that has all the classic properties including unlimited food, drink and sex, *Brave New World* suddenly comes out as an anti-Utopian novel. The Utopian society described in the Fourth Book of Jonathan Swift's *Gulliver's Travels* is viewed in the same way: '(The Houyhnhms) may have all the reason, but the Yahoos have all the life.' Voltaire's Candide voluntarily leaves Eldorado because it is boring. The Utopian writer's sole wish is to make his inhabitants happy, even if it should kill them, and this is what makes it so easy to change a Utopian novel into a horror story simply by substituting one of the numerous well-behaved citizens for a dissenter. What the Utopian writer really would need to populate his ideal community would be, I think, the robots envisaged by Karel Capek in his play *R.U.R.*

The Utopian tale as a genre points to some of the best and worst traits in Man—the best, since it voices hopes for the future and a desire to change society into something better and more perfect; the worst, since it gives no room for doubt that there exists a small Fascist in every man, or at least in every Utopian. For the Utopian tale and its first cousin, the anti-Utopian or Dystopian tale (so closely related that the difference usually only can be measured in the attitude of the reader), are based upon a yearning for absolute power over all men, since the altruistic Utopian naturally knows exactly how the world

Above: Watching distant wars on television—from 'Le vingtième siècle'
Right: Also from 'Le vingtième siècle', a flying summer house

ought to be organized; and now he tells the unenlightened how wonderful everything will be if only we will give him absolute dictatorial powers. The Utopian idea can also be exemplified with Ludvig Feuerbach's thesis about God as the product of Man's imagination, that Man compensates shortcomings in his life by creating an absolute ideal world which does not, and cannot, exist in the real world. Today we have a new Utopianism in the New Left which, although they might not be aware of it, is regarding the ideal commonwealth with the eyes of

Rousseau, as a direct democracy exercised by carefree peasants beneath the peaceful limbs of a pastoral oak or at some mass meeting à la Chine where everyone has the right to express an opinion and where finally a decision is made which is the smallest common denominator for the wishes of all concerned. This is of course—as are all Utopian ideals—an impossibility. Niccolo Machiavelli, the famous Italian statesman, points out in the first book of his *Discourses* that:

All those who have written upon civil institutions demonstrate (and history is full of examples to support them) that whoever desires to found a state and give it laws must start with assuming that all men are bad and ever ready to display their vicious nature, whenever they may find occasion

Above: Paris at night—from 'Le vingtième siècle'
Left: Departure of first interplanetary expedition—from 'Le vingtième siècle'
Overleaf: Strange ideas in 'La guerre au vingtième siècle'

for it. If their evil disposition remains concealed for a time, it must be attributed to some unknown reason; and we must assume that it lacked occasion to show itself; but time, which has been said to be the father of all truth, does not fail to bring it to light.

This was written about 1512, a few years before the first publication of Sir Thomas More's *Utopia*. And although More, like all Utopians, starts with assuming that all men are saints or at least will be as soon as they become converted to More's views, we find everywhere hints that More and his Utopian colleagues knew very well what Machiavelli meant. No Utopian would ever break the laws of Utopia, but if he did, punishment would be swift and horrible. More does not mention what happens to the ungrateful louts who fail to see the light and love the country of Utopia; most probably they were killed at sight. The Greek philosopher Plato, in *The Republic*, his description of a Utopia where all the people would be treated like cattle and only Greek philosophers would have any freedom of thought and speech, suggests that it would be best to murder all potential dissenters, preferably while still in the cradle. This is something that is understood by all Utopians, and the yearning for a docile people thinking only the right thoughts has led to some

curious Utopias.

Slightly more than one century after *Utopia*, Francis Bacon wrote *The New Atlantis* (1672), a work clearly inspired by Plato. Here, the narrator's ship is blown off course during a journey from Peru to China and comes to an unknown island in the South Pacific, whose inhabitants live in a kind of enlightened monarchy. They have submarines, airplanes, microphones, air conditioning and large research centres, in all, all the paraphernalia of the Victorian scientific romances. About the same time as *The New Atlantis*, the Italian Dominican monk Tommaso Campanella wrote the Utopian novel *La città del sole* (The City of the Sun), in many respects the antithesis of Plato's *Republic*. This is also a socialist state, where the government takes care of everything, including the citizen's private life and the upbringing of the children. It is all very efficient and incredibly boring. Being a monk, Campanella may have found a lifetime in his creation refreshing—but we are not all monks.

The first really modern Utopias appeared with the early industrial revolution—when the French revolution, which had appeared to promise so much but had given so little, became the gateway to a new world, more cruel than the old one. One of the most interesting of the new Utopians, the French socialist Charles Fourier, published a large work entitled *Théorie des quatres mouvements* (1808), describing a new society somewhat resembling Campanella's *La città del sole*, with some parts of More's *Utopia* thrown in for good measure.

Above: Paris air traffic in 1952, from 'Le vingtième siècle'
Left: Notre Dame, Paris, converted into an airbus station—from 'Le vingtième siècle'
Right: Norwegian anthology of horror

Fourier envisaged many thousand 'phalanges', socialist groups of up to 2,000 people living in large buildings, 'phalansteries', with central kitchens, schools, gymnasiums, nurseries and so on. The idea did not catch on—a few small phalanges were actually founded but were not very successful. The same goes for most of the many communist societies that appeared in the United States in the early nineteenth century—the Economists, the Zoarites, the Amana, the Icarians and many others. Most of them died out quickly, when it became evident that Utopia is in fact not a good place to live in, while others, like the Amish, are dying slowly but surely, still stubbornly clinging to the ways of a world that passed more than a hundred years ago. One of the best-known of these communist Utopias, the Shakers, is now all but dead, with only about ten members still alive. Perhaps the most interesting of all New World Utopias actually put into practice, the New Harmony Movement founded by Robert Owen in Indiana in 1825, 'to introduce an entire new system of society; to change it from an ignorant, selfish system to an enlightened social system which shall gradually unite all interests into one, and remove all causes for contest between individuals,' failed, despite great enthusiasm, within five years.

The late Victorian era was the scene of an unparalleled technical and scientific development which in a few decades completely changed the Western world. From

Nattjegere

En antologi over vampyrer og varulver.
Redaksjon og etterord ved
Peter Haars og Per G. Olsen.

Spirale

SCIENCE FICTION-FANTASTIQUE

aout-sept. N°5 -Prix:

HENNEBERG
LEM
MODZ
MURCIE
VIGIL

1

ANNO I
APRILE '76
L. 700

Sped. abb. post. Gr. 3/70

ROBOT

RIVISTA DI FANTASCIENZA

In questo numero:
racconti di

**Fritz Leiber
Damon Knight
Thomas Disch
Harry Harrison**

**Intervista con
Harlan Ellison**

**Ritratto di
Fritz Leiber**

Buck Rogers

Monster Movies

**I temi classici
della SF**

**SF e letteratura
popolare**

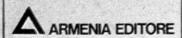ARMENIA EDITORE

Above: Italian SF magazine 'Robot'

Left: French SF magazine 'Spirale'

Above: Swedish SF magazine 'Vetenskapen och Livet'

Right: Electricity conquers all—from Robida's 'La vie électrique'

1870 appeared many of the inventions that have formed our present world—petrol and battery-powered cars, streamlined trains, heavier than air airplanes, wireless telegraphy, electric bulbs, wireless telephoto, cinematography, television, telephone, wire recorder and phonograph. Telegraph cables crossed Atlantic, the Curies achieved their epoch-making discoveries of the properties of radioactive materials. This was Jules Verne's century, a time of unbridled optimism while the shadows thickened so imperceptibly that few appeared to notice them. This fairyland lasted until 1912, when the greatest achievement of the machine age, the unsinkable passenger liner *Titanic*, collided with an iceberg and sank. Two years later, World War I broke out. The dream of the machine fairyland was shattered.

It was inevitable that this period should give birth to a veritable flood of enthusiastic Utopian tales where the dawning new era was extolled in confident terms. Jules Verne was the foremost soloist in this choir, but behind him stood thousands of lesser talents who described the probable future to the best of their abilities. In the same way as explorers and missionaries explored the white spots on the map, these authors explored, according to their individual tastes and abilities, the states and worlds that one day might be a part of the White Man's Burden. In the industrialized countries, England, France, Germany and, later on America, science fiction was published on a scale that remained unsurpassed until World War II.

Probably the most fantastic of all these innumerable works were two books by the celebrated French painter and lithographer Albert Robida (1848–1926), *Le vingtième siècle* (The Twentieth Century, 1882) and *La vie électrique* (The Electric Life, 1891–92), telling about the life in the 1950s with television, space flight, revolutions, incredible wars (and the proud display of unusual war machines at the great World Fairs), women's liberation and so on. The text in these books is far from spectacular—Robida was an illustrator, not an author—but the illustrations are incomparable, describing with sardonic wit and humour the wonders of the twentieth century in a way that no one either before or after has managed to surpass. These two books are an unusual mixture of Utopianism and anti-Utopianism, the future regarded with a laugh as it were, showing in exquisite detail the old world swept away by modern technology, the worldwide pollution from the wondrous factories, the chemical and bacteriological warfare, the radio correspondents treating the paying public to all the gory sights of the battlefields, the spectacle of young girls being auctioned off to lecherous old men, the architecture of an age where everything can fly, including houses, churches and pet dogs. His forecasting took on a more sinister tone with the publication of *La guerre au vingtième siècle* (War in the Twentieth Century) in 1883, in his magazine *La Caricature*, later expanded into a book with text and illustrations, in 1887, and these grim pictures from the kind of total war that later would be all too familiar are still eminently horrifying, even for a generation that has been living in the shadow of nuclear war. This was certainly no Utopian work. The other two were, though, and remain the best examples of the *fin de siècle* view of the future, executed with much charm by a man who didn't really trust the future at all.

Nowhere, however, and at no time, has the Utopian

Above: Robert Owen's proposed Utopian 'New Harmony' city (1825)
Right: May Day demonstrations in the future—drawing by Oscar Andersson

tale been more popular than in Russia during this time and immediately after the Revolution. Utopian novels and short stories were written and published by the hundreds. And for good reasons, I would imagine. Russia was at this time trying to create a modern Utopia, seemingly straight out of the pages of Edward Bellamy's *Looking Backward* or Thomas More's *Utopia*, and books about this happy event poured out in millions throughout Russia. The Russian Futurists, with authors and poets like Vladimir Mayakovskiy at their head, wrote magnificent Utopian novels and plays, and the Futurist architects created architectural wonders that still remain unsurpassed. This was science fiction and Utopias coming true—for a while. As the Soviet science fiction expert Boris Lyapunov points out, in his excellent survey of Soviet science fiction, *V mire fantastiki* (In the World of Science Fiction, 1975):
During the years when the Soviet regime was created, the pathos of revolutionary struggle was the fundamental

theme of our young literature. This was also the case with science fiction. The fights on the fronts of the civil war had not yet ceased, and the peaceful work of reconstruction had not yet been started, but science fiction authors already dreamt of a better future, of the coming victories of science and research, and they propagandized for scientific knowledge with artistic means. (. . .) At this time, social Utopias also began to appear, carrying on the tradition of Russian Utopian novels under the new order of things. As time went by they became more and more filled with concrete and variegated technical-scientific contents, painting more full-bodied pictures of the future. These works are characterized by an endeavour to picture the perfect society as the true end of the Revolution, although characterized by a certain fragmentary and schematic form (. . .) and an over-simplified understanding of social problems.

This, of course, goes for almost all Utopian tales and might be the fundamental reason why Utopias never can work when put into practice. Utopia is perfect; Man is not. Not even Communism managed to create Utopia—or, to quote Comrade Leonid Ilyich Brezhnev at the 25th Congress of the CPSU: 'We have not yet attained communism.' Vladimir Mayakovskiy soon realized this, and criticized the Utopian Socialistic world in his famous anti-Utopian plays *Banya* (The Bath House, 1939) and *Klop* (The Bedbug, 1929). Mayakovskiy's progress, from the enthusiastic revolutionary and director of propaganda who wrote the revolutionary poem *150,000,000* (1920—the title refers to the Russian population) to the disillusioned anti-Utopian, is a much too long and complicated story to tell in this brief survey of science fiction, and especially in a chapter dealing with the antithesis of Mayakovskiy's most celebrated works. It is enough to point out that Mayakovskiy, probably the most brilliant of a whole generation of brilliant revolutionary poets, finally turned away in disgust from Utopia. As, indeed, all intellectuals have done, sooner or later.

There is an interesting parallel here with the Chinese author Lao She (Shu She–yü), who in 1932 wrote an outstanding anti-Utopian novel, *Mao ch'eng chi* (Memoirs from Cat Country), an attack against the very ideal Mayakovskiy and other Futurists had once presented as the ideals of Mankind. *Memoirs from Cat Country* is a vitriolic dystopian novel about the first expedition to Mars (made by Chinese scientists), who find that the Martians are a degenerate people, drugged by narcotics and constantly trying to enrich themselves at the expense of others. When they are attacked by another country, the soldiers accept bribes from the enemy and flee, victims of a monumental egotism that places their own survival above everything else. The novel is a classic and has lately endeared the author to Soviet authorities who have been using it in their current cold war with China. Chinese authorities are understandably less enthusiastic about it, and the novel has not been published in China since the Revolution. Lao She was, notwithstanding, a leading person in China after the Revolution (he lived for some years in America but returned to China after the Revolution), member of the People's Assembly, vice-chairman of the Chinese writers' association and editor of the powerful magazine *Beitszin Venji*. He died in 1966, at the age of 67, and a recent Soviet edition of this novel, in the celebrated *Contemporary SF Library*, happily points out that Lao She was probably murdered during

the Cultural Revolution. Be that as it may, the novel has been published in numerous editions in the Soviet Union, less, I fear, for its obvious literary qualities than for its value as a weapon against the Chinese version of Communist Utopianism.

Returning to the Revolutionary zeal of Soviet science fiction, however, we should not forget Vladimir Odoyevskiy, the founding father of Russian science fiction, who in 1840 published parts of his novel *4338-oy god. Petersburgskiye pis'ma* (Year 4338. Letters from St Petersburg), a scientific Utopia of the type which Edward Bellamy and H. G. Wells later on would write, including all the time-honoured paraphernalia of modern Utopias: gigantic transport roads, electric trains, air ships, plastics, artificial food, telephone and television. This is Power indeed over man and nature, as shown in the finale when the scientists successfully disintegrate a comet that threatens to collide with Earth. Odoyevskiy's novel may have been the first to realize the impact of cheap, abundant energy on civilization and our world, which alone makes the novel interesting. (Jules Verne did it all over again later on, as did H. G. Wells, André Laurie and Kurd Lasswitz, but Verne was only twelve when the novel was published, and the other three were not even born). Odoyevskiy was the first author who realized, however vaguely, to what extent modern science would change the world, and why these changes were inevitable. In a sense, his work was the only true Utopian novel of that century, and certainly the only one which foresaw

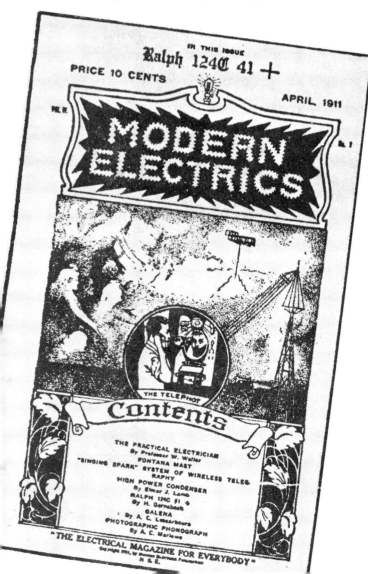

what would actually happen. He did not, however, foresee Communism in Russia; instead he predicted a harsh totalitarian government, which has made some recent Soviet science fiction scholars less than happy with him.

If Odoyevskiy's novel is of great interest for the science fiction scholar, Nikolai Chernyshevskiy's novel *Chto delat'?* (What is to be done?) is of considerably more interest in writing of Utopias as powerful images of a possible future. Written in 1862 and smuggled out of prison, it was not officially published in the Soviet Union until after the 1905 Revolution—but it was widely disseminated, everyone read it, and would-be revolutionaries used it for underground education until the October Revolution. Its massive impact can be compared to that of Edward Bellamy's *Looking Backward*—but it had a much more profound effect in Tzarist Russia than Bellamy's novel ever had in laissez-faire England and America. Chernyshevskiy envisaged a future Communist Utopia, somewhat reminiscent of Fourier's communal Utopia with its productive collectives (phalanges). In this novel, cheap and abundant energy also led to the new social order, to a Communism more like present-day Cambodia's than the Russian Soviets. What the protagonist of the novel, Vera Pavlovna, saw in her famous fourth dream of this beloved Soviet science fiction classic was the dream of the perfect socialist society, with inhabitants as perfect as the world in which they lived. The machine would make Mankind free to pursue Utopian goals. An interesting point is that Chernyshevskiy also realized that women must be totally liberated in order to pursue that goal. This was in sharp contrast to other Utopias of the time, where women were regarded as some sort of cattle to be kept at home and out of sight while the men performed their heroics among the Utopian machinery.

I am restricting myself to political and sociological Utopias as far as the Soviet Union is concerned, since these alone appear to be of some interest in relation to the tumultuous times in which they were written. We have too many machine-oriented Utopias everywhere else and, indeed, also in the Soviet Union, where the flood of political Utopias turned into a raging deluge after the October Revolution. Very little is readable today; Edward Bellamy's *Looking Backward* is as good an example as any of this sort of gadget Utopian tale. Combining Charles Fourier's production collectives with Robert Owen's dream of a more perfect world based upon machine productivity, and the classic Utopianism of Sir Thomas More, they created uniformly boring Schlaraffenlands of the type that later was to erect a mouldering mausoleum over itself in the form of the American publisher and editor Hugo Gernsback's pitiable Utopian novel *Ralph 124C41+* (1911), in which the intrepid editor-cum-author managed to take away all the sociological, political and intelligent parts and substitute them with machines and monsters without end. If you have read *Looking Backward,* you have read ninety per cent of all the classic Utopias. If you have read *Ralph 124C41+,* you have read the worst and most unforgivable parts of them.

Let us not waste time with all this. It is sufficient to say that in numbers alone the Soviet Union has produced more Utopian novels over the past hundred years or so than any other country in the world. (I have heard

Left: Cover of 'Modern Electrics' which featured the first instalment of Gernsback's 'Ralph 124C41+', perhaps the worst example of Utopianism yet written
Above: Russian Futurist author Vladimir Mayakovskiy

written before this one, novels that contained all the modern wonders the World Fairs displayed before an awed public, but whereas earlier mechanical Utopias in practice were nothing but catalogues of forthcoming miracles, Bellamy described his Utopia as the end result of an industrial and moral socialist revolution, an evolution that affected not only the machinery.

Looking Backward was in all respects the right book at the right time. It was first published in 1888, when the workers were organizing themselves against their employers, when the stratification of society had led to two irreconcilable groups of rich and poor, of sweaters and sweated, who prepared themselves for a seemingly inevitable clash. Bellamy's book gave voice to the hopes and dreams of a whole class; it promised a way out from Hell, and its success was as might be expected. *Looking Backward* was one of the most widely read books around the turn of the century, published in many millions of copies in more than twenty languages throughout the world. (It is still a bestseller in the United States. A current paperback edition has seen eleven printings since 1960.) An even better proof of the cogency of the novel is the flood of similar Utopian novels that immediately deluged the market, advocating other social systems, attacking Bellamy's socialism or just trying to make money while the market was good. Titles such as *Looking Forward, Looking Beyond, Looking Ahead, Looking Further Backward, Looking Within* and *Looking Backward And What I Saw* tell much about where these enthusiastic authors got their inspiration. Between 1889 and 1900 forty-six such Utopian novels were published in the United States alone, and an unknown number in other countries. Even H. G. Wells was swept along by the mounting excitement and wrote in 1889 the novel *When the Sleeper Wakes*, in which the protagonist, in imitation of Bellamy's hero, sleeps into the future, but unlike his precursor finds himself owning the entire world. Everything is now ruled in his name by a council which finally, after much cloak-and-dagger intrigue and lofty rhetoric, is crushed, after which the true Utopia can begin. In the States, Bellamy's book is even considered one of the most influential books of the century, overshadowed only by Karl Marx' *Das Kapital*.

And what is Bellamy's version of Utopia? Generalizing somewhat, one can say it is More's *Utopia* plus electricity; large parts of Bellamy's ideal state are stolen virtually unchanged from More's work, for example the distribution of goods and the socialist system, the latter in Bellamy's case strengthened by the neat trick of making every citizen a private in the Worker's Army, complete with all the traditional military paraphernalia. The leaders of Bellamy's ideal state are all Colonels and other nice people. More, on the other hand, went farther than Bellamy with public ownership, and while More's Utopia was a hideous patriarchal state, women in Bellamy's future actually have some kind of intrinsic value (though they cannot become Colonels). Otherwise, Bellamy's Utopia is filled to bursting point with all the usual Victorian future props; airplanes, motorcars, radio, moving sidewalks and so on. His citizens own not only the necessities of life, but also its abundance, even though they do not share the happiness of More's citizens in owning chamber-pots of pure gold. Bellamy is more detailed than More in his description of his fairyland, and the novel is also more literary, particularly in its introduction of a

rumours of enormous numbers of Utopian tales being published in China after the 1949 Revolution, but so far I have not seen a single one of these works and thus prefer, at least for the time being, to take the information with a pinch of salt.) I wish Soviet Utopias were better than those produced in less enlightened countries. They were not. Gone is the mercurial Vladimir Mayakovskiy who celebrated the victorious Revolution with his grandiose Utopian pageant, *Misteriya-buff* (Mystery-Buffo, 1918), in which the working classes get rid of their masters and finally attain the Utopian paradise. Instead we get battalions of iron-grey Utopian Commissars with their heads filled with cogwheels, dynamos and new ways of increasing production.

The great modern classic in Utopian literature was, however, written by a man who never before or since touched upon science fiction: *Looking Backward 2000–1887* by Edward Bellamy, a fantastic story describing in minute (and boring) detail a socialist paradise of the year 2000. It is without question the most important Utopian work in the Western world since More's *Utopia,* and also the first truly modern Utopian work of the West, since Bellamy realized that Utopia does not belong to our time but in the future. Many Utopian novels had been

rather silly love story between the hero and the beautiful Utopian woman Edith Leete, a young lady with soft blue eyes and stainless steel morals. (The morals are always strong in Utopian novels.) They listen together to orchestral music in the evenings and regard each other with heated eyes while the electric moon of the modern Utopia benevolently shines down upon them.

Bellamy's Utopia, like all others, is based upon one fundamental assumption: than no one will want more than his own share, which is partly why these ideal states seem so incredibly naive. We all know that most people are not only far from content with only their own share, but are also quite willing to steal everyone else's share as well, and this is why Utopia can never work. In More's and Bellamy's Utopias, everything is owned in common, and if a citizen needs anything he has only to walk to the nearest warehouse and take whatever he happens to need. Everybody is equal—almost. More's Utopia rests upon the collective working power of an abundance of slaves, and Bellamy's rests upon machines. but slaves are not that plentiful any more, nor is cheap energy. H. G. Wells may have realized this, since his second Utopian novel, *A Modern Utopia* (1905), describes a modern welfare state governed by a rational elite called *Samurai*, and the result is a world ruled by efficiency, proving, as many of Wells's subsequent works did, that he had no fondness for socialism in its classic sense, or even for democracy. This message is also brought forth in two later works, *Men Like Gods* (1923) and *The Shape of Things to Come* (1933), in which scientific progress and evolutionary processes, whose end results are so gloomily predicted in his early works, are held forth as the bases for desirable brave new worlds, strange as it may seem when one knows that Wells once was an active member of the British Fabian Society, a socialist movement. In these novels, Wells suddenly returns to the time-honoured system proposed by, among others, Francis Bacon in *The New Atlantis* and Plato in *The Republic*: a meritocracy with Science (of Philosophy) as an obedient servant standing behind the Masters. It is Utopia in all respects, chemically free of everything that possibly could make life worth living.

I am happy to say, though, that science fiction is now slowly recovering lost ground, and the best example of the traditional Utopia described in terms of modern sociology is no doubt the American author Ursula K. LeGuin's award-winning novel *The Dispossessed* (1975), an 'ambiguous Utopia' (to borrow the author's own subtitle), in which two apparent Utopias, a Capitalist one called Urras, and a Communist one called Annares, confront each other. Urras is rich and slightly decadent, Annares is poor, strict and tough, a small moon of Urras to which the socialist minority of that planet once emigrated in order to create their own Utopia. The novel is interesting in many ways, particularly since LeGuin realizes that Utopia is unattainable and both these Utopias bear within themselves the seeds of destruction. Urras becomes too weak and decadent, whereas the Communism of Annares becomes more and more rigid. LeGuin also realizes that any society is inhabited by human beings, with all their faults, and even though she occasionally falls into the usual Utopian trap of preaching through the protagonist of the novel, the scientist

Shevek who embodies the best of these two worlds, this novel is certainly among the best and most mature modern Utopias in the traditional style.

LeGuin is sermonizing, of course, as all true Utopians are. Few authors have the courage or the audacity to regard Utopia as something natural, as we would regard our own twentieth-century world (certainly a Utopian paradise for a nineteenth-century factory worker). A favourite of mine in this context, that manages to treat Utopia as something completely natural while still retaining the ambiguity of the Utopian dream, is a recent novel by a British newcomer to the science fiction field, Tanith Lee's *Don't Bite the Sun* (1976), describing an adolescent girl searching for identity in a mad, mad world where only the improbable is normal, where even life and death are outmoded concepts, where Mankind has attained everything it has ever strived' for. Make-believe work is available for those who want it; bodies can be changed at will; if you die you are revived. Nothing, literally *nothing*, is impossible. By concentrating not on the society, as any tranditional Utopian writer would have done, but on its effects on the girl of the story, Tanith Lee has created what might be the first really convincing description of a true Utopia, dwelling less on the Utopian hardware than on the inner world of a lost and bewildered child. It is very much a story about our own world and age, as all good Utopias are in the end, but here it is better executed than usual.

The other side of the Utopian coin is shown by Robert Sheckley in a short story, *The Store Of the Worlds* (1959), describing with chilling plausibility the true Utopia. It turns out to be what we would call a very, very ordinary life with the usual amount of small, unimportant annoyances, an uneventful life peacefully moving on towards old age and ultimate death, without the protagonist ever realizing that he is living in Utopia.

Somewhat similar in theme, if not in scope, is a recent novel by the British sf author Bob Shaw, *Orbitsville* (1975), in which Man's expansion in space is halted by a gigantic Dyson sphere (in this case a sphere with a diameter equivalent to Earth's orbit around the sun, the inner shell of which is inhabitable), the equivalent of billions of virgin worlds eminently suitable for Man, offering Mankind unlimited food and life space. The eternal and changeless savannahs of Orbitsville give Mankind the Utopia of invariability, an eternal stability, Nirvana at last.

The most unusual of the modern Utopias is undoubtedly the Argentine author Jorge Louis Borges's story *Tlön, Uqbar, Orbis Tertius* (1940). Borges belongs to the same avant-garde group in fantastic literature as Julio Cortazar, Raymond Roussel, Boris Vian, Alfred Jarry and Robert Sheckley, and his Utopia is, consequently, quite different from the usual ones. In 1936, Borges wrote:
I suspect that a general scrutiny of fantastic literature would reveal that it is not very fantastic. I have visited many Utopias—from the eponymous one of More to Brave New World—and I have not yet found a single one that exceeds the cozy limits of satire or sermon and describes in detail an imaginary country, with its geography, its history, its religion, its language, its literature, its music, its government, its metaphysical and theological controversy . . . its encyclopedia, in short; all of it organically coherent, of course, and (I know I'm very demanding) with no reference whatsoever to the horrible injustices suffered by Captain

Modern Utopia, US style. Frank R. Paul's illustration in 'Amazing Stories Quarterly', Winter 1928

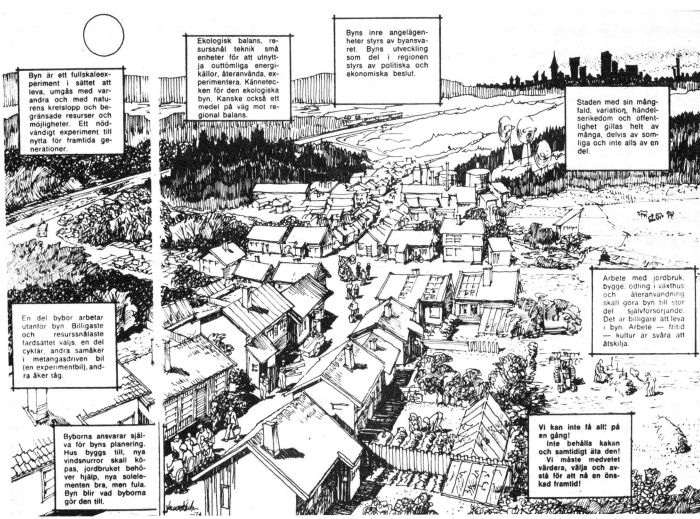

Above: Village-type Utopia, one of the latest crazes in the industrialized world—from Swedish magazine 'Vi'

Right: City of the future, of the type envisaged by Owen and Fourier more than a century before

Far right: Konrad Lehtimäki (1883–1937), known chiefly for his novel 'Ylös helvetistä' ('Up from Hell'), 1917

Alfred Dreyfus.

Borges' Utopia is certainly different. In the story, he first comes across it in a pirated edition of *Encyclopaedia Britannica*, where he finds an entry on a supposed country in Asia Minor called Uqbar. The entry mentions that the epics and legends of Uqbar never refer to reality but to the imaginary regions of Mlejnas and Tlön. Borges then finds an encyclopedia of Tlön, giving some strange information about what is said to be an entire planet, and in the story he proceeds to explain this strange Utopia, surely one that would have delighted Alfred Jarry or Raymond Roussel. Whereas our common concept of reality is materialistic, Tlön's philosophy teaches that the only realities are mental perceptions. In Tlön, objects multiply by thought and vanish when they are forgotten. It is a world somewhat reminiscent of Boris Vian's *L'écume des jours* (1947), where all emotions are materialized and forcibly change the outer world. (When the protagonist is unhappy it starts to rain, flowers wither and die, volcanoes spew out fire, the air turns grey and thick with sorrow around him.) Tlön is a Utopia where Berkeleyan idealism is victorious, where mind triumphs over matter—in sharp contrast to traditional Utopias,

where Mankind always ends up as a small cog in the great Utopian machinery. Borges understands, as does Robert Sheckley in his recent novel *Options*, that reality is taking place within the brain of the observer, not outside him. Reality is what he thinks is reality, no more, no less. In Tlön, inner and outer space are the same thing. He ends the story by gleefully pointing out that Tlön is starting to intrude on our own world. Strange objects from Tlön are found, our orderly man-made conception of the universe is breaking up, our very memories are replaced by others. Utopia is coming, and it is of a kind that none ever dreamt of.

The best known present-day Utopia is, of course, J. R. R. Tolkien's epic trilogy *The Lord of the Rings* (1954–55) which has by now sold millions of copies, creating a genuine sub-culture of its own which describes this fairyland Utopia in minute detail through records, posters, fan magazines, clubs, films and so on. As an Utopia Tolkien's world is strictly traditional and pre-industrialized, Arcadia all over again, a fitting opiate for a generation born and raised in the polluted industrial cities of our age. It is based directly on Anglo-Saxon and Nordic mythology, with Midgard (Middle Earth) as the centre of the world. In this Midgard live the small, peace-loving, pipe-smoking and tea-drinking Hobbits in their cozy dens amid elves, trolls, dragons, white and black magicians and all the other standard attributes of the fairy tale. The mythology is painstakingly constructed (Tolkien was the author of a number of scholarly works on Nordic and Old English literature) and above everything hovers a gossamer veil of nostalgia, goodness and the victory of justice and righteousness over all evil forces.

This means that Tolkien's books are rather conservative in their outlook, more so that most Utopias. Tolkien's Midgard is in many ways not so much a creation of unbridled imagination as a conservative man's Utopia, where an old white-haired philologist can expect to study to his heart's content without being disturbed by the coarse populace and their annoying cries of justice, food, freedom, human rights and other trivialities.

Utopia is wish-fulfilment, or course, and science fiction in general has carefully steered away from it during the past thirty or forty years—with the notable exception of Tolkien's celebrated trilogy. One of the last undiluted Utopian novels, James Hilton's *Lost Horizon*, was first published in 1933, and described a valley paradise in Tibet, called Shangri-La. It is very naive and contains nothing but a longing to escape from everything. It has been reprinted innumerable times and has recently been made into a movie for the second time, which I find somewhat disquieting. For if pure, undiluted escapism is that popular, as attested by Tolkien and Hilton, it must certainly suggest that something must be seriously wrong with our society. A lot of evidence appears to point to that, especially the fact that people who can afford it now are moving out from the cities in increasing numbers, creating their own small Utopian communities that, they hope, will be self-sufficient. The affluent and the hippies can do this, since the cities and the factories and millions of workers stay behind to support them. Reading about these Utopian villages with their balanced ecology, their communal meetings and their joint ownership of almost everything, it seems that the Utopian wheel has turned full circle and the present-day Utopians are back to the early nineteenth-century Utopians again. Ecological balance is certainly good, as is communal spirit, low-energy transportation and all the rest; but, like More's Utopian citizens, these idealists appears to have forgotten the one thing that makes Utopia an impossibility. Reading the detailed descriptions of the various ideal communities now planned, I remember Chesterton's words:

The weakness of all Utopias is this, that they take the greatest difficulty of man and assume it to be overcome, and then give an elaborate account of the overcoming of the smaller ones. They first assume that no man will want more than his share, and then are very ingenious in explaining whether his share will be delivered by motorcar or balloon.

NIGHTMARES

Utopia is what is good for others. Dystopia, or anti-Utopia, is what others (erroneously) think is good for you. You are, of course, always the sole judge of what is what, which is why so many science fiction works can be Utopian for one reader and the opposite for another. The word 'Utopia' means literally 'No place', and 'Dystopia' might be translated as 'Bad place.' Utopia is really the dream of unlimited power over Man and Nature, with this power used to ends acceptable to you. Dystopia is some fool using these powers in another way. This makes the Dystopian tale useful for political pamphlets, and it has indeed been used as such with great success, both East and West. In the West, where most science fiction authors still struggle within the rigid framework of the science fiction ghetto, targets for Dystopian works are habitually very vague—overpopulation, the computerization of society, pollution, advertising—and authors appear consciously to avoid criticizing government practices which stand in sharp contrast to Europe, particularly in countries with a less than perfect democracy in our sense of the word, such as Soviet Union, Spain or Turkey. It is significant that even during the McCarthy witchhunt in the United States during the 1950s, when almost every outspoken intellectual was dragged before the House Committee of Un-American Activities, no single science fiction author was ever subject to scrutiny by that remarkable organization—of course, since North American science fiction authors never really seriously questioned the (North) American Way of Life. South American science fiction is more tough, attacking topical problems in a way that would be unthinkable in the north. It is also significant that the only science fiction attack against former President Richard M. Nixon was launched not by an acknowledged science fiction author, but by an outsider to the field, Philip Roth, with the magnificent novel *Our Gang* (1971), certainly the most furious attack on a head of state ever made in a science fiction disguise.

British and American science fiction authors of today were reared in pulp magazine tradition, a heritage difficult to shake off. Pulp magazines were exported to Europe, together with the science fiction ghetto, after World War II along with other goodies of the Marshall plan, and Germany in particular has suffered from these—there is practically no Dystopian science fiction being written there now, only way-out space opera stuff with broad-shouldered heroes fighting obnoxious aliens richly endowed with tentacles. (In all fairness, though, it should be pointed out that political dissenters are not very popular in Germany, authors of literary works advocating unpopular political views can be jailed, and we all know about the infamous German Berufsverbot laws. This does not encourage Dystopian criticism.) Eastern Europe is now producing some of the best Dystopian works ever written. Leading Soviet authors within

the genre include Andrey Sinyavskiy and Yuliy Daniel, and there are also leading science fiction satirists such as Ilya Varshavskiy, Anatoliy Dneprov and the Strugatskiy brothers who are writing biting *Roman preduprezhdeniye,* or 'warning novels', the likes of which we haven't seen in the West since Frederik Pohl's and C. M. Kornbluth's *The Space Merchants* and *Gladiator-at-Law.* Sinyavskiy and Daniel wrote so scathingly and well that they were caught by the KGB and sentenced to hard labour for slander and vilification of the Soviet regime. However, that happened ten years ago, and Soviet satirists in the science fiction field today do not appear to have any troubles with the authorities. With so much Dystopian science fiction now not only being written but also published in Eastern Europe, it would appear that these Dystopias are at least tolerated, if not exactly encouraged, by the authorities. I understand that a few decidedly unprintable Dystopian science fiction novels are cur-

Left: **Laissez-faire Dystopia on Mars—everything owned by B. Gosh & Co.**
Above: **Machine Dystopia—illustration by L. Benett for Verne's 'Les cinq cent millions de la Begum' (1879)**

Morlocks herd elois to slaughter—from a 1960 film of H. G. Wells's 'The Time Machine'

rently circulating within the Soviet Union in *samizdat* (typewritten carbon copies).

Every age exorcises its own evils through literature, particularly through science fiction, and while present-day apocalyptic visions very seldom deal with something like the Yellow Peril, we have other themes that crop up more and more frequently. Just like Dracula, Frankenstein's monster and others reared their ugly heads in the United States during the Depression, groaning under the weight of more or less outspoken symbolism, and the German science fiction films of the Weimar Republic era shouted out its message of catastrophe and bloody change, today has more than its share of visions of impending catastrophes through our own misuses of ecological systems or nuclear power. I won't go into this particular aspect of the Dystopian vision, except to observe that the current over-abundance of catastrophe books, catastrophe films and catastrophe comics plainly indicates the fears of writers, film directors and artists, as well as the public, since catastrophe tales are invariably great moneymakers as well. The most celebrated of all catastrophe novels, the leading Japanese science fiction author Sakyo Komatsu's brilliant *Nippon Chinbotsu* (Japan Sinks, 1973), sold four million copies in Japan alone, and has since then been translated into scores of other languages. It has also been filmed in all its gory detail, showing exactly how Japan sinks completely in the sea, partly owing to Man's own misuse of his world. This is the greatest of all modern bestsellers in science fiction, which confirms my opinion that we are all suckers for eco-pornography.

That even the perfect Utopia is somewhat less that desirable was pointed out as early as 1741 by the Danish dramatist and author Ludvig Holberg in his novel *Nicolai Klimii Iter Subterraneum*. Perfect harmony is not only unattainable for human beings, he finds, it is not even desirable. In the novel, Niels Klim comes to a country called Nakir, the Sensible Country, the acme of perfection. All the inhabitants are astute and shrewd, serious, moral and self-sacrificing, a race of true Utopians in all respects. But the first enthusiasm is soon replaced by the realization that Nakir is dull and indifferent, its inhabitants phlegmatic and soulless. The country is simply sick, he observes, due to its lack of fools. 'I admit', sighs Niels Klim, 'that foolishness is a fault, but it does not seem to me to be very sensible to eradicate it completely from the country.' He comes to the painful conclusion that in a well organized community at least half of the inhabitants must be fools.

The Russian poet and Futurist Vladimir Mayakovskiy later made the same observation in his play *Klop* (The Bedbug, 1929), the story of the worker Pierre Skripkin Prisipkin whose marriage celebration turns into a free-for-all brawl during which most of the guests die and Prisipkin is frozen into a block of ice in the cellar. He is discovered in 1979 and is let loose in the perfect Communist Utopia. Unable to cope with this inhuman perfection, he finally ends up as an exhibition in the local zoo where people watch with terrified fascination as he slowly drinks himself to death, the inevitable fate of a less than perfect human being in the perfect society.

Mayakovskiy was ultimately hounded to death by a

sterile and servile bureaucracy. His contemporary Yevgeniy Zamyatin suffered a similar fate, although he, thanks to superior connections with the Party, managed to get permission to leave the country. Zamyatin (1884–1937) was a leading Communist, one of the organizers of the famous rebellion aboard the armoured cruiser *Potemkin,* one of the crucial incidents during the October Revolution 1917. However, like Mayakovskiy he soon turned away from the direction the Revolution was taking, and in 1920 he wrote what is still one of the most horrifying Dystopian novels, *My* (We). Set in The Only State of the year 2500 it is a furious attack against collectivism and the dictatorship of technocracy, describing in minute and frightening detail a perfect Utopia where the inhabitants are deprived of all individuality and where attempts to break away can be punished by painful death at the hands of the ubiquitous secret police. Privacy is a crime against the state, it is even forbidden to pull the blinds down on the windows except during the carefully regulated procreation hours. Lovers are selected by the state, on genetic principles.

This sounds like an updated version of Plato's *The Republic* or Sir Thomas More's *Utopia.* How true. It is the traditional Utopia, but with the subtle difference that in this case the story is told not by an awestruck visitor from our own sorry time or by one of the rulers, but by one of the local inhabitants, the rocket engineer D-503, who has reasons to feel unenthusiastic about the setup. Suddenly we have a frightening Dystopia on our hands, a gigantic concentration camp where everything is regulated from cradle to grave, in the best Utopian tradition, where even the word 'I' is forbidden as being too reactionary and individualistic. 'Yesterday there was a Tzar and there were slaves,' Zamyatin wrote in 1919. 'Today there is no Tzar, but the slaves are still here. Tomorrow there will only be Tzars. We walk forward in the name of the free man of tomorrow, the Tzar of tomorrow. We have gone through the epoch when the masses were oppressed. We are now going through the epoch when the individual is oppressed in the name of the masses.'

As offshoots of sorts of this famous novel are several novels by an American advocate of unbridled laissez-faire capitalism and self-appointed crusades against altruism and self-sacrifice, the inventor of Objectivism, Mrs Ayn Rand. With an apparent ignorance of economics, sociology or politics, she has proceeded to outline her philosophy of selfishness in a number of books among which are at least two Dystopian novels. The earliest of these, *Anthem* (1938), is liberally borrowed from Yevgeniy Zamyatin's *My* and H. G. Wells's *The Shape of Things to Come,* with some crack-barrel philosophy for good measure in yet another of these badly thought out tales about the oppressed individual in an authoritarian society. Another, *Atlas Shrugged* (1957), is a 1168-page novel describing what would happen if we don't give industralists and millionaires more privileges.

There are of course thousands of Dystopias like those of Mrs Rand's books; the difference lies in the fact that she has had considerable success in the United States with her message of total selfishness. All of this goes to prove once again that Utopia is unattainable since Utopia demands unselfishness and altruism, something that at

The traditional fascist Dystopia—policemen hunt for prey in a 1955 film of Orwell's '1984'

least the many followers of Mrs Rand are not prepared to offer anyone.

Let us turn to something else.

There are several ways of designing an anti-Utopian world of horror and make it stick. The good old way, still useful it would appear, is the trusted secret police, the knock on the door at three o'clock in the morning, torture and execution. George Orwell, in his classic *1984* (1949) goes one step further, creating a 'Thought Police' to monitor disobedient ideas and television cameras to spy upon people's private lives. Very good, but also very inefficient. Aldous Huxley created what is still an unsurpassed Dystopia in *Brave New World* (1932), where people do not even realize that they are slaves; unlimited food, drink and sex keeps them happy, and an army of sub-humans, cloned from good working-men stock, keep the wheels rolling. It is a super-affluent anti-Utopia of the Western type, a bawdy, hedonistic one, and just as soulless as Orwell's Nazi-type prison camp. One excellent Dystopia of this type is Arkadiy and Boris Strugatskiy's novel *Khishchnye veshchi veka* (The Final Circle of Paradise, 1965) in which a do-gooder named Ivan Zhilin works as a secret agent for the United Nations Security Council in a 'Land of Fools' in Central Europe. The

motto of this happy country is 'The most important is not to think, but to enjoy', and this the good people do, especially with the Strugatskiy version of Huxley's happiness drug *Soma*, an electronic device called the *Drozhka* which makes the user completely and totally happy. Happy and obedient like so many sheep. Somewhere lurking in the background is also a band of 'Intels', bad guys who destroy the drozhkas whenever they can, arguing that they are changing people into mindless animals. The government does not mind, and instead does its best to kill off the Intels. The government succeeds, the Intels—the intellectuals—fail, as did Mr Savage in Huxley's novel.

Then someone invents an even better electronic device, the *Sleg*, which makes the user believe he has attained everything he ever wished for. Zhilin tries to rouse the population against this trick of a rotten government and fails miserably since everyone is too busy building his own sleg to pay any attention. Even Zhilin's colleagues turn into sleg slaves, happily dreaming themselves away into a world where everything they want comes true.

The Roman emperors offered their subjects 'bread and circuses' in order to keep them happy and away from poli-

Above: Arkadiy and Boris Strugatskiy
Right: Two recent covers of the Strugatskiys' books
Overleaf: The end of it all—from the Japanese film version of
Komatsu's best-selling catastrophe novel 'Japan Sinks' (1973)

tics. In the modern Dystopia they do it all with electronics.

Man has always had a deep-rooted urge to retreat into a make-believe world of simplified actions and emotions, as attested by television, films and sport events in our own Dystopian age. The Soviet Nobel Prize winner Aleksandr Solzhenitsyn has commented upon this in the play *Svet, kotoryy v tebe* (The Light within You) from 1973, set in a future Soviet run by science and a self-fulfilling dream of affluence. The protagonist, Alex, returns from nine years in prison to a society where biocybernetics—the possibility of governing the population by drugs—is rapidly doing away with human relations, making people more fit for a modern society. Actually, Solzhenitsyn is a tragic example of a would-be Utopian suffering in the hands of other Utopians. After his expulsion from the Soviet Union, Solzhenitsyn has created his own self-contained Utopia near Cavendish, Vermont, on a secluded 50-acre estate surrounded by a

barbed-wire fence and guarded by electric-eye devices and closed-circuit television. This is a true Utopia, or nightmare, into which no one is admitted. 'What do you want?' asks a disembodied voice when a visitor ventures too close. 'There is nobody to talk to. You can't come in.' This might be Solzhenitsyn's dream of the perfect Utopia, but I dare say the rest of us are quite happy to stay out of it.

Solzhenitsyn's closed world is hauntingly reminiscent of the British author E. M. Forster's classic short story *The Machine Stops* (1928), where all law-abiding citizens live in small hexagonal cells, living their pseudo-lives in front of the radio without ever venturing outdoors. The British journalist Michael Frayn has lately modernized this sort of existence somewhat in his novel *A Very Private Life* (1968), where the affluent part of humanity lives in self-contained worlds of its own, heavily guarded houses complete with all modern amenities. Food, drink and entertainment are piped in, waste is piped out into a barren outer world which is so polluted that no one could survive there very long. Even babies are made to order in factories somewhere.

Frayn has previously written a very funny Dystopian novel, *The Tin Men* (1965), where everything is computerized, even sex and the writing of pornography. And why not? Surely that would come if the moralists succeed in stealing all our emotions away from us.

The Norwegian writer Axel Jensen made one of the most pointed comments on this sort of future in his novel *Epp* (1965), set in a future home for old people, the modern 'automat pensioners', who are supposed to live quietly in their small cubicles, eat and drink according to the regulations and die without bothering anyone. Contact between the pensioners is frowned upon, and they spend much time dreaming up complicated schemes to cut up doors between the cubicles. This could be a comment on the current Utopian concept of family communities, now being set up in increasing numbers by bearded young men and dove-eyed young women as a way of Getting Away From It All. These modern Utopias are nothing more than the Very Private Lives of Michael Frayn in a more rustic overcoat, a way of keeping the mundane world out and the like-minded friends in, of course, and just as dependent upon the despised outer world as the guarded houses of Frayn's novel or Solzhenitsyn's reality. Today, debate in Sweden is much concerned with the question of 'life quality', meaning presumably joy in life and work. These Dystopian communities and societies would probably offer 'life quality' in ample measure, according to the current yardstick used by technocrats and revolutionaires alike—but would it be worth living?

This question is asked again and again in modern science fiction, with the rather obvious answer that it would not. The Finnish author Erkki Ahonen, one of the most unusual of the modern generation of Scandinavian writers, has dissected these fears in two notable novels, *Paikka nimeltä Plaston* (A Place Named Plaston, 1968) and *Tietokonelapsi* (The Computer Kid, 1972). In *Plaston* a young Finn is brought to the distant planet Plaston where the machines have created the perfect Utopia,

New York 1999. Transport for food-processing, from 'Soylent Green' (1973), the film of Harrison's 'Make Room! Make Room!'

93

reducing Man to a useless appendix, soon to be removed. In *Tietokonelapsi*, a child is raised by a computer. None of these futures are particularly pleasant.

A more subtle way of approaching Dystopia is of course through over-production, paradoxically an acute problem of the West in this very day and age despite the fact that the majority of the people on Earth are literally starving to death. The American authors Frederik Pohl and C. M. Kornbluth have commented upon this in several good novels and short stories, describing the corporation future awaiting us all in the future consumer society, with Frederik Pohl's *The Midas Plague* (1951) as an early and excellent example. Here, over-production has totally reversed all values of affluence and poverty, with the poor people forced to consume like mad while the affluent can afford to live simply. (This not very wide of the truth today although on a different scale.) The dilemma is finally solved by installing consumer circuits in the robots, making perfect, insvatiable consumers this way. A more recent example of this theme, though treated in a totally different way, is a short story by the Soviet author Boris Zubkov, *Etot neprochny, neprochny, neprochny mir* (This Transient, Transient, Transient World, 1966) in which all consumer goods have a planned obsolence and literally fall to pieces after a short time, forcing the consumer to buy more and more, thus keeping the wheels of production rolling. The story tells of a man who fearfully runs home through this consumer-oriented nightmare, past government controllers who make sure citizens do their duty and consume twenty-four hours a day, holding a piece of forbidden property clutched to his breast. A real stool, made of strong and durable wood . . .

Apart from obvious threats like the ones above, the spectre most often revived in present-day science fiction is that of over-population. Curiously enough, these fears are not expressed so much where they should be most rampant (in Northern Europe, which is the most over-populated part of the world) as in the United States. The theme of overpopulation is not new—one of the best examples can be found in a novel from 1928, *Aventurile domnului Ionel Lacustra-Termidor* (The Adventures of Mr Ionel Lacustra-Termidor) by the Romanian novelist Felix Aderca. He vividly describes the planet Earth in the year AD 8000, so over-populated that some of its inhabitants have settled 'in a species of bamboo cages spread like a network above the ocean between the continents'. It sounds bad, and it is, particularly when the wicked Norwegians drown them all to get more *lebensraum*.

Despite the warnings of the British political economist Thomas Malthus, who early in the nineteenth century predicted that the population would rise faster than the production of food, with catastrophic results, governments rather encouraged than discouraged larger families in a world that already had too manz mouths to feed. Science fiction authors in general seemed to be blissfully unaware of the problem. If they deigned to think aboutit,theyaplarently ttough it could be solved by emigration to other planets. The mounting problem was studied seriously first in the 1950s. The British chemist Harrison Brown then pointed out in his book *The Challenge To Man's Future* that:
There is a possibility that stabilization of population can be achieved, that war can be avoided, and that the resource transition can be successfully negotiated. In that event mankind will be confronted with a pattern which looms on the horizon of events as the second most likely possibility—the completely controlled, collectivized industrial society.

Aldous Huxley had described such a society in *Brave New World*, and this theme has been used over and over again, presenting the near future as a discreet dictatorship with the whip hidden somewhere behind the Coca Cola bottles and the population fooled into believing they are free. Huxley used drugs and sex to keep the people occupied; the mercurial American author Robert Sheckley goes one step further in his unusual novel *The Tenth Victim* (1966), where the governments organize legal hunts in which people of both sexes amuse themselves with playing big game hunters, killing each other in what surely must be the most nightmarish farce ever written in science fiction. The British author Mark Adlard promises even worse things in the novel *Volteface* (1972), in which automation has rendered the workers virtually useless and the working population is kept occupied with make-believe jobs. Real work is a rare privilege. The swarming billions live packed close together in small cells, dreaming away their lives in front of the television. Perhaps more plausible is American Author Harry Harrison's novel *Make Room! Make Room!* (1966), New York in the year 1999, unrelieved even by the few amenities of Mark Adlard's Dystopian vision; a world with too little space, too little money, too little work, too little food and too many people, where only the strongest survive and the weak starve and die. This is the total laissez-faire society, more believable than perhaps any other recent Dystopia, and therefore more frightening, because this world already exists in the poverty-stricken and overpopulated cities of the world, in Calcutta and Tokyo. What frightens us is that Harrison has placed it right here in the Western world, in New York. If the suffering of Indians does not touch us, that of the New Yorkers will.

However, no work of Dystopian science fiction succeeds in describing such a hauntingly and frightening, as well as probable, world of coming horrors as the series of short stories, commonly known as the Donomaga Cycle, by the late Soviet science fiction author Ilya Varshavskiy (1919–1973). Ilya Varshavskiy was probably the leading science fiction author in the Soviet Union and certainly among the two or three best in the world. Very few of his 80-odd short stories have been translated into other languages, alas, but he remains one of the most popular Soviet writers in this field. He was mainly a humorist in the O. Henry style, a brilliant satirist, as attested by his collection of short stories, *Chelovek, kotoryy videl antimir* (The Man who Saw the Anti-World) from 1965, a volume crammed with tongue-in-cheek stories about robots, bio-electronics, time travel paradoxes etc. The Donomaga stories are different—terrifying glimpses from the country Donomaga (which probably is understood to be one of the industrialized Capitalist countries, but just as well could be set in Chile or the Soviet we meet in Aleksandr Solzhenitsyn's books). Most of these stories are collected in the books *Solntse zakhodit v Donomage* (The Sun Goes down in Donomaga) from 1966, and *Lavka snovideniy* (The Dream Bench) and describe this imaginary, or perhaps not so imaginary, country where the rulers keep absolute control over science and finance, where people are subjected to inhuman experiments in biochemistry, where everything is regulated, where human feelings have been substituted by electronic

Ilya Varshavskiy, author of the most chilling modern Dystopian tales

Overleaf: Dystopia created by juvenile delinquents. Stanley Kubrick's film 'A Clockwork Orange' (1971), based on Anthony Burgess's novel of that name

devices monitored by the ruling elite and where everybody—except the rulers—has to conform to certain standards in all aspects of life. Varshavskiy describes monstrous experiments being done in the laboratories and prison camps of this country, and points out that the people of Donomaga are nothing more than guinea pigs for experiments that become more and more terrifying.

Stories similar to these have appeared in the United States (like Frederik Pohl's *Tunnel under the World*, and J. G. Ballard's brilliant short story *The Subliminal Man*), but no one has created a Dystopian world so rich in detail as Ilya Varshavskiy. It is even more frightening because too much of what he says is true, and more might be hidden beneath the heavy cloak of official secrecy in East and West. Varshavskiy tells us these stories are set in the Capitalist world; but they do of course tell us more about the fears of a Soviet intellectual in the Soviets than about the horrors of Capitalism, just as Frederik Pohl's and J. G. Ballard's horrifying stories about a Capitalist future ruled by Commercialism tells us more about the Western world than perhaps we want to know.

Let us stay with the Soviet version of the Dystopian society for a moment. Generally, modern Soviet science fiction authors tend to describe the Dystopian future as a harsh dictatorship of the Fascist junta type, with prison camps, secret police etc, somewhat like the Stalin era and the experiences too many Russians were subjected to during World War II—this in contrast to the prevalent Western attitude towards Dystopia as a consumer-orientated autocracy where the rulers are just as inhuman, but do their job with the aid of advertising bureaux and multi-national corporations rather than the kind of dictatorship we find in, for example, Chile. Since the Dystopian story always mirrors the fears and forebodings of the author's time and place, this is to be expected, of course, and the fact is that today we find a much more open and fruitful discussion of contemporary political and sociological trends, both East and West, in this type of science fiction than in almost any other kind of fiction. I might also point out that science fiction authors East and West appear to have very little trouble getting their stories through the official or unofficial censorship (with the exception, of course, of certain Latin American countries where all outspoken critics of the system either have fled their countries or gone into hiding or have been killed).

The leading Soviet science fiction authors today—and very probably the leading science fiction authors in the world—are the brothers Arkadiy and Boris Strugatskiy, incomparably witty and intelligent, but also quite Dystopian in their views on the world and the future facing us. Lately they have become more and more interested in the problem of Man's right to interfere with other civilizations in order to make them happier (or make them adhere to your own views on democracy or whatever), and these works, so very different from the prevalent Western attitude in science fiction of looking at aliens as either monsters or supermen to conquer and teach civilized manners, are one hopeful sign that science fiction as a tool for social discussion and debate at last may be leaving the pulp ghetto. Their short story *Popytka k begstvu* (Escape Attempt, 1962) deals with a Soviet army officer, Saul Repnin, who escapes from a Nazi concentration camp in a manner reminiscent of Jack London's *The Jacket* to a seemingly Utopian future which, alas, turns

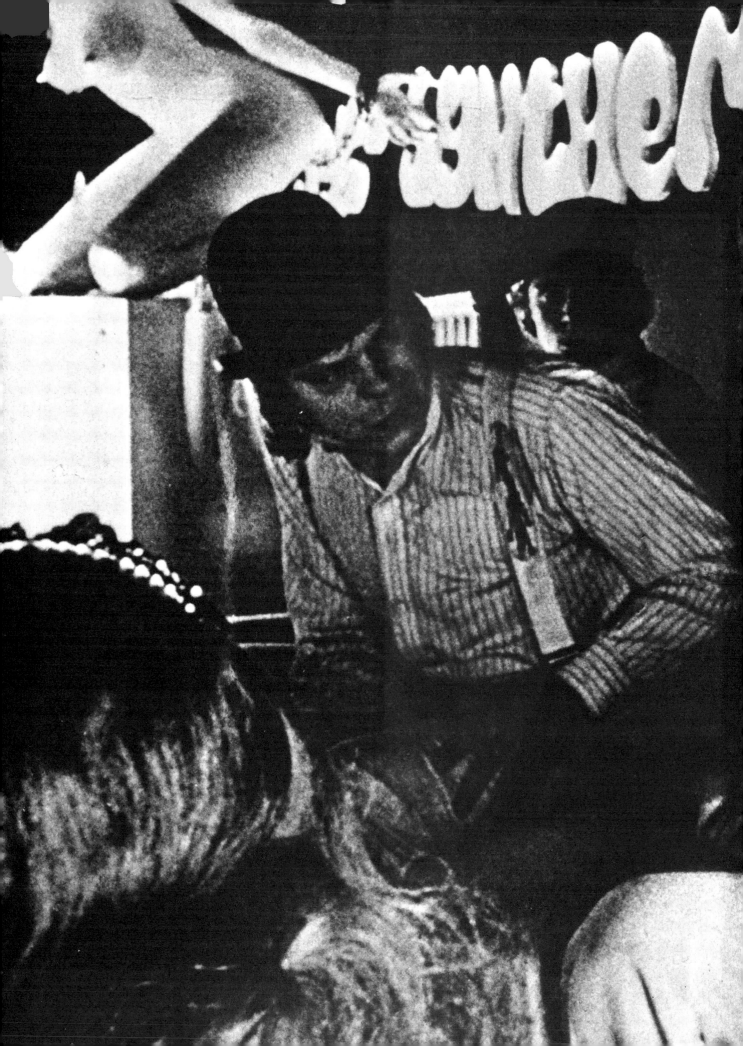

Left: The Soviet author Yevgeniy Zamyatin
Above: Danish artist Palle Nielsen has made an unsurpassed Utopian story in his 'Orpheus and Eurydice' suite, of which this is part
Overleaf: From the 1975 US film 'Rollerball', where the population, under the control of the major corporate conglomerates, is treated to entertainment of an increasingly violent sort

out to be thoroughly fascist, with the same old prison camps all over again, organized slavery, something like Medieval Britain ruled under fascist laws. In the good old pulp magazine days the good Saul Repnin would have saved the world singlehanded, and probably got the princess for his efforts, but the Strugatskiy brothers know more about politics and human nature than that. Repnin tries to save the world by himself, and fails of course. Instead, he returns to the Nazi concentration camp and dies trying to kill a Nazi officer. The moral might be that you should solve your own problems before you try to solve others'.

The problem is put forward even more strongly in their celebrated novel *Trudno byt bogom* (Hard to be a God, 1964), in which observers from a Communist future go to a distant planet with the familiar fascist feudal social order. They see a warlike fanatism, ignorance and oppression and want to help the people. However, interference leads to disaster: they unwittingly help in the creation of a kind of fascist dictatorship which cannot be defeated without killing most of the people on the planet. It is obvious that a society must mature from within and that it cannot be helped from the outside.

The conquest of space and contacts with other civilizations raises the question of relations between societies on different levels of scientific and sociological development. One point concerns the right of a stronger group to interfere with the social system of a weaker one. We all know how this ticklish problem has been solved, particularly in American science fiction—with the ray gun. This simple solution has not been unknown in Soviet science fiction either, but it is remarkably rare. The Strugatskiy brothers may seem somewhat cynical about this; though history appears to prove their point. When we export our own value judgments and try to force them upon others, the results are always discouraging.

What it all boils down to is the conviction that Change is evil, and that everything will surely turn to the worse if we change anything. This belief pervades all Dystopian science fiction, and in this respect it is anti-progress, even reactionary. We know what we have, but not what we will get. The first commandment of the Dystopian thinker must always be that everything you invent or discover, be it intentional or accidental, will ultimately be used against you. And beneath this, of course, is the deeply rooted conviction that we ourselves are our own greatest enemy.

MONSTERS AND SUCH

Once, at a science fiction convention in England, I caught sight of one of these cheap paperback science fiction novels produced in England in the early fifties when they really knew how to produce sub-standard novels. I fell in love with it at first sight, bought it and carried it home to my native Sweden with covetously trembling hands. I knew the novel would be bad to the point of idiocy, without any redeeming qualities; also, the nauseating cover hurt my eyes, and the book as such reeked of cheap pulp paper, imprisoned for untold years in a damp dungeon. I loathed the book, but the title was wonderful.

The novel was *Mushroom Men From Mars,* by one Lee Stanton, published in 1951 when science fiction everywhere was at an all-time low. Nowhere was the overall quality of paperback science fiction half as low as in England, however, and this reeking book must surely constitute an all-time bottom mark in the annals of the genre, I thought. It turned out that I was wrong, but no matter.

We don't need to know more about this atrocity than the magnificent title, the acme of twenty-five years of increasingly silly Anglo-American monster tales. Surely mushroom monsters from Mars are no more improbable or stupid than all those other monsters we have been subjected to in pulp magazines and Hollywood movies.

I said I thought *Mushroom Men From Mars* was the all-time bottom mark in the genre, and that I was wrong. In my opinion one of the most beautiful examples of this is, alas, another British product, proving that Britain has not only some of the best but also some of the worst science fiction authors anywhere. This particular novel, *Galaxy 666* (1963), by someone who has preferred to hide behind the pseudonym Pel Torro, offers, among many, many other delights, a description of a group of monsters that surely never can be outdone by anyone in this universe or the next:

The things were odd, weird, grotesque. There was something horribly uncustomary and unwonted about them. They were completely unfamiliar. Their appearance was outlandish and extraordinary. There was something quite phenomenal about them; they were supernormal; they were unparalleled; they were unexampled. The shape of the aliens was singular in every sense. They were curious, odd,

Above: Cover of 'Mushroom Men of Mars'
Right: A mid-18th-century Russian 'lubok'

102

ФИГУРА СОННАГО ЧЮДА КОТОРОЕ СОБРЕЛИ ВГИШПАНИИ
СОЛДАТЫ НАСХОТЪ ХОДЕЧИ ВЛЕСУ И ОНЫМЪ ЧЮ
ДОМЪ ПОДАРИЛИ ОНИ КИНЦЕРОА ВНИЦИИ КОТОРОИ ЕГО
ПОСАДИЛЪ НАТАКОИ ГАЛИОТЪ СОФЛОТА КОТОРОИ СРЕБРО[м]
НАГРУЖЕНЪ ВГИШПАНИЮ И НЕДАВНО ПРИБЫЛЪ ОНЫ ТУДА
БЛГОПОЛУЧНО. ИСИЕ ЧЮДО ПОСЫЛАЕТСА НН[Ѣ] ЧР[Е]ЗЪ ГАЛ[ЇЮ]

WHAT WE OUGHT TO DO IN CHINA.

Above: 'The Yellow Peril; or What to do about inferior races'—'Punch' magazine, 22 December 1860
Right: Belief in monsters was not restricted to Medieval times—a 'true story' from the 1870s

queer, peculiar and fantastic; and yet when every adjective had been used on them, when every preternatural epithet had been applied to their aberrant and freakish appearance, when everything that could be said about such eccentric, exceptional, anomalous creatures had been said, they still remained indescribable in any concrete term.

Let us leave this eloquent example of pulp science fiction for better pastures.

Monsters have always been extremely popular in folklore and popular literature, as witnessed by the brief survey of *Märchen* and Gothic tales elsewhere in this book. In medieval times one of the most popular literary forms was the bestiary, books filled to the bursting point with imaginative descriptions of incredible monsters, and every self-respecting church was liberally decorated with expressive paintings of monsters of all sizes and shapes, devils, dragons, succubi and other fruits of a perverted imagination. Some of the finest examples of this love of monsters can be found in the Russian *luboks* of the eighteenth century, usually hand-coloured copper and wood engravings sold by travelling salesmen at markets. In their outspoken naïvité they speak volumes about what the common man imagined of the inhabitants of distant countries. In a sense, the monster part of present-day science fiction is little more than updated *luboks*, describing in awed voices the strange and terrible things awaiting us in distant worlds. And many people still believe in mons-

ters, as people once believed in the creatures painted in the *luboks*. The interest is still shown by popular beliefs in the Abominable Snowman, the Sasquatch, the various flying saucer visitors, the Loch Ness monster and so on.

In the fifth century A.D., St Augustine produced a beautiful example of popular belief in monsters, in *De Civitas Dei* (The City Of God), 16 : 8 :
It is further demanded whether Noah's sons, or rather Adam's (of whom all mankind came) begat any of those monstrous men that are mentioned in profane histories; as some that have but one eye in their mid forehead; some with their heels where their toes should be; some with both sexes in one, and their right breast a man's, and the left a woman's, and both begetting and bearing children in one body; some without mouths, living only by air and smelling: some a cubit high, called pygmies by the Greeks; in

INTER WITH A SEA DEVIL

some places the women bear children at the fifth year of their age, dying at the eighth; some that have but one leg, and bend it not, and yet are of wonderful swiftness, being called Sciapodes, because they sleep under the shade of this their foot; some neckless, with the face of a man in their breasts; and such others as are wrought in chequer-work in Sea Street at Carthage, being taken out of their most curious and exact histories. What shall I say of the Cynocephaloi, that had dog's heads, and barked like dogs?

The first science fiction story, in our meaning of the term, was a biting reply to this sort of tall tale, the Syrian satirist Lucian of Samosata's very funny *Vera Historia* (A True History), written sometime between AD 150 and 180. He starts off with naming some of the best known authors of dubious travel stories and goes on to say that ... *as I had nothing true to tell, I took to lying. But my*

lying is far more honest than theirs, for though I tell the truth in nothing else, I shall at least be truthful in saying that I am a liar. I think I can escape the censure of the world by my own admission that I am not telling a word of truth. Be it understood, then, that I am writing about things which I have neither seen nor had to do with nor learned from others—which, in fact, do not exist at all and, in the nature of things, cannot exist. Therefore my reader should on no account believe me.

Whereupon he proceeds to tell the tallest of all tall tales, with flying ships, dragons, living lamps, spidermen, men with big faces and numerous other strange beings, even including what some consider to be the first space opera story, a fantastic battle in space between unusual armies from the Sun and the Moon. Lucian's novel is a classic, also great fun to read, which is more than one

Left: The classic tentacled Martian monster appears for the first time. Illustration for H. G. Wells's 'The War of the Worlds' (1897)
Above: In 1934 Flash Gordon started fighting evil flying saucers. Thirteen years later people started seeing the 'real' things

can say of most stories dealing with extraterrestrial beings. Many of his ideas were later borrowed by other writers of fantastic fiction, notably Savinien Cyrano de Bergerac and Münchhausen.

Writers of fantastic stories were mostly content with keeping themselves to this Earth, however, and with widening horizons the number of gruesome monsters dwindled rapidly, finding instead a new home in the Gothic horror tales. On the other hand, some speculated on the inhabitants of other planets, as exemplified by the Dutch physicist and the astronomer Christiaan Huygens, who (and this is a pleasant change from the sort of attitude towards extraterrestrials we habitually meet in science fiction) wrote in his *New Conjectures Concerning the Planetary Worlds, Their Inhabitants And Productions* (1670):

Were we to meet with a Creature of a much different Shape from Man, with Reason and Speech, we would be much surprised and shocked at the Sight. For if we try to imagine or paint a Creature like a Man in every Thing else, but that has a Neck four times as long, and with great round Eyes or six times as big, and farther distant, we cannot look upon't without the outmost Aversion, altho' at the same time we can give no account of our Dislike ... For 'tis a very ridiculous Opinion, that the common People have got, that 'tis impossible a rational Soul should dwell in any other Shape than ours ... This can proceed from nothing but the Weakness, Ignorance, and Prejudice of

Men.

Johannes Kepler, in his story *Somnium* (1634), described Selenites quite different from Earth people, since they were adapted to their own environment. They were thinking and reasoning creatures, not the sort of Bug-Eyed Monsters later made so painfully familiar through magazines and films. One of the first stories about alien visitors to Earth, Voltaire's *Micromégas* (1752), is an amusing story of two travellers, one from Saturn and one from Sirius, who descend upon Earth in order to search for intelligent life. They find nothing at first, since both are giants who expect intelligent life to have at least the same stature as themselves. But at last they find a ship with a number of philosophers who are voluble but fail to convince the visitors that Earth harbours intelligent life.

Moving on to what we might consider modern science fiction and the sort of invading aliens we are more accustomed to, we find first a few quite fascinating stories by J.-H. Rosny aîné, one of the leading French science fiction authors of his time and in many respects a more interesting one than his contemporary, Jules Verne. His first story, *Les Xipéhus* (1887) describes a primitive tribe in the land which is to become Mesopotamia, who are suddenly confronted by alien creatures shaped like translucent cones of living matter, filled with magnetic energy. These extraterrestrial beings, the Xipéhus, are mineral life and so completely different from men that no communication between the two species is possible, and when they suddenly appear in large numbers they threaten the very existence of Man. They are intelligent, too, and appear to reason just as Man has when discovering a new island or continent: 'As long as the aborigines don't disturb us, fine. If and when they do, destroy them.' They are certainly not evil in any sense of the word, just

anxious to survive. They are finally defeated and killed, but until that point the story is one of the more mature and intelligent in the monster genre. Rosny later wrote a more unusual story about alien creatures, *Un autre monde* (Another World, 1895), in which he describes, through a narrator who is a mutation and can see parts of the spectrum invisible to the normal human eye, an entire new world of animals living and dying all round us but on a higher wavelength, as it were. We cannot see them and they, probably, cannot see us, they pass through us without anyone noticing, and our houses and other artifacts are just parts of their constantly changing environment. It is a powerful, strange story, which also gives the best and most moving story of a superman (the mutation) until Alfred Jarry and his still unequalled novel *Le Surmâle* (1902).

Then, of course, came the great classic of the monster science fiction sub-genre, and the one that started the stampede of loathsome, tentacled monstrosities who started propagating like mad rabbits shortly after the novel appeared in an American pulp magazine in 1927. I am referring to H. G. Wells's *The War of the Worlds* (1897), archetype of so many tales of slimy aliens planning to do a Song My of the entire planet Earth.

The Martians of H. G. Wells's novel were solely out to conquer, with the help of superior war machines that left the British cannon as helpless as the assegai was against the Maxim gun during the colonization of South Africa. It is a bitter novel; Wells was an avowed socialist and anti-imperialist and the novel was a comment upon the British way of carrying the White Man's Burden (which mostly consisted of solid gold, jewels and other goodies). Contrasting the common man's futile struggle against the invincible war machines of the Martians, he manages to give a vivid picture of what the Africans, the Indians, the Tasmanians and others must have felt when British forces moved in on their lands. When the Martians are defeated in the end, it is not thanks to the brave Britons—the example of the British colonies proved that no nation could hope to fight off an enemy with modern weapons—but because the aliens were not immune to Earth bacteria. Today, with the example of South-east Asia before us, we might consider a victory for Man despite the Martian war machines; but in Wells's time only superior fire power counted.

It took only a year before lesser talents started climbing aboard the wagon to fight the slimy extraterrestrials. In 1898 a magazine serial appeared in the United States, *Edison's Conquest of Mars*, by a homegrown talent, Garret P. Serviss, who sent the leading American hero of the time, Thomas Alva Edison, in a space ship to Mars to wreak vengeance upon the rotten Martians who had dared do this to Earth. The less said about this pitiable effort, the better; suffice it to say, that Mr Edison did what Mr Serviss and the magazine readers expected of him, namely doing to the Martians what the Martians could not do to us.

A more interesting offspring of Wells's book is, I think, a recent novel by Arkady and Boris Strugatskiy, *Vtoroye nashestviye marsian. Zapiski zdravomyslyashchego* (The

Left: US 1953 film, typical of the time, 'Invaders from Mars', and (below) 'The Incredible Shrinking Man'

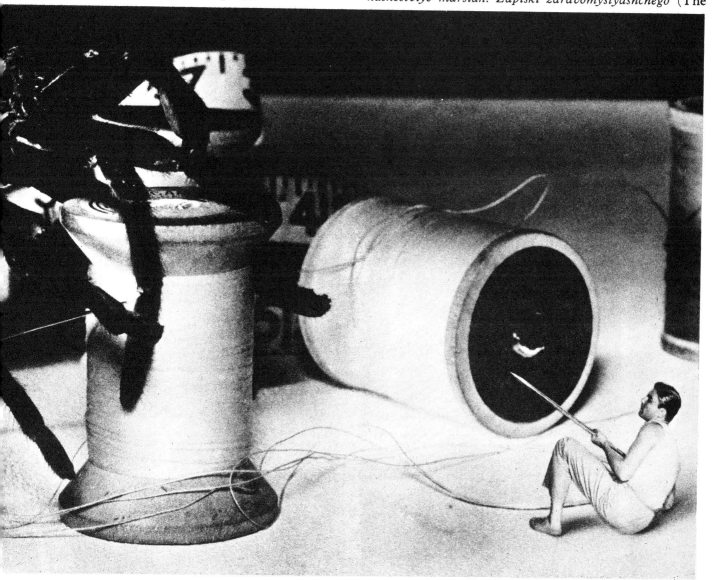

Second Martian Invasion. Notes by a Sound Thinking Person, 1967), a variation of *The War of the Worlds* in which the Martians, after the preliminary shootings, manage to convince the British that they are just ordinary businessmen here to buy certain commodities. The commodity turns out to be gastric juices. The Martians pay well and in cash; lots of people are willing to sell their gastric juices, demand creates supply. The point of the novel is that there are always people willing to collaborate, for a profit, even if it means acting like some sort of milch cow for the invaders. The Martians are even considered to be the benefactors of mankind, when they eradicate drug addiction on Earth (in order to help the production and raise the quality of the gastric juices). Mankind willingly succumbs to the invaders, not through force of arms, but through its own greed and short-sightedness.

Meanwhile, back in the early twentieth century, J.-H. Rosny aîné's and H. G. Wells's example spawned more domestic and extraterrestrial monsters. The Yellow Peril reared its ugly head in hundreds of different disguises, serving as the Monster in quite a number of novels from the 1890s on, notably the Australian author Guy Boothby's well-known novels about the enigmatic Dr Nikola, always trying to undermine the white man's supremacy, and the British author Sax Rohmer's many books about the vile Oriental known as Dr Fu Manchu, a baddie if there ever was one. These were remnants from an earlier age, however, even though both Dr Nikola and Dr Fu Manchu remained popular for quite some time. Human fiends were all very well, but the public's appetite demanded stronger stuff, preferably with as many tentacles as possible. The public got it.

Arthur Conan Doyle wrote a few classics, including the novel *The Lost World* (1912), in which the slightly mad Professor Challenger finds prehistoric animals in an inaccessible part of the world, and the short story *The Horror of the Heights* (1913), in which the invisible beings of Rosny's *Un autre monde* were exchanged for grotesque giant animals, somewhat resembling jelly-fish, living in the stratosphere. In 1911, an awed world could read the first true flying saucer tale, including Venusians picking up an Earthman in their flying saucer and telling him all about how they are keeping an eye upon Man. This story was Bertram Atkey's *The Strange Case of Alan Moraine*, published in the British *Grand Magazine*, and it could pass for a typical flying saucer 'true tale' any day. Still, these stories were rather crude, with the exception of those by Rosny and Wells, and very little of note was published until the French author André Maurois wrote his *Fragments d'une histoire générale* (Fragments of a World History, 1926), three stories about the near future including two in which extraterrestrials play an important part. In the first, world leaders are faced with an international crisis and world war and turn desperately to a gigantic hoax, telling the world that the people of the Moon are secretly attacking the Earth and that a full-scale invasion can be expected very soon. All resources are pooled to fight off the alien invaders and the danger of world war is averted. A weapon is invented in the form of a heat ray, and 'retaliation' is put in hand with a lot of patriotic noises and flag-waving. Then it turns out that the Moon *is* inhabited, and three days later the Selenites strike back.

The second story is even more cynical, describing the

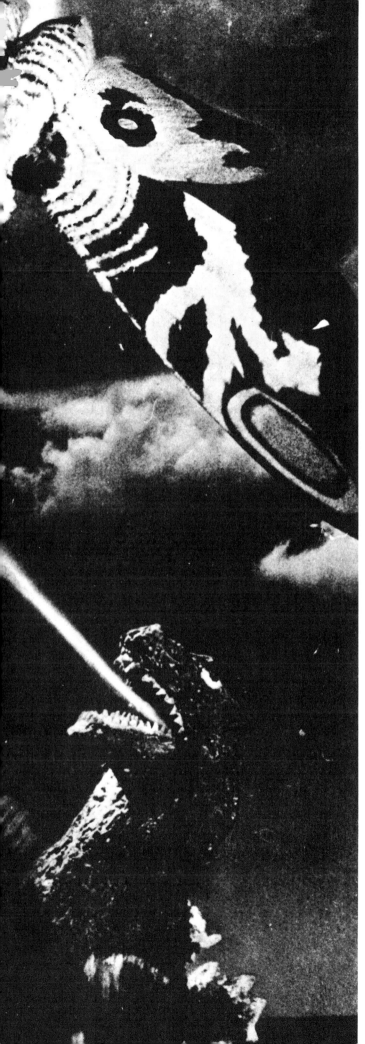

VALLEY OF DOOM: By Halliday Sutherland

FANTASY 1/-
THRILLING SCIENCE FICTION

Enthralling Scientific Adventure
WINGED TERROR
By G.R. MALLOCH
And Other Great
Imaginative Stories
JOHN BEYNON · RUSSELL FEARN
ERIC F. RUSSELL · WILLY LEY

Left: the most famous and loved of all film monsters, the Japanese Godzilla, fighting his old enemy Mothra, in 'Godzilla tai Mothra' (1964)
Above: Gigantic insects have always been extremely popular, as attested by this March 1939 cover of the British magazine 'Fantasy'

experiments of a Uranian scientist, Mr A E 17, that finally result in a scholarly book, *The Life of Man*, a standard work on the subject of all the civilized planets in the solar system. (Earth is not included.) Making the sort of experiments with human beings that any scientist would do with unknown species of animals, he comes to some amusing conclusions, attributing Man's various activities to instinct and denying all claims that Man has a creative intelligence. His comments regarding the life in the big cities of Earth are wry and pointed and would be very good reading for any biologist or anthropologist. (This updated version of Voltaire's *Micromégas* was later on updated once again by the British author Arthur C. Clarke as the short story *Report On Planet Three*.)

The first North American science fiction magazine, *Amazing Stories,* appeared in 1926. Since only a handful of science fiction writers existed in the United States at this time, all of them inferior to the best in Europe which had had a much longer tradition of science fiction, *Amazing Stories* had to make do with reprinting mostly old French, German and British science fiction, and *The War of the Worlds* was once again published in the August 1927 issue, starting a flood of American monster tales that was soon to deluge their science fiction. This is where the typical science fiction monster is born, rearing

111

The Green Slime are coming!

Tentacled monsters in 1968 Japanese film

its slimy tentacles against an unsuspecting world, seemingly born only to drag the shrieking heroine round the universe with the square-jawed hero in hot pursuit. Wells and others had given some purpose to their monsters, but the monsters that now deluged science fiction, at least in the United States, had no purpose whatsoever other than offering cheap thrills to unsophisticated readers. Borrowing heavily from *Märchen* and Gothic tales, updating the aliens only by more tentacles and moving them out into space or letting them come to Earth from space to do their evil deeds (while, at the same time, noble Earth heroes murdered loathsome alien creatures on *their* home worlds), American science fiction magazines preached the gospel of uninhibited violence. Once again, as in the Gothic tales, we have the externalization of evil, the pure black and white of the fairy tales, only this time in a pseudo-scientific setting, vulgarizing all those works of science fiction from which the ideas came. Two typical examples of this form of science fiction are mentioned at the beginning of this chapter. There are many more, each worse than the other. Until the advent of *Amazing Stories,* science fiction had been enjoying a good reputation as a useful tool for social criticism and also for its literary quality; this flood of pseudo-scientific poorly written tales, abounding in racism, violence, puerile sex and primitive views of society, soon destroyed the last vestiges of that reputation. Science fiction became 'that Buck Rogers stuff.' The mushroom men of Mars emerged triumphant from the carnage.

One American writer managed briefly to make some impact upon pulp magazine science fiction with a few short stories dealing with extraterrestrials, depicting them not as monsters but as individual beings and definite personalities, not evil, but *different.* This was, of course, what European science fiction had been doing all along, with J.-H. Rosny aîné and André Maurois as leading examples, but American readers knew only what was published in their own local magazines, and for them Stanley G. Weinbaum's debut, *A Martian Odyssey* (1934), descended like a ton of bricks. Still, even in Weinbaum's story, only Earthmen are really worthy of respect, they steal and loot with impunity, and only collaborating aliens are good aliens.

It is interesting to compare this attitude towards extraterrestrials, usually murderous and at best patronizing, with developments in Europe, particularly the emergence of the new super power, the Soviet Union. The Soviet Union had not quite the American tradition of pulp magazines of the cheap *Amazing Stories* sort, nor the tradition of Wild West stories, from which writers got much of their inspiration. What they had inherited, and this was almost as suffocating, was the Utopian tradition from the Revolution, the demand that science fiction should be first didactic and educational and only secondly entertaining. This was in contrast to the demands of American magazine editors, that popular fiction should be entertaining, and nothing else. Another fault

Spider monsters and heroine on Japanese film poster

The Japanese 'Kingu Kongo no Gyakushu' (1967) film poster

in common with the American example was the emphasis on vulgarized political ideas. In America science fiction advocated free enterprise and Capitalism; the Soviet counterpart advocated Communism and collectivism. Extraterrestrial visitors in Soviet works of this time usually exemplified either the dangers of Capitalism or the blessings of Communism. And some of these hated Capitalist monsters were just as richly endowed with tentacles as their Western Communist parallels. (The word 'Communism' was seldom used by American writers when describing extraterrestrial monster civilizations, but the many descriptions of insect-like communities, blind obedience to leaders and de-individualized lives are very revealing.) The hate expressed towards the aliens particularly in American science fiction, however, is very seldom found in Soviet science fiction of this time. Novels such as M. Prussak's *Gosti zemli* (Guests of Earth), A. Volkov's *Chuzhiye* (The Alien Ones) and I. A. Bobrichev-Pushkin's *Zaletnyy gost'* (The Guest who Came Flying) are typical examples of aliens visiting Earth not as enemies but as strange guests, bearing tidings from sometimes incomprehensibly different worlds. One of my personal favourites is a later short story by Marietta Chudakova, *Prostranstvo zhizhni* (Life Space, 1969), describing a strange man who might or might not come from another world or another dimension or another time, whose life span is limited not by time but by space. As he grows older the area in which he can move gets smaller and smaller until he finally dies when

he inadvertently steps outside his life space. It is a strangely moving story, giving hints of a life enormously different from ours.

Apart from obvious political reasons for the abundance of horrible monsters attacking civilization during the 'golden years' of American science fiction up to the mid-1950s, the principle of which was attained with a particularly nasty film, *Invasion of the Body Snatchers* (1956), where monsters from outer space try to create a new world order in which everybody is equal but, of course, finally defeated and exterminated by the hero, one of the main reasons for this sorry state of things must be the fact that most American writers were reared on the local cheap fiction magazine tradition, which called for WASP heroes, villains easy to hate, and simple sexual interest, with lots of gore, naturally. Science fiction in the United States faithfully followed the pulp magazine formula, as witness the greatest names of the time—Edgar Rice Burroughs, E. E. Smith, Edmond Hamilton and others. The magazines were edited by people who might have loved science fiction but also had to bow to publishers who wanted nothing but fast profits. Monsters and wild adventures always sold, and with one editor forced to edit perhaps two or three or four magazines simultaneously, no one can wonder that the results were often disastrous. The Soviet Union did not have these particular problems; instead, science fiction authors and editors had to keep a wary eye on the various

Ghidra, Godzilla and Mothra try to destroy Tokyo (1965)

113

politruk who thought that science fiction should try to solve technological problems of the near future, as well as presenting readers with 'positive' heroes. This was the time in Soviet science fiction when, according to a rueful comment in a story by Soviet science fiction author Nikolai Tomas, 'fantasizing was allowed only within the limits of the Five-Year Plan for the national economy'. American authors had blood-sucking publishers and over-worked editors to cope with; their Soviet counterparts had the Commissars. The difference—and here I am speaking as a citizen of a non-aligned nation which nevertheless was exposed to the various offerings of this time—was that the producers of American science fiction were *exporting* their junk. The ones in the Soviet Union and other Socialist countries kept their junk for themselves. Only the best of the Soviet science fiction sneaked out, like Yevgeniy Zamyatin's *My,* Aleksey Tolstoy's *Ayelita* and Ivan Yefremov's *Andromeda.* These novels offered no monsters and very little preaching. Over the Atlantic, science fiction of the period offered both in ample measure.

With time, of course, strong-willed and single-minded editors appeared, forceful enough to effect a change. Good editors, such as John W. Campbell and, in the Soviet Union, Bella Kluyeva (to mention two of the most well-known), found new authors by the dozen and also had enough muscle to develop them into the new generation of writers so urgently needed.

I am happy to say that the attitude towards extraterrestrials and other monstrous beings has changed dramatically during the past two decades, thanks to the efforts of such editors. One of my favourite stories of monsters, and

certainly one of the most chilling treatments in modern monster lore, is a short story, *Mimic,* which appeared as early as 1942. Written by Donald A. Wollheim, who for more than thirty years has been one of the shapers of modern science fiction, as editor and as publisher, it might be called the first really modern terror tale, telling of a kind of insect that has adopted a protective mimicry suitable for its survival in a modern city. It looks like a human being.

'Nature practises deceptions in every angle,' Wollheim says in the story. 'Evolution will create a being for any niche than can be found, no matter how unlikely.'

Wollheim's remarkable insect—and the even stranger predators that feed upon it in the modern cities—is just a strange creature trying to survive, far removed from the kind of murderous monsters so sadly common elsewhere. The same attitude towards strange beings who have not had the fortune of being born as square-jawed, broad-shouldered WASP space heroes, is shown in another of the new breed of monster stories, Murray Leinster's *First Contact,* which appeared in the May 1945 issue of *Astounding Science Fiction.* In this ingenious story, Earthmen and aliens solve the ticklish problem of acquiring some alien know-how without revealing the whereabouts of their respective home worlds by switching space ships. No blasters, no tentacles, just a complicated problem that has to be solved by two species which respect but do not

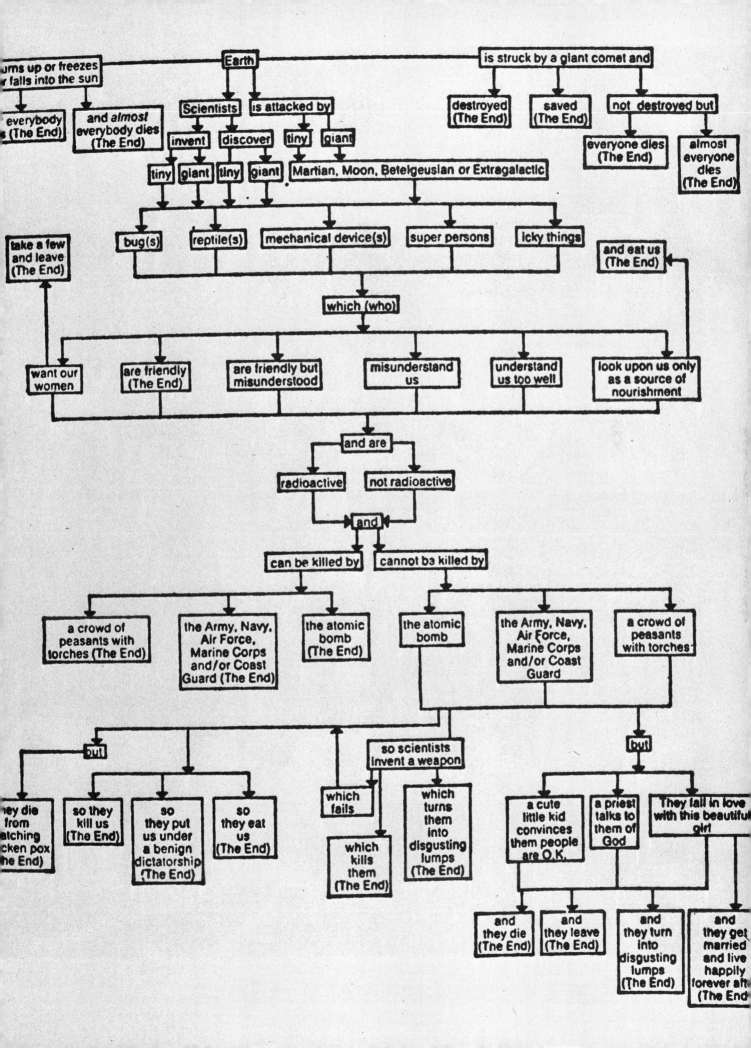

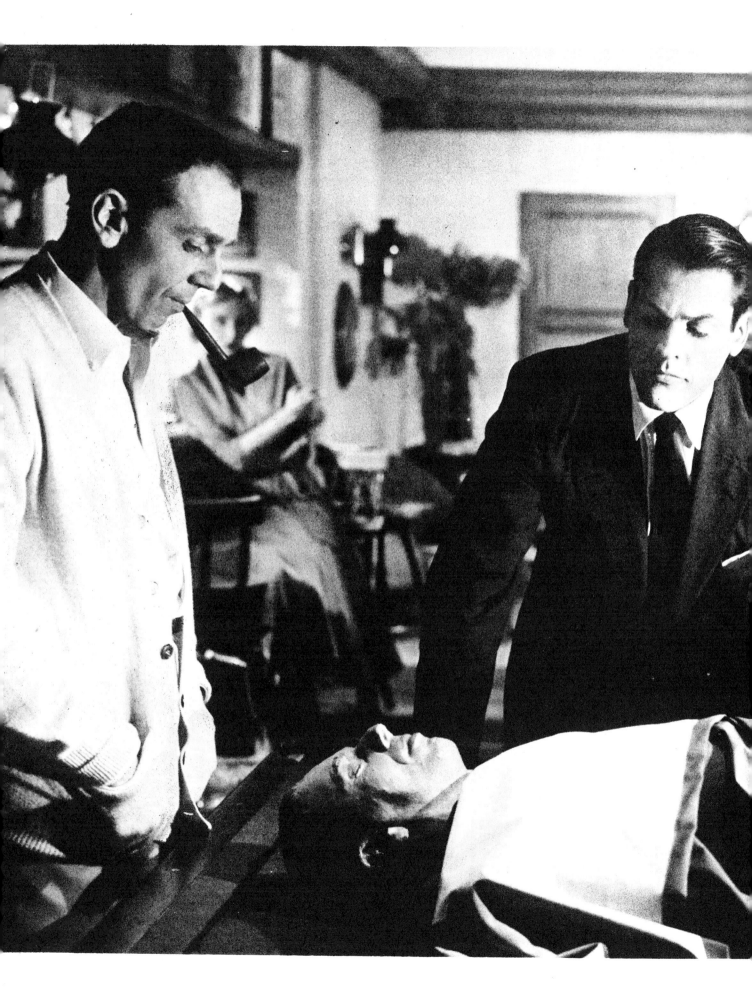

INVASION OF THE SAUCER-MEN

CREEPING HORROR
...From the depths
of time and space!

Left: Appraisal of one of the alien Communist monsters planning to take over Earth, from the film 'Invasion of the Body Snatchers' (1956)
Above: One of the most unintentionally funny films in the monster field

quite trust each other. In an interesting aftermath to this story, the Soviet science fiction author Ivan Yefremov later wrote a novel, *Serdtse Zmei* (The Heart of the Snake, 1959) in response to Leinster's story, suggesting an entirely different way of solving the problem.

Not much later the brilliant American writer Harry Harrison wrote what is one of the best variations of the man-against-monster theme, the novel *Deathworld* (1969), first published in John W. Campbell's magazine *Astounding*. The story is set on a planet inhabited by the worst kind of monsters imaginable. Every animal, every insect, every growth on this planet seems to be possessed by one single thought: to kill as many human beings as possible. The colonizers have dug themselves in behind impenetrable steel barriers and venture out from these forts only in armoured tanks fitted with flame-throwers, machine guns and cannon. The children are taught to handle guns at the age of four years, and are ruthlessly drilled to act quicker than quick when attacked. The colonized arm themselves to their teeth as the attacks become fiercer and harder to repel.

Actually, the planet is not particularly hostile; but all living things there are very, very sensitive to aggressive emotions.

We have an interesting parallel of sorts to this in the American author John Gardner's moving novel *Grendel* (1971), in which the despised and hated monster eyes man with revulsion and dread. Grendel is the archetypal monster from the eighth-century epic *Beowulf*, one of the most famous of all classic literary monsters. Here, Gardner lets him speak for himself, and Beowulf's views on mankind are nothing short of devastating. The gulf between Man's opinion of himself and his actions make Grendel sick. When he finally realizes that Man needs him as the epitome of Man's own evil, that only through Grendel can Man hope to see his own destructiveness, cowardice and loneliness, he becomes truly 'evil'. This is probably the best portrait yet of the archetypal monster in modern literature, and also probably the best comment on the abundance of monsters and alien creatures in science fiction and related literature.

Grendel is of course a monster similar enough to human beings to make communication and understanding possible, merely (or perhaps not so merely) a vehicle for the author's theories and opinions. Taking a step towards the strange worlds of if, we find a beautiful short story by the British author J. G. Ballard, *The Drowned Giant* (1965), describing in dry, precise prose, almost like an academic lecture, the sudden appearance of a dead giant on a beach, the local people's reactions and the subsequent putrefaction and disappearance of the gigantic carcass. This short story, reminiscent of the French 'pataphysicists, conveys a feeling of latent power, of the strangeness from Outside thrust upon us.

It cannot be compared with the acknowledged masterpieces in the field, though. The intelligent ocean in the Polish author Stanislaw Lem's novel *Solaris* (1961) remains one of science fiction's most striking and original concepts, an alien entity that is irrefutably *alien*, on a par with Arthur C. Clarke's magnificent novel *Rendezvous with Rama* (1973), in which a strange extraterrestrial space ship suddenly appears in the solar system, passing through on its way to an unknown goal. Extensive investigation by Earth scientists aboard this gigantic space craft, almost a small planetoid in size, fails to reveal any living beings. There are quite a number of strange robots doing incomprehensible things, but no intelligent life. What Clarke manages to do here, and he might be the first science fiction author since Olaf Stapledon to achieve it, is to depict something so totally different from us that it is virtually unexplainable. The finale of the novel, with the strange space ship disappearing into the

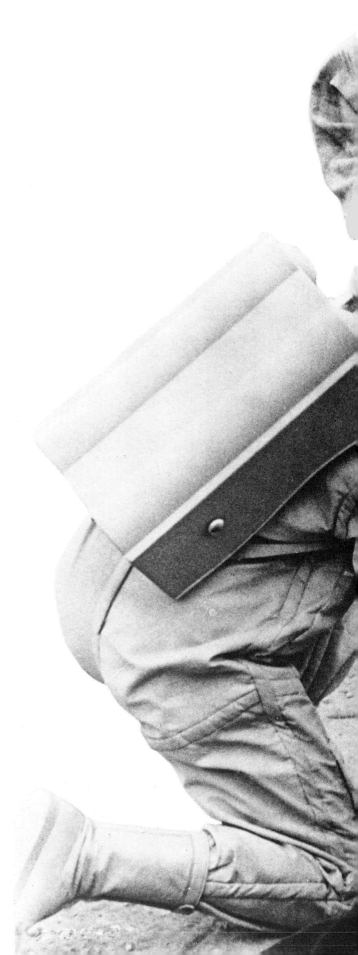

Scenes from 'The Andromeda Strain' (1971), where the monsters are microbes, attacking Man and ultimately being defeated by the brave WASP scientist

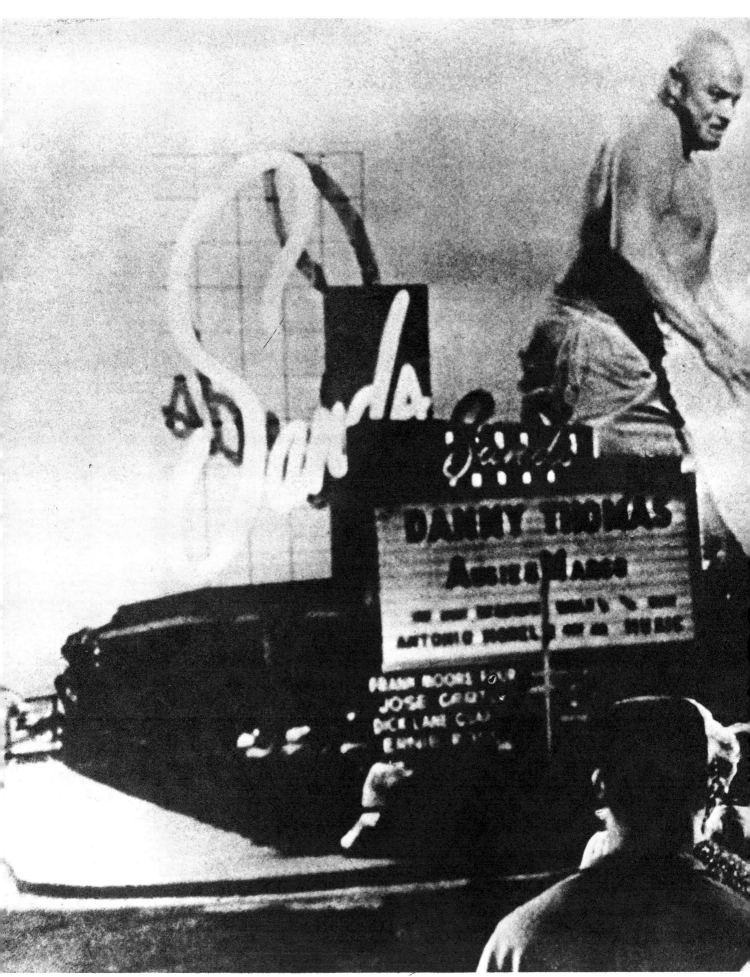

endless void after a brief refuelling at the Sun without even having noticed the humans, is magnificent and worthy of Clarke at the peak of his powers.

The finest and strangest description of an alien entity, however, must be the Star Maker, the creator of universes, the truly supreme being, in the British author and philosopher Olaf Stapledon's novel *Star Maker* (1937). It is a strange novel, if novel it can be called, only hinting at the true nature of the Star Maker, since his nature cannot be completely understood or explained. It is a description of a god, or the works of a god, and as such this is surely the best and most powerful of all stories dealing with the alien, the strange and the incomprehensible.

And who are these aliens, these extraterrestrials, these monsters, half beasts and half gods whom Mankind forever fights? I think the answer should be obvious. H. G. Wells gave much of the answer in *The War of the Worlds*, the culmination of hundreds of future-war novels

**Left: Here, in the film 'The Amazing Colossal Man' (1965), an ordinary man grows out of proportion and threatens the world
Above: Walt Kelly's comic strip 'Pogo Possum'**

that catered for the masochistic needs of British readers during the second part of the nineteenth century. England, which had started by governing Wales, Scotland and Ireland by the sword and then proceeded to bring British civilization to the rest of the world, obviously knew what Wells was talking about in this, the most popular of all monster tales. American readers obviously knew, born as they were in a nation which still reeked of the blood of millions of Indians murdered by the European settlers. A celebrated film, *Forbidden Planet* (1956), presented the true monster, the Monster of the Id, the monster of Man's own subconscious, the mirror image of Man, Dr Jekyll totally free at last. We all know who the eternal monster in science fiction is.

Or, in the profound words of the cartoonist Walt Kelly, in the comic strip *Pogo Possum:* 'We have met the enemy and he is us.'

ROBOTS AND MECHANICAL MEN

In all ages *hubris*, the sin of presumption, has been the greatest of human crimes. Any successful attempt to rise above man's station and become equal to the gods is regarded with grave dislike by all gods and religious leaders. The idea that the gods will surely smite anyone who rises too high played an important part in, for example, the classical Greek view of life. Even today we find the idea that there are things we are not meant to know; it is not good to poke around too much in the secrets of Nature. We know what happened when Prometheus stole the fire from the gods and when Icarus tried to fly. Such knowledge is dangerously close to hubris and should be discouraged. The prerogative most jealously guarded by all real gods is the creation of living beings, and the artificial creation of human beings must thus be particularly blasphemous and exciting. The creation of artificial life has therefore always been one of the most popular pastimes of alchemists and scholars.

We all know that the creation of life is the simplest thing in the world, as underlined by our present over-population, but science and imagination must take the hard way, using their own methods. This artificial human being, or homunculus, golem, mandrake, android, automaton, robot or whatever, can be traced back to Classical times. King Minos of Crete is supposed to have had a most useful brass robot, built by Zeus, which patrolled Crete's shores at night and earned his keep by pouncing on any intruder and dragging him into a bonfire from which only the faithful robot returned unharmed.

Similar descriptions of automatons can be found everywhere in ancient times. Albertus Magnus (1206–1280) is said to have spent twenty years building an automaton 'of metals and unknown substances according to the stars' which, he claimed, could walk and talk and carry out the menial tasks of a manservant. It talked a little too much, though, and one day the incessant chatter of the automaton so annoyed Magnus's disciple Thomas Aquinas that he destroyed it. Pope Silvester II used, according to the legend, a 'brazen oracular head' to keep himself informed about everything that took place around him. It might have worked only too well as a spy instrument. A Bull of 1326 prohibited the making of prophetic 'heads, arms, eyes, jointed fingers and mechanical pointers' throughout all Christendom.

An unusual scene in the film 'Forbidden Plant' (1956), where the robot handles not the heroine but some luckless male; and an advertisement for the first film version of 'Frankenstein'

The comic panel contains the following text:

THE CREATURE AWAKES. IT AWAKES TO PAIN... AND WILD RAGE. ALL NERVE CENTERS ARE EXCITED AT THE SAME TIME, WHILE EXCRUCIATING SPASMS TEAR MUSCLES AND CARTILAGES, CAUSING FEATURES TO BECOME DISTORTED AND MISSHAPEN..., IN UNBEARABLE **AGONY!** FROM THE DEEPEST OF HELLS..., BY THE UNHOLY COPULATION OF MADNESS WITH HORROR....

MEIN GOTT!! HE'S AWAKEN!!

NO! NO!! ARRRGGH!

SNAP! KRUNCH!

DINKENSTEIN IS BORN...!!

GASP

KRAK

SNAP!

CRASH!

AIIIIEEEEEEEEEEEEEE!

ARGH

Above: Today, Frankenstein's monster has become incredibly vicious, as shown in this comic strip by Carlos Maria Federici (1976)

Right: A scene in Jarry's 'Le surmâle', sculpted by Jacques Carleman (1902)

These fine things are more mythical than real, however, and real automatons did not appear until the early Industrial Revolution, when clockwork automatons became immensely popular in Europe. The French engineer Jacques Vaucanson, who had created three famous automatons, a flautist, a drummer and a mechanical duck that both ate and defecated *(un canard dirégateur)*, was in 1739 asked by King Louis XV if he also could construct a creature in which the blood circulated. Vaucanson immediately started making an 'automaton which in its movements should imitate the bodily functions, the circulation of the blood, the breathing, the digestion, the muscle movements, sinews, nerves, etc.'

These creations, however, were nothing more than amusing mechanical toys. The tales spread in Germany at this time of the android called Golem, created by the Jews to defend themselves against their tormentors, were more like the classic artificial men in *Frankenstein* and *R.U.R.* But more of these later.

The first true modern literary robot appears to have been the robot woman Olympia in E. T. A. Hoffmann's novel *Der Sandmann* (1816), later famous as one of the three tales in Jacques Offenbach's opera *Les contes d'Hoffman* (1881). Olympia is a beautiful young woman made of cogwheels and springs who almost dances a young man to death before she can be turned off. Other German writers of the Romantic era had earlier written stories dealing with artificial men and women, but these were what we would call androids or golems, not true robots. In Achim von Arnim's celebrated novel *Isabella von Ägypten* (1812) the protagonist, Bella, is for a short time supplanted by a magic *Doppelgänger,* and in the strange world of black magic and folklore where Bella and her royal lover dwell, we also find living dead and a

black dog sacrificed in a rite which turns it into a mandrake, a little monster endowed with artificial life. Unlike the sinister Golem of Jewish folklore, this mandrake is a ridiculous little caricature of mankind, vain and quarrelsome. To make things more interesting, the fair Bella loses her head over the mandrake, lavishing her love on him and for a time even forgets her human lover. Hoffmann later used a similar theme is *Klein Zaches* (1819), where the mandrake is somewhat less attractive. The fair and dangerous Olympia in *Der Sandmann* is almost a repetition of Bella's lover, and also almost too similar to the Spinnpuppe in Clemens Brentano's *Das Märchen von den Märchen* (1812), a witty artificial female being with a personality of her own. Brentano actually put a robot in his very funny tale *Gockel, Hinkel und Gackeleia* (written about 1816, but not published until 1838, and then only in a heavily censored version), but this admirable automaton is finally discovered to be powered by a tiny mouse somewhere under her skirts.

Hoffmann's mechanical woman was pure, unadulterated horror, reflecting the fears of a humanist during the Industrial Revolution who could not and would not understand the new age. This was, of course, also the case with Mary Shelley's famous novel *Frankenstein* (1818), where the monster was not a robot but a golem or android of the usual sort, with the additional twist of having his ugly head crammed with romantic notions straight out of the writings of Mary Shelley's lover, and later husband, Percy Bysshe Shelley and their friend

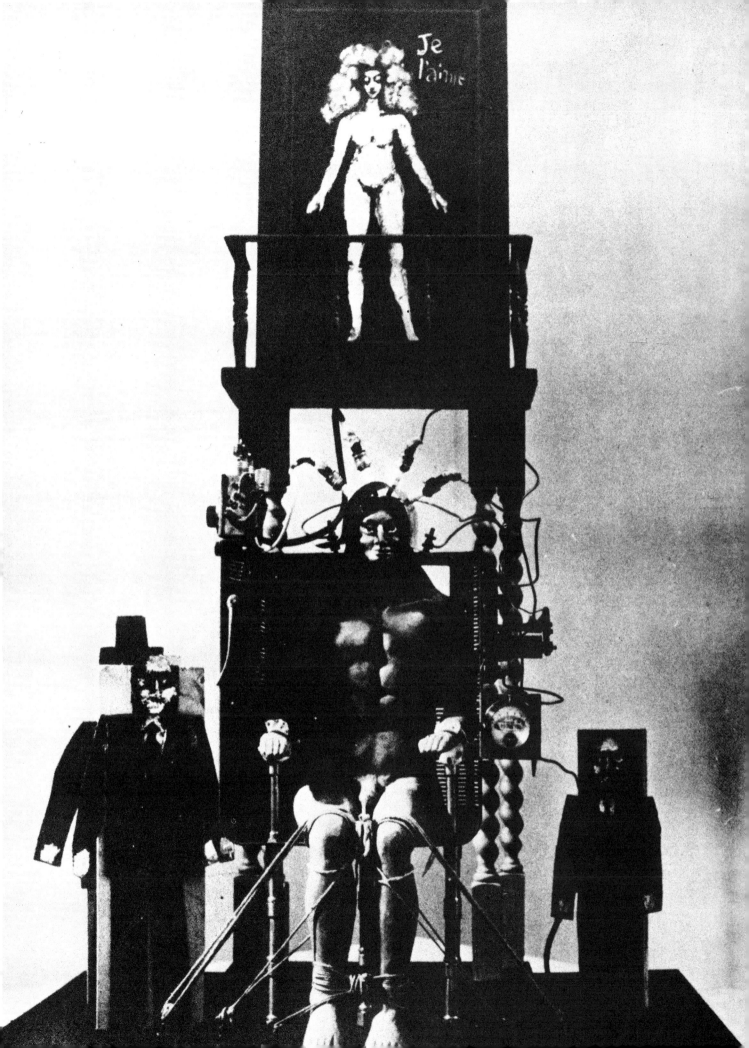

Lord Byron.

Some critics think *Frankenstein* was the first science fiction tale ever written. It was obviously not, but this merging of the traditional British Gothic tale with the German *Märchen* tales proved successful and popular *Frankenstein* is more related to *Das Märchen von den Märchen* than to the gadget-type science fiction story *Der Sandmann,* but Mary Shelley managed to tread the dangerous path between the sublime and the pathetic so well that the Monster, which is the true protagonist of the story, holds the reader's interest to the last page with his rather Shelleyan farewell to life and man. One feels pity for the Monster, and Victor Frankenstein stands out more and more as a cowardly hypocrite who refuses to bear the responsibility for his acts and give his creation the small amount of happiness he wants.

This is what made *Frankenstein* a revolutionary work is this particular field. Mary Shelley described the Monster, the Alien, the Unknown factor as it were, as a creature with feelings and emotions, a creature which could be hurt and who acted logically. This had seldom been the case before and, alas, it is still very unusual. The many film versions of this novel, of which the less said the better, have almost totally concentrated upon the Monster aspect of the story, with disastrous results. Starting with a 1910 Edison film in which the awed movie goer could watch 'the creation of the Monster in a cauldron of blazing chemicals', to quote the official press

Two scenes from Mel Brooks's brilliant parody, 'Young Frankenstein' (1975), in which he used the sets of the 1931 US version

release, Victor Frankenstein's poor monster has sunk deeper and deeper into the murky depths of commercialism, finally ending up in quickies like *I Was a Teenage Frankenstein* (1957) and *Frankenstein Versus the Space Monsters* (1965); but the inevitable parody, Mel Brooks's *Young Frankenstein* (1975), was brilliant. I might sound somewhat parochial here, but the only decent movie version of Mary Shelley's novel I have seen is a recent Swedish one, *Victor Frankenstein* (1976), produced by Calvin Floyd, with the noted Swedish actor Per Oscarsson as the Monster. It is a deeply moving film, capturing much of the *Weltschmertz* of the novel, and interesting also in that Per Oscarsson as the Monster wears unusually little make-up. This is a far cry from the

127

FOURTH EDITION.

BEADLE'S HALF DIME Library

$2.50 a Year.   Entered at the Post Office at New York, N. Y., at Second Class Mail Rates.   Copyrighted in 1882 by BEADLE AND ADAMS.   October 3, 1882.

Vol. XI.   Single Number.   PUBLISHED WEEKLY BY BEADLE AND ADAMS, No. 98 WILLIAM STREET, NEW YORK.   Price, 5 Cents.   No. 271.

THE HUGE HUNTER; or, THE STEAM MAN OF THE PRAIRIES.

BY EDWARD S. ELLIS.

AUTHOR OF "THE BOY MINERS," "SETH JONES," "BILL BIDDON," ETC., ETC., ETC.

"BEGORRAH BUT IT'S THE OULD DIVIL, HITCHED TO HIS THROTTIN' WAGING, WID HIS OULD WIFE HOWLDING THE REINS." EXCLAIMED MICKEY.

Left: Illustration by L. Benett for Verne's 'La maison à vapeur', with a steam-driven elephant running away from his flesh and blood cousins
Above: The very first US robot
Overleaf: Two scenes with Paul Wegener as Der Golem from the films of that name (1915 and—inset—1920)

Golem-type make-up used in the poor 1931 American version of the novel.

Frankenstein was an immediate success, infusing Weltschmertz and the Sturm und Drang tradition with the classic horror tale, and its popularity soared, partly owing to Peggy Wiebling's highly successful dramatization in 1850. This was still an example of the Romantic notion of the subject, though, heavily influenced by the German Romanticists of the late eighteenth century, it was acknowledged as Literature. Then the United States, rapidly on its way to become the leading industrialized nation in the world, took over the artificial man. The first true North American robot novel appeared in 1865, and a comparison between its description of the artificial being with Mary Shelley's brooding Monster speaks volumes about the difference in outlook and feelings between the Old and the New World:

*At that instant, a shriek like that of some agonized giant came home to them across the plains, and both looked around, as if about to flee in terror; but the curiosity of the Yankee restrained him. His practical eye saw that what-*ever it might be it was a human contrivance, and there could be nothing supernatural about it . . .

It was about ten feet in height, measuring to the top of the 'stove-pipe hat', which was fashioned after the common order of felt coverings, with a broad brim, all painted a shiny black. The face was made of iron, painted a black color, with a pair of fearful eyes, and a tremendous grinning mouth. A whistle-like contrivance was made to answer for the nose. The steam chest proper and boiler were where the chest in a human being is generally supposed to be, extending also into a large knapsack arrangement over the shoulders and back. A pair of arms, like projections, held the shafts, and the broad flat feet were covered with short spikes, as thought he were the monarch of base-ball players. The legs were quite long, and the step was natural, except when running, at which time, the bolt uprightness in the figure showed different from a human being.

In the knapsack were the valves, by which the steam or water was examined. In fron was a painted imitation of a vest, in which a door opened to receive the fuel, which, together with the water, was carried in the wagon, a pipe running along the shaft and connecting with the boiler.

The lines which the driver held controlled the course of the steam man; thus, when pulling the strap on the right, a deflection was caused which turned it in that direction, and the same acted on the other side. A small rod, which ran along the right shaft, let out or shut off the steam, as was desired, while a cord, running along the left, controlled the whistle at the nose.

The legs of this extraordinary mechanism were fully a yard apart, so as to avoid the danger of its upsetting, and at the same time, there was given more room for the play of the delicate machinery within. Long, sharp, spike-like projections adorned the soles of the immense feet, so that there was little danger of its slipping, while the length of the legs showed that, under favourable circumstances, the steam man must be capable of very great speed.

This sublime example of the sort of pulp magazine writing which for many years was to plague science fiction, appeared in a dime novel by Edward S. Ellis, *The Steam Man of the Prairies* (1865). The steam man is an eminently American creation, machinery throughout, without any sort of emotions, since this is purely a machine made for utilitarian purposes. He was made to work, and he worked without ever complaining as long as he had water in his boiler and wood in his furnace. Gone is the Weltschmertz of Mary Shelley's *Frankenstein*, gone are all pretensions of literary quality, gone also are all moral and philosophical questions adumbrated in earlier stories about robots, automatons, golems and mandrakes. This is a machine, solely. And while Mary Shelley's monster forty-seven years earlier had run away from mankind, pondering upon the eternal questions of whence and why, this modern robot is used for nothing better than to kill Indians with.

I won't go into all the various reasons why the old concept of the artificial man suddenly turned into something so feeble; it is enough to point out that the robot never really recuperated from his transfer to North American soil. Mary Shelley was blissfully dead (she died in 1851) and was spared this atrocity.

The robot man caught on, and quite a number of more or less imaginative plagiarisms came on the market, all of them to be found in the various dime novel series that flooded the country. *The Huge Hunter* appeared in several

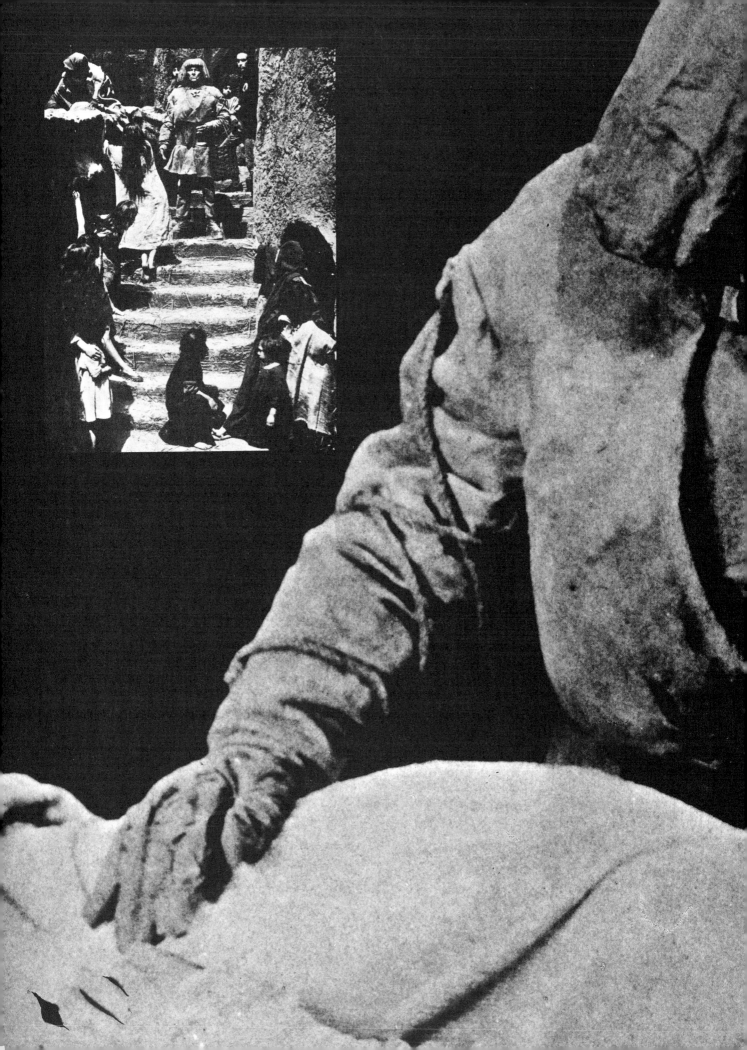

editions, under new imaginative titles, and a competing dime novel publisher, Frank Tousey, started a whole series based upon this theme. This series, chronicling the improbable adventure of Frank Reade, boy inventor, proved very popular and appeared in 191 issues, stealing science fiction themes and ideas wherever it could find them. The first three Frank Reade Stories were unabashed plagiarisms of the original Ellis story—*Frank Reade and his Steam Man of the Plains, Frank Reade and his Steam Horse* and *Frank Reade and his Steam Team.* Later came stories like *Frank Reade, Jr and his Steam Wonder,* after which the whole shebang was modernized somewhat with the advent of *Frank Reade, Jr and his Electric Boat.*

The robot clanked on in North America, getting more silly and murderous with every passing day, and it would probably have stayed within the realms of the penny dreadfuls had it not been for two now classic works, one novel and one play, that saved this ingenious tool for social commentary from the American pulp jungle (or, rather, saved the robot in Europe. Nothing really happened in the United States until the late 1940s).

The novel was the Hungarian author Frigyes Karinthy's *Utazás Faremidóba* (Voyage to Faremido) which first appeared in 1917 and purported to be the true tale of Lemuel Gulliver's fifth voyage. This time Gulliver is travelling in an airplane when he is suddenly snatched away and finds himself on the planet Faremido, inhabited solely by robots calling themselves *solasis,* who regard organic life as a hideous disease which must be destroyed. Such organic life, including human beings, is called *dosire* and is held in very low regard by the *solasis.*

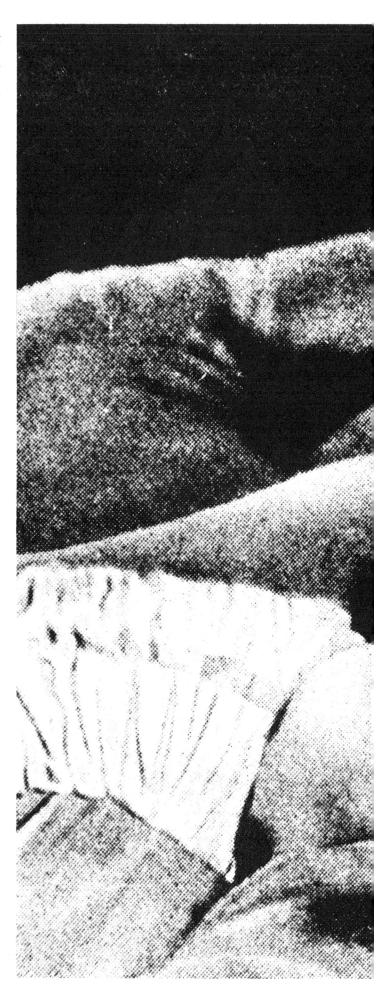

Above: Karel Capek, author of 'R.U.R.' (1920)
Right: Brigitte Helm as the artificial woman in the 1930 film of Hanns Heinz Ewers' 'Alraune'

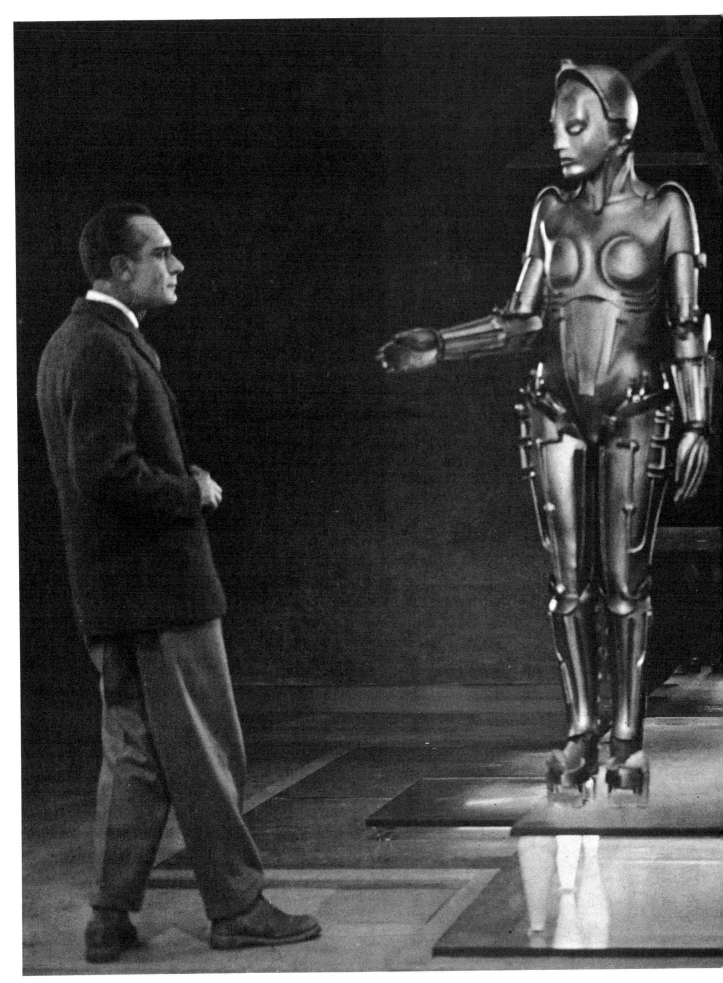

Organic life, say the *solasis,* is the malady of the universe. They examine Mr Gulliver thoroughly and come to·the conclusion that he is a *dosire* of rather low order, show him around for a while in their perfect robot society and then send him back to Earth. All was a mistake—they thought his airplane was an Earth *solasis* with a severe case of *dosire* poisoning; no one had even imagined a machine, as *solasis,* without a will of its own. Very confusing for the poor robots who are very happy to see Mr Gulliver go.

This is obviously a much too mature work to have appeared out of nothing (it certainly had nothing to do with the Edward S. Ellis tale) and Karinthy was merely an exponent for the utter fascination of the intellectuals in Europe for the machine which, they felt, one day would rule the world. Earlier tools had been extensions of the human arm; now man was becoming a cog in a machinery that worked with a rhythm of its own. From the middle of the nineteenth century, writers and artists had a boundless admiration for the machine, but this attitude changed about the turn of the century. Feelings became more complex, turning into a mixture of enthusiasm and frustration. In the visual arts, Duchamp, Picabia, Man Ray and Picasso created bizarre female machines, de Chirico painted strange robot-like mannequins. The celebrated French author Villiers de l'Isle-Adam wrote one of his most witty and scathing satires, the novel *L'Eve future* (The Eve of the Future, 1886), about the magnificent android Hadaly, the first modern robot in science fiction, given life by a barrage of electricity in Menlo Park, USA, by Edison (!). Hadaly, still the best and most fascinating robot in science fiction, was later stolen, body and soul, by the German writer Thea von Harbou for her novel and film *Metropolis* (1926). And, of course, the creation of the artificial human being with the aid of electricity was also used in the 1931 film version of *Frankenstein.* (Earlier film versions of that novel had been using Mary Shelley's own recipe with chemicals to animate the monster, but obviously Villiers de l'Isle-Adam and von Harbou gave the American film industry an idea or two). In Germany, perhaps the most intriguing and fascinating of all modern tales of artificial men, Gustav Meyrink's *Der Golem,* appeared in 1915. Based upon old Hebrew tales about the artificial man Golem, the saviour of the Jews, it was a psychological and literary masterpiece, and is still the leading classic within this particular literary field. It was filmed three times during World War I with Paul Wegener as the monster, and has since been filmed no less than eleven times, the latest version being a 1966 French version. *Der Golem* not only preceded the classic American *Frankenstein* by sixteen years, it also brought to the screen the monster figure used later on, with a few insignificant changes, by Boris Karloff in *Frankenstein.* At least one of Paul Wegener's Golem films appeared in the United States, *The Monster of Fate,* in 1917. Borrowing liberally from this film, from *L'Eve future,* and from *Metropolis,* the film director James Whale made *Frankenstein* in 1931 into a money-making success. Of course. Some of the greatest literary and cinematic personalities of modern time had done everything for him.

Left and overleaf: Scenes from Fritz Lang's classic film 'Metropolis' (1926), based on Thea von Harbou's novel, with Brigitte Helm being reproduced as the robot Maria

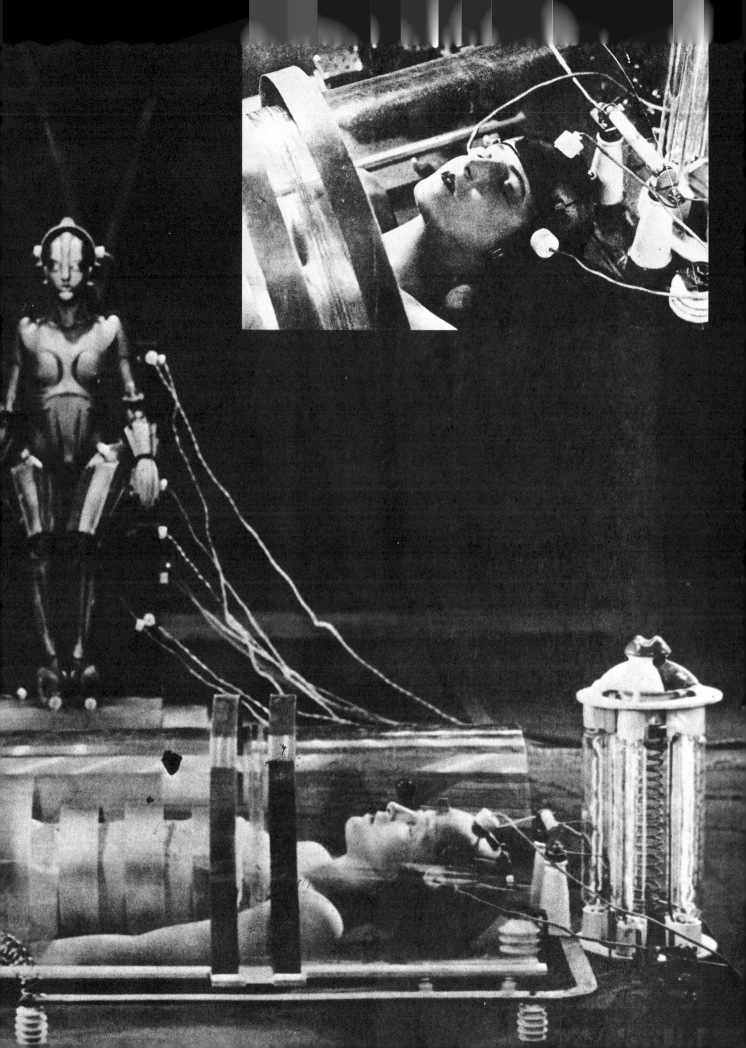

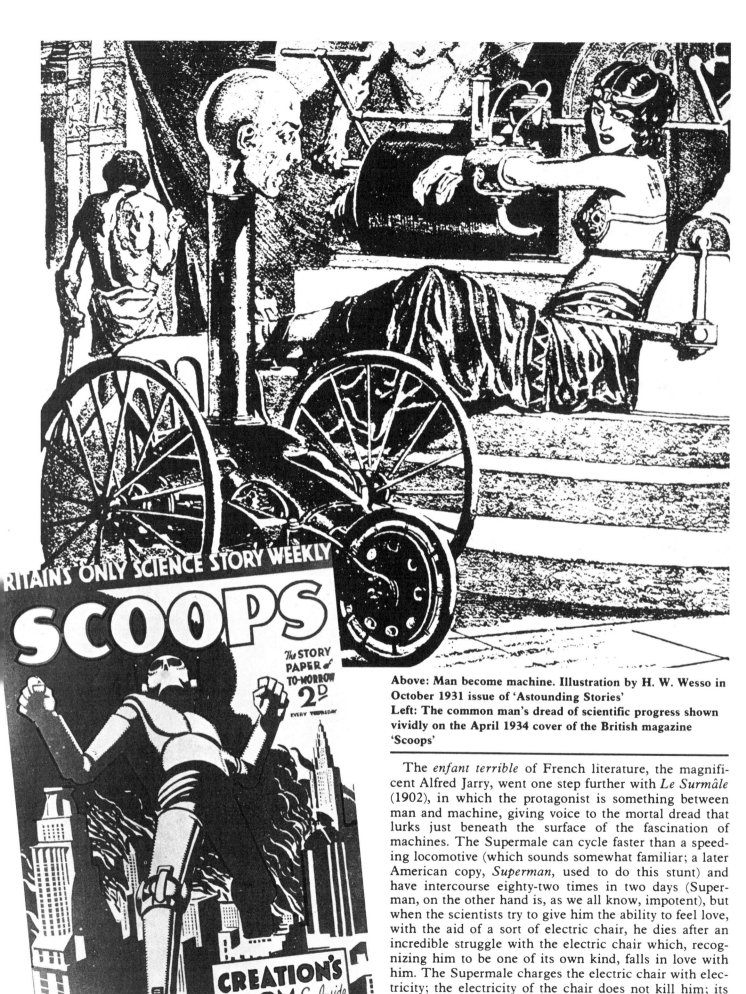

Above: Man become machine. Illustration by H. W. Wesso in October 1931 issue of 'Astounding Stories'

Left: The common man's dread of scientific progress shown vividly on the April 1934 cover of the British magazine 'Scoops'

BRITAIN'S ONLY SCIENCE STORY WEEKLY

SCOOPS

The STORY PAPER of TO-MORROW 2D EVERY THURSDAY

CREATION'S DOOM See Inside

The *enfant terrible* of French literature, the magnificent Alfred Jarry, went one step further with *Le Surmâle* (1902), in which the protagonist is something between man and machine, giving voice to the mortal dread that lurks just beneath the surface of the fascination of machines. The Supermale can cycle faster than a speeding locomotive (which sounds somewhat familiar; a later American copy, *Superman*, used to do this stunt) and have intercourse eighty-two times in two days (Superman, on the other hand is, as we all know, impotent), but when the scientists try to give him the ability to feel love, with the aid of a sort of electric chair, he dies after an incredible struggle with the electric chair which, recognizing him to be one of its own kind, falls in love with him. The Supermale charges the electric chair with electricity; the electricity of the chair does not kill him; its pure, unselfish love does.

Jarry's friend Raymond Roussel (1877–1933) wrote an even more bizarre tale of artificial life with his now classic novel *Locus Solus* (1914), surely one of the strangest science fiction novels ever written. The Locus Solus of the title is a manor (owned by the strange scientist Martial Canterel), filled with unbelievable wonders, including an enormous diamond containing, among other things, a smiling, dancing robot and a large number of small automatons. The diamond is a creator of art, particularly in the form of music issuing from the hair of the dancing robot Faustine.

A few years later the German author Hanns Heinz Ewers mixed *Märchen* folklore with modern science in a more traditional classic in this field, the novel *Alraune* (1919). The usual scientist creates a homunculus, or android, called Alraune, after the mandrake root legend from which she was modelled. She is a strange, soulless being, incredibly beautiful and with a fatal attraction for all men. The hero falls under her sexual spell and is gradually wasting away only to be saved at the last minute when Alraune learns the truth of her being and kills herself. The novel was an immediate bestseller and has formed the basis for at least three highly successful films. She also met the other monster hero of the time, Golem, in the film *Alraune und der Golem* (1919), a sort of *Bride of Frankenstein* sixteen years before that film.

Which leads us to the modern classic among robot tales, which might have been influenced by Ewers's novel and the one that, paradoxically, really opened wide the floodgates for a deluge of killing machines. The creator of this one was the Czech author and playwright Karel Capek, 'the father of Czech theatre', whose play *R.U.R., Rossum's Universal Robots,* opened in Prague in 1921 and became a tremendous success. Capek called his creations *robots* (from the Czech *robota*, worker), and the name quickly caught on. However, and this might have amused Capek, the word robot today implies any mechanical device, capable of at least some limited 'thought' process, be it a nuclear rocket, a mechanical man or an industrial robot which can perform simple, repetitive tasks. Capek's robots were, like Mary Shelley's monster, created chemically and would today be called androids.

R.U.R. is set in the near future, on an island where robots are manufactured by the hundreds of thousands and sold as workers, servants and soldiers. Eventually, the manufacturers promise, these robots will take care of all menial work, and Utopia will open its gates for everyone (except, I suppose, for the robots).

'Young Rossum invented a worker with a minimum amount of requirements,' one scientist tells Helena Glory, president of the Humanitarian League. 'He rejected everything that did not contribute directly to the progress of work—everything that makes man more expensive. In fact he rejected man and made the Robot. My dear Miss Glory, the Robots are not people. Mechanically they are more perfect than we are, they have an enormously developed intelligence, but they have no soul.'

They certainly have no souls at the beginning of the play, but in time Miss Glory persuades one of the engineers to raise the 'irritability' of the robots. Her reasons are purely humanitarian: she is scared—as anyone would be—of the chillingly effective, totally unemotional robots who unprotestingly go to their death when they get old and useless. 'I thought', she explains to her friends, 'that they would understand us better if they were like us . . .'

The robots do understand, they understand only too well. Tired of being exploited they revolt against their masters and kill everyone except one man whom they order to rediscover the secret of the creation of life. He fails, and the robots, who are sexless, seem to be doomed. However, in the end of the play a male and a female robot appear and it is implied that they will start a new humanity, with luck better than the old one.

The huge success of the play spawned imitations everywhere, and the robot soon became a staple commodity in science fiction, stomping around in increasingly sillier pulp magazine stories and killing everyone in sight. Exceptions to the rule appeared, but they were few and far between, such as Lester Del Rey's delightful short story of *Helen O'Loy* (1938), who ends up marrying her inventor and living happily ever after. Otherwise, the robots were all bad. Even in comparatively serious novels, like the Romanian author Cezar Petrescu's *Baletul mecanic* (The Mechanical Ballet, 1931) and the Swedish Elfred Berggren's *Robotarnas gud* (The God of the Robots, 1932), it all ended with the robots destroying their masters.

The situation got so bad that speedy countermeasures were called for. Science fiction already had its wicked guys, the extraterrestrials, who were always handy when externalized evil was needed. Also, the recurring theme of the robots revolting against their masters was decidedly Dystopian.

It was up to one single writer to defuse this too successful tool of the science fiction factory; and he did it so well that the robot has never again reared its ugly head in earnest. I am referring, of course, to the American writer Isaac Asimov and his Three Laws of Robotics, which are now standard rules in the genre:

1. *A robot may not injure a human being, or, through inaction, allow a human being to come to harm.*
2. *A robot must obey the orders given it by human beings except when such orders would conflict with the First Law.*
3. *A robot must protect its own existence as long as such protection does not conflict with the First or Second Law.*

This immediately made all robots incapable of behaving like true human beings, and Asimov set about writing a number of robot stories in which robots appeared to break one or several of these laws, or got into tight corners as a result of them, later collected in two books, *I, Robot* (1950) and *The Rest of the Robots* (1964). This again made robots suitable as good company, but it also made them somewhat boring and predictable. Asimov may have realized this when he wrote the 'ultimate' robot story, *That You Art Mindful of Him!* (1974), in which he neatly turns the whole concept upside-down, allowing the robots to exterminate human beings at will without breaking the holy laws of robotics.

Some robots, however, persist in being decidedly unfriendly towards Man, particularly those created by aliens whose Laws of Robotics apparently do not include Earth humans among those to be protected at all costs. An outstanding example of this is the novels by Fred Saberhagen about the Berserkers (*Berserker*, 1967; *Brother Assassin*, 1969, and *Berserker's Planet*, 1975) who

Left: Man and machine. Illustration by Charles Schneeman in 'Astounding Science Fiction', December 1942
Above: Pinocchio warming his feet

are gigantic killing machines, programmed by a long since vanished civilization to search out and destroy all intelligent life in the universe—tough going, since the Berserkers are virtually indestructible, as well as almost immortal, but the humans have triumphed at the end of each and every novel, at least so far. Better still is the leading space opera series (in quality, if not in quantity), the Spanish *La Familia Aznar* by 'George H. White' (Pascual Enguidanos Usach), who for ten years, from 1954 to 1963, delighted Spanish-speaking readers with stupendous space battles between alien robots and intrepid human heroes. Incredible armies of robot soldiers and metal spiders fight the armies of Earth in *Guerra de autòmatas* (War of the Automatons, 1954); electronic brains hunt human explorers on the strange planet Ragol, where the robots have risen against their human masters and killed them, in *Cerebros electrónicos* (Electronic Brains, 1954); and the heroic humans, led by the Aznar family, even repeatedly fight the murderous robot planet Valera (in *El coloso en rebeldia* [The Recalcitrant Colossus, 1956] and other novels in the series). Actually, the robot planet Valera keeps appearing in this series, and seems to be the only entity for which the author entertains any kind of warm feeling. The various members of the Aznar family are more expendable and die one after another as the series progresses, by

their own hand or with the help of aliens or human beings. Only the immortal robots press on and actually win the occasional famous victory against the humans.

A similar love-hate relationship with the robot warriors, coupled with the robots' low regard of non-artificial life, can be found in the Hungarian Péter Lengyel's fine novel *Ogg masodik bolygoja* (The Second Planet of Ogg, 1972) in which armies of no-good robots, known as Memnons, are doing their best to kill off the inhabitants of the peaceful world Eela. They are thwarted in the end, of course, but one gets the distinct impression that the author is much more interested in his murderous robots than in the not very exciting humans, despite his repeated assurances to the contrary. Similar feelings are surfacing in the German space opera series Perry Rhodan, where the great hero and his faithful friends spend most of their time fighting the dreadful Positronicon, the Mechanical Mind, The Soulless Regent of the robot planet Arkon—apparently without much success, since that Machine Nemesis always pops up again, ready for new mischiefs on a galactic scale.

As I write this, one of the most popular television programmes in Japan is an out-and-out animated robot series called *Majinger-Z*, featuring enormous robots equipped with everything imaginable in the way of weaponry, from photon-beam cannon, hurricane blowers and various missiles to photon energy rockets, 'crash punchers' and a secret weapon only used in really tight situations. They fight invaders from space, human heroes, natural catastrophes and, when nothing else comes along, each other. Good, clean fun, and immensely popular.

This is very far from the most loved of all automatons, the Italian Carlo Collodi's *Pinocchio* (1881–82), the wooden doll made by old Mr Gepetto which comes alive and is hounded through life in a manner reminiscent of Frankenstein's monster. It is a fairy tale in the most bloodthirsty Grimm tradition, a Gothic novel thinly disguised as a fairy tale where Pinocchio flees through a world of inhuman poverty, insensitivity and downright cruelty. Not even his good fairy can always be trusted. Disobedience is punished immediately and Pinocchio's dream of becoming a 'real' boy is granted only with the reservation that he will be changed back into a wooden doll again if he doesn't behave. Things have certainly changed since then. With the modern robot embodying, in some perverted way, Man's super ego, projecting the sort of uninhibited brute presumably lurking inside all men, or at least inside all science fiction authors, nothing remains sacred from these monsters. Soon not even our wives and daughters will be safe from their lecherous designs, at least if we are to believe a recent American film, *Demon Seed* (1976), where a computer creates havoc when it decides to procreate with its creator's wife. Frankenstein's monster was never like that. He civilly asked his creator to make a monstress for him. On the other hand, since Frankenstein flatly refused to help his monster out, the computer in *Demon Seed* might have a point.

Incidentally, the Hungarian science fiction author Ervin Gyertyán has made a rather outspoken defence for the robot as sexual object in his very funny (and rather unchaste) novel *The Splendour and Decline of Cyberneros* (1963), dealing with the perfect love partner for the connoisseur, the untiring Cyberneros, 'designed for meeting even the most variegated demands.' The same theme appears in a delightful short story by the Soviet author

Aleksandr Shalimov, *Vse nachalos s Evy* (It all Began with Eve, 1964), in which beautiful female robots are manufactured and sold as servants and pets to needy customers. It soon becomes a question of morals, however, and also a question of jealousy when furious women start tearing their husbands' robot mistresses to pieces. At this point, the manufacturer starts manufacturing male robots as well and also manages to get all robots legally declared human beings. Soon no one can tell the difference between robots and 'real' human beings without opening (and killing) them, and the situation becomes chaotic.

Robots also take over man's time-honoured position as creator and inventor. The Polish writer Stanislaw Lem, in particular, who has written more robot stories than most authors in the field, has gleefully put forward the robot as inventor and creator with a vengeance, notably in his stories about the strange robots Trurl and Klapaucius. While not a great author, Lem nevertheless makes good, solid and funny points in these stories, collected in three volumes, *Ksiega robotów* (Book of Robots, 1961), *Bajki robotów* (Fairy Tales for Robots, 1964) and *Cyberiada* (The Cyberiad, 1965). In one short story, *Kobyszcze* (In Hot Pursuit of Happiness, 1971) Trurl decides to define true happiness and constructs, among other things, an Ecstatic Contemplator of Existence, designed to give accurate readings of happiness experienced. It is calibrated in hedons, or heds for short, with one hed being 'the quantity of bliss one would experience after walking exactly four miles with a nail in one's boot and then having the nail removed.' One kilohed would be what the elders felt when they beheld Susanna at her bath, and one megahed the joy of a man condemned to hang but reprieved at the last minute.

I read this as a wry comment on the theoreticians of the world, those content with systematizing life instead of experiencing it. And, of course, this is an effective method of defusing the robot.

The American writer Ron Goulart has created his own sub-genre of science fiction, the Goulart novel, with a predictable assortment of malfunctioning robots, uppity androids, scatterbrained heroes and females with small brains but enormously developed breasts. Most living things in the Goulart novels are robots, from birds, dogs and horses to humanoid robots and androids. Goulart has written dozens of these novels, all of them slight variations on a standard theme that obviously is highly appreciated by his fans. It is indeed a robot world to outdo all other robot worlds. Personally, I find it quite boring after the first dozen novels or so.

With the dividing line between human and robot becoming increasingly thinner, we are reapproaching Alfred Jarry's Supermale. In the Chilean author Hugo Correa's bitter short story *Alter Ego* (1967) the ultimate robot is finally created and can be bought by anyone. Its human owner and master can see through its eyes, feel with its body, taste with its mouth. But, jaded by overpowerful sensations, only one experience remains for the robot's owner. Using the robot as an extension of his own body, he kills himself.

The robot can be too good, too obliging; it can help us

Robots abducting nice girls: illustration by Virgil Finlay in November 1952 'Fantastic Adventures'; in a Turkish edition of Asimov's collection of short stories about robots 'I, Robot'; and hanging the hero before dealing with the girl

ISAAC ASIMOV

ROBOTLAR

MJ Milliyet
YAYINLARI

BILIM-KURGU DİZİS

ANC IMAGINATION

JUNE, 1954
35¢

STORIES OF SCIENCE AND FANTASY

SLAVES TO TH
METAL HORDE
—by MILTON
LESSER

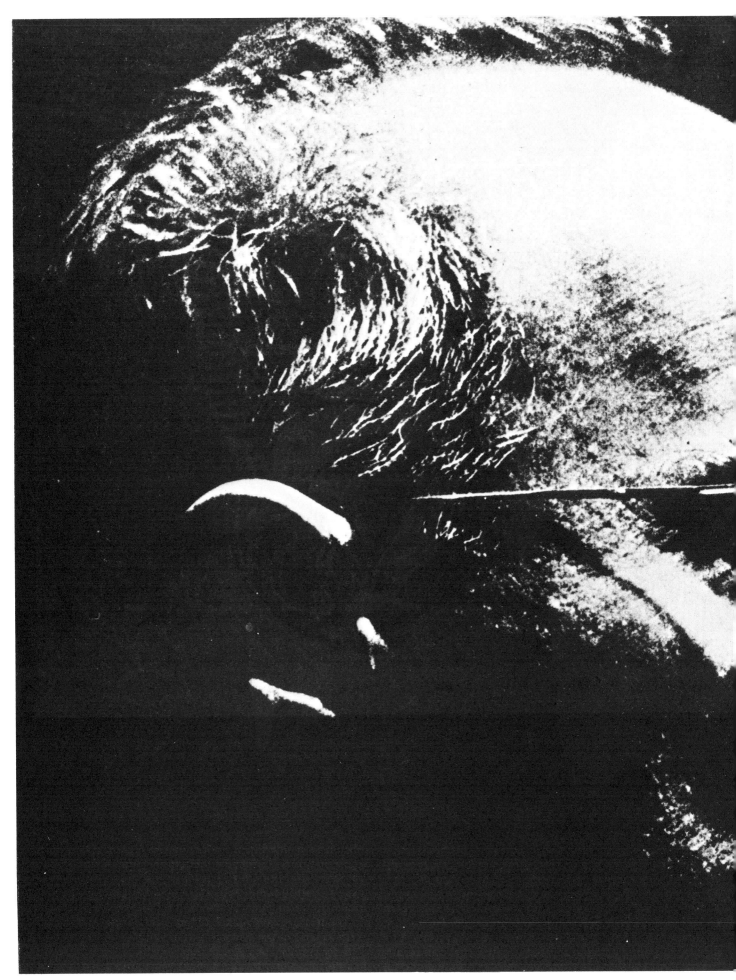

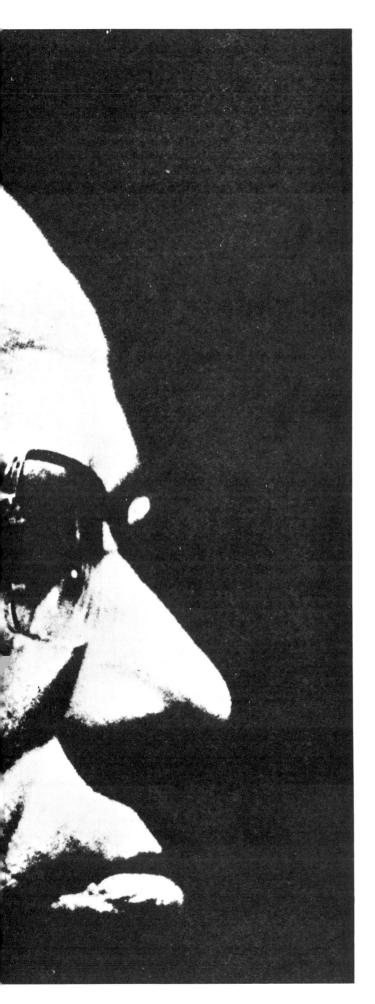

Left: Stanislav Lem, the prolific Polish robot story writer
Above: With Western and SF films among the most stereotyped in the film industry, it was inevitable that someone should try mixing the genres. Yul Brynner appears here as a robot cowboy in 'Westworld' (1973)

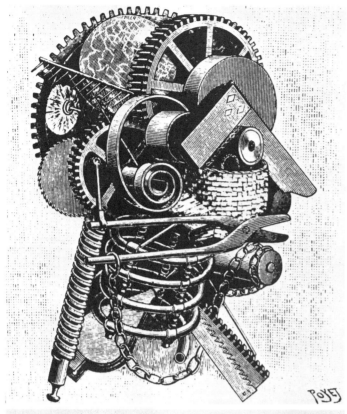

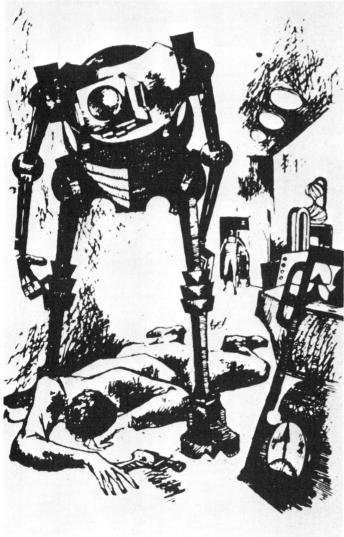

Left: Machine turning into man: 'The Inventor', late
19th-century illustration by Poyet; and man and his
master—drawing by the Bulgarian Nikifor Ruskov
Above: Robot mending his leg—'Amazing Stories', January
1939
Overleaf: Walter Pidgeon in 'Forbidden Planet'

usually even after that. Science fiction writers and readers are basically quite conservative, even reactionary, which may be a good sign—we have too many starry-eyed Utopians in our midst, always willing to go along with anything new. That the affluence and leisure made possible by the ever-present and obedient robots can be highly dangerous is clear in the leading German science fiction writer Herbert W. Franke's novel *Der Orchideenkäfig* (The Orchid Cage, 1961), in which two groups of human explorers come to a distant planet and break into an ancient mechanized city with no visible inhabitants. The city fights them all the way, but one of the groups of explorers finally gets hold of a nuclear weapon and destroys the city. The result is surprising—the humans are dragged before a court of computers who decide they have committed murder and sentence them to death. It appears that the builders of the city are hiding somewhere beneath the ruined city, and the humans finally get permission from the robots to visit them. They find long rooms with strange orchids, the evolved, still living bodies of the builders of the city, dreaming never-ending dreams of happiness and glory, faithfully served by their robots.

Too cold, too logical, too wise. Eternal Nirvana might be the best for all of us, but is hardly the thing we are longing for. From the viewpoint of a machine, though, it might be just that. In Karel Capek's *R.U.R.* the robots were given human emotions, courtesy of Miss Helena Glory, which at least helped them, if not their former masters and owners.

Science fiction writers have realized this, and the android, the chemically created man, is these days as much a staple commodity in the genre as the robot. The android does not toil under any Laws of Robotics. Like Capek's liberated robots he is free, or at least wants to be free, an unpredictable animal, just as good or as bad as ordinary human beings. They can be rather nasty, too, when demanding their equal rights, as in the Danish science fiction author Niels E. Nielsen's moving and compassionate novel *Herskerne* (The Rulers, 1970), in which the androids, created during and for enormous experiments in genetics, demand their rights from their former rulers. Upon being denied this, they go to war, a particularly horrible one since the humans see them as machines or at best animals with no right to life or happiness, while the androids fight, backs to the wall, against defeat and extermination. The situation of the androids here—and in most science fiction stories where they appear—is that of the Jews in Nazi Germany, the Indians in America and the Blacks in South Africa—and here, at last, science fiction appears to have found a fitting symbol for our own times and indeed for ourselves. The traditional robots are too stupid or too good or too bad, according to their programming. The androids are really human beings; what is good in Man is good in them; what is dark in the human character is dark in theirs. With the return, as it were, of the Frankenstein's monster android to science fiction, with all that implies, I think the genre will find a good and solid future ahead.

a little too effectively and perhaps too far, until we can no longer keep up with it. Fears of an all-powerful machine are coming back, though in a different disguise—not always as blatant as in the celebrated Clarke and Kubrick film *2001—A Space Odyssey* (1968) where the robot brain HAL decides it must kill off its human crew so as not endanger the mission. Perfectly logical, of course. The robot could be the grave digger of the human race, as in Clifford D. Simak's modern classic *City* (1952), chronicling man's last 10,000 years on Earth, with the last robots faithfully nursing the last remnants of the human race until even the memory of Man is gone and Earth is taken over by the dogs, and later on by the ants, because the ants alone are unselfish enough to create a lasting civilization—the robots could do it, too, but they are too much like Man. They remain, taking care of Man's inheritors, creating a Utopia the like of which could never appear as long as Man remained.

The robot seems to be a mixed blessing, at least in science fiction, where any invention is automatically assumed to be dangerous until proved otherwise, and

GALACTIC PATROL

Qadgop the Mercotan slithered flatly around the afterbulge of the tranship. One claw dug into the meters-thick armour of pure neutronium, then another. The terrible xmex-like snout locked on. Its zymolosely polydactile tongue crunched out, crashed down, rasped across. SLURP! SLURP! *At each abrasive stroke the groove in the tranship's plating deepened and Qadgop leered more fiercely. Fools! Did they think that the airlessness of absolute space, the heatlessness of absolute zero, the yieldlessness of absolute neutronium, could stop QADGOP THE MERCOTAN? And the stowaway, the human wench Cynthia, cowering in helpless terror just beyond this thin and fragile wall . . .*

In all fairness, this enthralling example of breathtaking intergalactic high adventure was never meant to be taken seriously, although written by the unquestioned king of the Space Opera writers. It appears in E. E. 'Doc' Smith's eventful novel *Children of the Lens* (1947) as part of a literary masterpiece written by one of the greatest space opera heroes, Kim Kinnison, who spends his spare moments between smashing suns and saving the universe writing glorious space adventures. Life is, however, stranger than Kinnison's fiction, at least in E. E. Smith's novel, for later in *Children of the Lens* Kim Kinnison and his fiancé Karen encounter even worse things when they learn that Karen

had been en rapport with one of Civilization's bitterest, most implacable foes, that she has seen with clairvoyant and telepathic accuracy the intrinsically three-dimensionally-indescribable form assumed in their winter by the horrid, the monstrous inhabitants of that viciously hostile world, the unspeakable planet Ploor!

The awed reader later learns that the Kinnisons successfully blast the unspeakable planet Ploor to cinders and that Kinnison's novel ends up as a smash hit. Probably he receives both the Nobel Peace and Literature Prize from a grateful world, although this is not mentioned in the novel.

He must have been awarded these prizes, because the fundamental fact of any self-respecting space opera tale is that the hero is, literally, the greatest, bravest, most handsome and most intelligent man in the entire universe, a wonder of a man who can out-think and out-draw any being in this universe or the next. He is ruthless when the need arises, but he is also always willing to risk his life for blue-eyed and fair-haired WASP females in distress. In E. E. Smith's novel *Skylark DuQuesne* (1965), the final novel in the stupenduous Skylark saga, the hero single-handedly destroys an entire galaxy of fifty thousand million suns, each of them with an undisclosed number of inhabited planets, without raising an eyebrow: *(The Chlorans) died in uncounted trillions. The greeny-yellow soup that served them for air boiled away. Their halogenous flesh was charred, baked and dessiccated in the split-second of the passing of the wave front from each exploding double star, moments before their planets themselves began to seethe and boil. Many died unaware. Most died fighting. Some died in terrible, frantic efforts to escape. . . .*

But they all died.

However, E. E. Smith assures us, 'No human world was destroyed.' This shows that the hero is a nice guy after all, although forced by circumstances to out-do all mass-murderers in history. Whereas the Wild West, or Horse Opera, hero defends the white race and Western civilization with his trusty six-shooters, the space opera hero carries the White Man's Burden on his broad shoulders around the entire universe, killing off everything that appears too alien. The difference lies not in attitude or philosophy, but in scale; at bottom, we still have the age-old desire to externalize evil, to create adversaries that are truly and unquestionably evil. It is too easy to feel compassion for Indians, Chinese or Vietnamese—thorough evil, as embodied in Satan or the Alien, comes closer to the mark. Thus, the space opera tale vindicated a bloodlust that is all too common in this day and age.

This sort of gore and sadism, set against a backdrop of galactic wars, mile-long space ships and alien civilizations, all of them bent upon the destruction of humanity, had its heyday in American pulp magazines of the 1930s. Basically a spin-off from the dime novels of the late

Above: Kapitän Mors in a meteorite shower (1910)
Right: The lecherous Martian defeated—Stanley Wood's illustration for George Griffith's 'Honeymoon in Space' (1899)

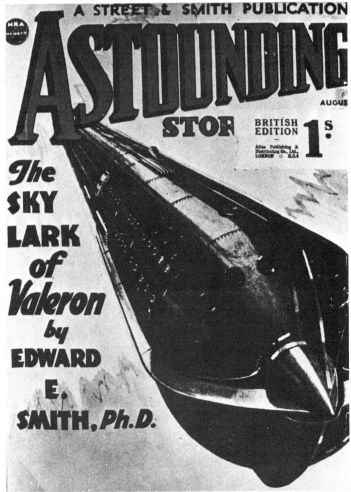

Magazine covers from USA and Spain, including one of E. E. Smith's colossal spaceships and 'La bestia capitula' ('The Beast Surrenders'), volume 58 in the Aznar Family series

nineteenth century, with their bold heroes and incredibly evil adversaries, the space opera writers exchanged the Wild West or battlefields of World War I for interstellar space, made heroes and villains superhuman and created universes dripping with blood in which Man marched triumphant, brandishing his atomic cannon and blasting away at everything in sight. It was little more than an updating of the popular future war stories of the 1890s, the undisputed king of which was George Griffith. H. G. Wells brought in tentacled aliens for added thrills in *The War of the Worlds* and also introduced the theme of super-science. North American pulp writers went further, showing in gory detail the dangers that threatened the American Way of Life during the Depression. These tales were incredibly crude, by literary standards, and highly improbable, by any standards, but this modern mixture of Horatio Alger Jr and the Brothers Grimm caught on and was thriving well into the 1950s when the Korean War spawned hundreds of films and novels describing intrepid WASP heroes saving civilization against terrifying invaders from outer space. The 1960s and 1970s have seen a revival of this kind of fiction, with new editions of E. E. Smith's novels and a number of new space opera heroes galloping through space. Attesting this new popularity of space opera, we have television series such as the British *Space: 1999* and the American *Star Trek* which, despite their ingenious presentation

FUTURO

novelas de CIENCIA Y FANTASIA

LA MAQUINA

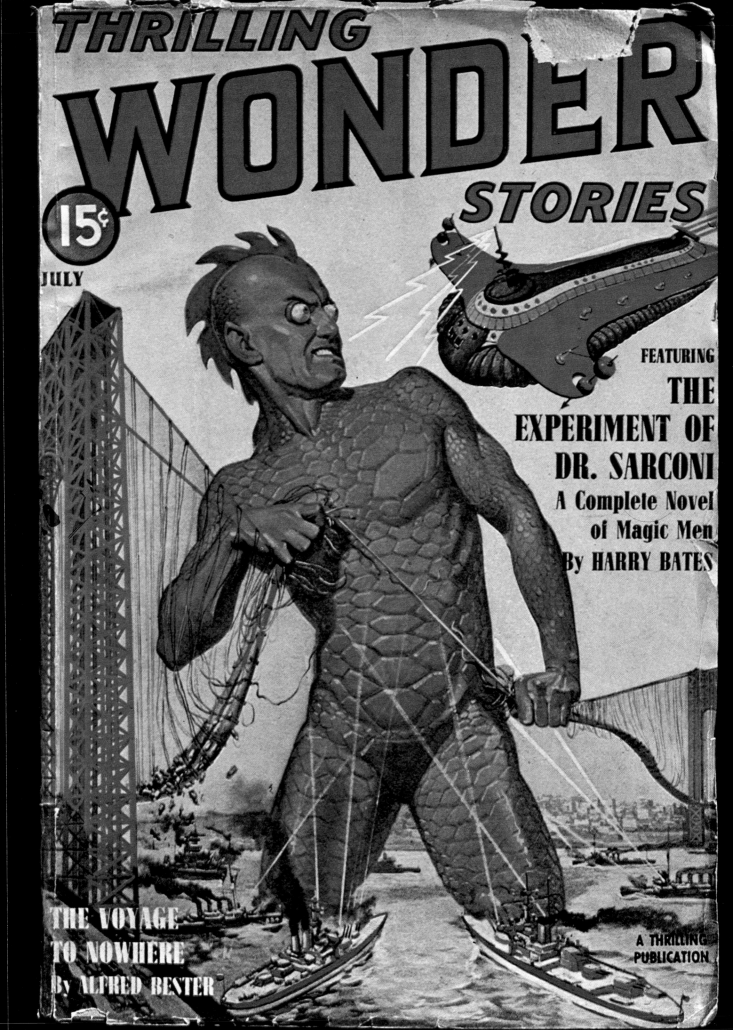

Nr. 575
DM 1,-
Österreich S 7,-
Schweiz Fr. 1.20
Italien Lire 240
Belgien frs.16,-
Luxemburg frs.15,-
Frankreich FF 180
Niederlande hfl. 120
Spanien Ptas 25,-

Perry Rhodan
der Erbe des Universums

Neu!

Die grosse WELTRAUM-SERIE
von K. H. Scheer und Clark Darlton

Stadt im Lavameer

Spuk auf der Welt der Asporcos –
die Mutanten laufen Amok

Mit
Rißzeichnung
»Forschungsschiff
der Accalauris«

Pulp magazine covers, include a fine Perry Rhodan one

SEPTEMBER

AMAZING STORIES

IN CANADA 30 CENTS

SKYLARK THREE

by Edward E. Smith, Ph.D

Other Scientifiction Stories by:

Harl Vincent

Fred M. Barclay

Isaac R. Nathanson

'Amazing Stories' cover and (right) volume 44 in the Aznar Family series

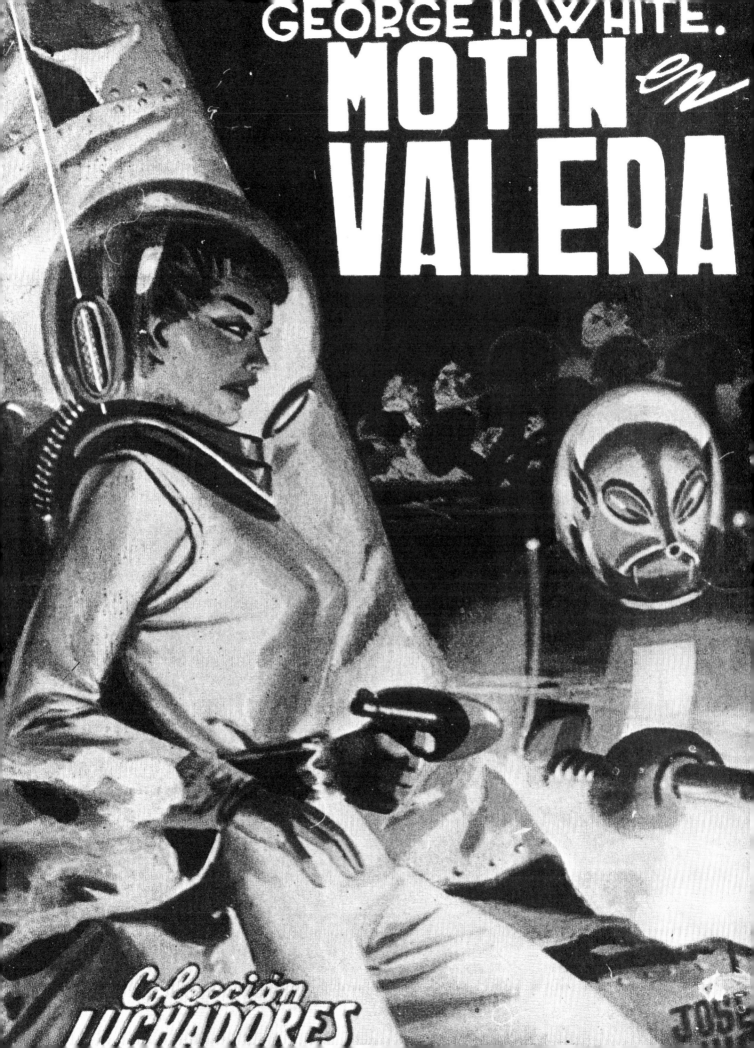

GEORGE H. WHITE.

MOTIN en

VALERA

Colección
LUCHADORES

Above: One of the usual stupendous space battles. Illustration by Frank R. Paul for John W. Campbell's 'The Black Star Passes', in 'Amazing Stories Quarterly', Fall 1930
Right: Space opera hero with friends. Illustration by Charles Schneeman for E. E. Smith's 'Gray Lensman', in 'Astounding Science Fiction', October 1939

and weak plots have found thousands of fanatical followers who are now holding regular conventions.

It all began, as I see it, with George Griffith's novel *Stories of Other Worlds*, first serialized in the British *Pearson's Magazine* in 1900 and the following year published in book form as *Honeymoon In Space*. The plot was a standard one already: a round trip to the planets of the solar system, in this case made by an extremely British hero and his bride. The hero is introduced as Rollo Lennox Smeaton Aubrey, Earl of Redgrave, Baron Smeaton in the Peerage of England, and Viscount Aubrey in the Peerage of Ireland. Better people than that did not exist in Victorian England. He also has a 'tall athletic figure and the regular-featured, bronzed, honest English face'. His wife, Zaidie, is no less beautiful:
It was a face which possessed at once the fair Anglo-Saxon skin, the firm yet delicate Anglo-Saxon features, and the wavy wealth of the old Saxon gold-brown hair; but a pair of big, soft, pansy eyes, fringed with long, curling, black lashes, looked out from under dark and perhaps just a trifle heavy eyebrows. Moreover, there was that indescrib-

'That a man!' says her husband through clenched teeth. 'Not much! Here, Andrew, open that door again and help me to heave this thing overboard . . .'

Here, then, is the mould in which all space opera stories have been cast. Details are different in modern space opera, but the basic attitude is the same. This is apparently what has made this particular branch of science fiction so popular and, in my personal opinion, rather dangerous. Racism and the glorification of violence is still the main ingredient of space opera, albeit usually discreetly hidden somewhere among the mind-boggling space armadas.

We find this already in the first great space opera series, the German *Der Luftpirat und sein lenkbares Luftschiff* (The Pirate of the Air and His Dirigible Air Ship), featuring the intrepid master villain, Kapitän Mors. This pulp magazine series, originating from Berlin, appeared weekly, starting in 1908, and delighted hundreds of thousands of Germans with at least 165 volumes, becoming in the process one of the most popular pulp magazines in the world, with sales up to 100,000 per issue, and the leading space opera series until the similarly German series Perry Rhodan appeared in 1961.

Kapitän Mors, the 'Pirate of the Air', formerly submarine commander, now a curious mixture of Jules Verne's Captain Nemo and world police of the Robin Hood type, upholds with his wondrous 'mysterious, dirigible air ship' order and justice on Earth, in the seas and, above all, in space. On the back cover of volume 102 of his fantastic adventures amid rascals and corrupt politicians, aliens and other trash, we can read:

And just as Verne's mysterious Captain Nemo once ruled the seas, Captain Mors now rules the air with his mysterious air ship.

And the world calls him the Pirate of the Air!

Why?

Captain Mors tears the ill-gotten gains from those who make enormous fortunes solely through the power of capital, and gives it to the poor and destitute. Thus he relieves poverty and misery with these treasures. The Pirate of the Air protects the persecuted innocents, he punishes insidious criminals . . .

Nothing can be hidden from him!

A number of the most wonderful adventures that any human being ever experienced take place before the readers' eyes. Abundant with touching situations, told with imagination and executed with boldness, the adventures of the Pirate of the Air guarantee entertaining and instructive reading.

Kapitän Mors is a genius 'centuries before his time.' His airship is powered by 'the terrifying solar energy', which is 'otherwise only . . . used by alien beings'. A real space opera hero, almost indistiguishable from latter-day ones, as demonstrated by the titles of some of the spine-chilling volumes in this series: *Der Kampf mit den Bewohnern des Kriegsplaneten* (The Battle Against the People of the War Planet); *Das Rätsel des unsichtbaren Planeten* (The Mystery of the Invisible Planet); *Der Tempel in der Mondlandschaft Plato* (The Temple in the Moon Landscape Plato); *Am Ende der Sonnenwelt* (At the End of the Solar System); *Auf dem Krystall-Mond des Saturn* (On Saturn's Crystal Moon); *Die Signalstation am Mondkrater Cassini* (The Signal Station in the Moon Crater Cassini); and *Im Urmeer des fernsten Planeten* (In the Original Sea of the Distant Planets). Monsters are

able expression in the curve of her lips and the pose of her head; to say nothing of a lissome, vivacious grace in her whole carriage which proclaimed her a daughter of the younger branch of the Race that Rules.

And rule it does, as this heavenly pair travels around the solar system with their obedient valet Andrew Murgatroyd, who spends his time alternately taking off his cap for his betters and loading the many cannon with which the space ship, the *Astronef,* is so amply endowed. Descending on Mars, they find to their surprise that the Martians detest having them wreak havoc and start defending themselves. Having destroyed an undisclosed number of unarmed Martian air ships, they land and Zaidie steps outside.

'If a seraph had come on Earth and presented itself before a throng of human beings, there might have happened some such miracle as was wrought when the swarm of Martians beheld the strange beauty of this radiant daughter of the Earth,' Griffith assures us, apparently correctly, for hardly has ten minutes passed before one of the brutish Martians makes a pass at Zaidie, whereupon she promptly shoots him. 'That's the first man I've ever killed,' she confides to her proud husband as the love-starved Martian lies twitching on the deck. 'Still, do you really think it really was a man?'

abundant, usually 'slimy' and 'terrifying', science consists of 'strange devices', Earth is 'Mother Earth', space is enormous, unending and filled with alien dangers that must be defeated at all costs.

All this reads just like the space opera series so popular in English-speaking countries particularly during the 1940s—the Captain Futures, the Kinnisons, and so on. The anonymous author of Kapitän Mors' adventures invented modern space opera singlehanded; everything that came after him was nothing but a pale copy—amusing in their bungling, illiterate way, but only copies.

Also, Kapitän Mors had one good feature that later space opera heroes lacked; he promised justice in a world and a time which had precious little of that commodity. Later heroes only offered blood, gore and monsters, plus some pseudo-science even worse than that of Kapitän Mors.

It is interesting that the next great space opera series, E. E. Smith's *Skylark* series, was begun in 1915 (although the first novel did not see publication until 1928), while Kapitän Mors was still at the peak of his popularity in German-speaking countries. I do not know whether E. E. Smith could read German and if so, ever

Flash Gordon in the original (above) and, more amazingly, according to 'Mad' magazine

read Kapitän Mors. Surely the similarities are too great to be overlooked. The difference between E. E. Smith and Kapitän Mors is mostly one of scale. E. E. Smith's *Skylark* (four novels) and *Lensman* (six novels) series contain all the time-honoured ingredients of space opera, everything on such a gigantic scale it is almost a parody with mile-long space ships, space fleets of hundreds of thousand ships, heroes brave and noble beyond all reason

Intrepid, handsome Captain Future. Above, he battles against evil alien monsters trying to abduct heroine—'Captain Future', Winter 1942

and villains straight out of the nethermost pits of Hell. In essence, they were written for boys by a writer that never quite grew up; E. E. Smith is like a child playing with stars and galaxies, without bothering for a second about credibility or morals or anything that possibly could take the fun out of the game. The *Skylark* and *Lensman* novels become confusing if read one after another; the magnificent space battles, villains, heroes, scientific marvels and incredible happenings in this or another dimension overwhelm the mind, and in the end it seems somewhat repetitious. It also becomes a bit boring. When the hero, Seaton, in *Skylark of Valeron* (1934), condemns some of his enemies to solitary confinement in a ball of force for seventeen thousand million years, after having turned the whole galaxy upside down catching them, one can't muster even half the enthusiasm this incredible feat is undoubtedly worth. In this case, space opera has somehow managed to slip out of the confinement of its own formula and emerged as absurdism.

In the late 1920s another American science fiction writer, Edmond Hamilton, started writing stories of superscience, juggling stars and planets and galaxies like a circus performer and creating, among other things, the *Interstellar Patrol*, a sort of police governing the entire

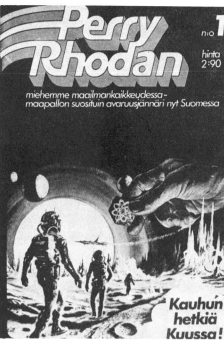

Original German Perry Rhodan (left), and British, Finnish and film versions. The film 'SOS aus dem Weltall' appeared in 1968

universe according to Terran (i.e. North American) laws. It was simply colonialism in a somewhat modernized overcoat, and this idea, also used by E. E. Smith in his *Galactic Patrol* stories, has since become a science fiction cliché. Hamilton fought so many wars of peace in interstellar space, smashed innumerable enemy worlds into atoms and saved Mother Earth so many times that he eventually earned the nickname 'World-Saver Hamilton'. For some years in the early 1930s Hamilton was competing for the place of leading American space opera author with John W. Campbell (1910–1971), who produced quite a number of incredible space opera yarns such as *The Mightiest Machine* (1934) and *The Brain Stealers of Mars* (1936), until in October 1937 he found his true vocation as editor of *Astounding Stories* (now *Analog*), and started an editorial career during which he advocated the ideas of a large number of cranks, notably former science fiction author, now prophet, L. Ron Hubbard, whose strange religion Dianetics, now Scientology, found its first home in *Astounding*. Campbell wanted to create super-science in real life; Hamilton was more modest.

Edmond Hamilton (1904–1977), a surprisingly mature and sensitive author who might have become one of science fiction's most important writers had he not spent most of his time and energy writing blood-and-thunder juvenile space operas is, however, most fondly remembered for one series of space opera novels, rivalling E. E. Smith's novels in popularity. Here, space opera really started tugging at its dime novel tail, and the attitudes of ordinary human beings towards the hero of these novels are nothing short of idolatry:

James Carthew's face set. He looked out through the eastern window of the tower room, at the full moon that was rising majestically in the heavens like a great silver shield.

'There is one man who can smash Doctor Zarro's plot, if anyone can,' he muttered. 'I did not want to call upon him before this, for he is not the kind of man to be annoyed with matters the regular authorities can handle . . .'

The secretary stiffened. His lips trembled.
'You mean . . . Captain Future?'

Correct. Captain Future, the most handsome, intelligent and great guy in seven universes, always ready to save the universe at the drop of a hat. Whenever destruction threatened Mankind during the 1940s, Earth authorities sent a distress call to Captain Future's secret abode on the Moon and Captain Future raced out, blaster at the ready, to rectify the situation. To be fair, he was not completely alone. Whereas the Kinnisons in E. E. Smith's *Lensman* stories could always count on a friendly alien intelligence to bail them out of tight spots, Captain Future, also known as Curt Newton, had a gang of loyal followers, each with his own specialty: Grag, an incredibly strong but not too intelligent robot; Otho, an android capable of changing his appearance in a matter of seconds; the Brain, a deceased scientist whose brain sloshed around in a glass box, always inventing new incredible scientific marvels whenever Captain Future needed them; and Joan, the Captain's fiancée, who seemingly made her living by getting abducted by various villains and monsters at appropriate times. The good Captain himself combined the best traits of his followers, creating a team that made any villain in known space tremble with fear.

The idea was not Hamilton's; he was commissioned to write the stories for a new pulp magazine, *Captain Future Magazine*, which was just an updated version of the old Frank Reade dime novels. Each story must be a crusade to bring an arch villain to justice, and in each story the hero must be captured and escape three times. This he faithfully did in twenty-seven Captain Future tales between 1940 and 1951, all but three of which were written by Edmond Hamilton. None of them were great literary achievements, but they were certainly filled to the bursting point with everything a youthful audience could wish for in the way of space wars, villainy and unbelievable deeds of heroism. A whole generation of American fans who read these stories during their formative years still think Captain Future is the greatest literature ever written.

In Spain and the Spanish-speaking countries of South

America, however, the greatest space hero was and is not one, but a family, the intrepid Aznar family, who from 1954 through 1963 fought the entire universe in 35 grandiose novels. Written by 'George H. White' (Pascual Enguidanos Usach, a Spanish writer living in Madrid), these novels were published in the *Luchadores del espacio* (Fighters of Space) series, usually under the heading *La Saga de los Aznar* (The Saga of the Aznars) or *Hazañas de la familia Aznar* (The Feats of the Aznar Family), and from an enormous 8,000 year galactic odyssey, amply imbued with Shakespearian tragedy and *machismo*, chronicling the suicides, misfortunes and triumphs of the Aznar family through numerous wars. The series enjoyed enormous popularity in the Spanish-speaking world, and is now being reissued in a somewhat modernized form, incorporating cloning, lasers, and other new science fiction tools.

The Familia Aznar series is unusual in many respects, at least compared to the American and German space operas. The author devotes page after page to explaining the scientific principles behind the various machinery and the biological make-up of alien races. His literary style is epic, romantic and fatalistic, at the same time, and the barbarous splendour of certain space empires is described with a skill very unusual in this genre. Lots of space is devoted to musings about the secrets of the universe, best exemplified perhaps by the robot planet Valera which hides a number of secrets which are only hinted at. The exploration of the universe is led, throughout this epic series, mainly by four families whose sons and daughters take over when their parents die—usually violently. They are the Ferrers (engineers), the Castillos (biologists and natural scientists), the Valeras (astronomers) and the Aznars. The Aznars are the real explorers, but also the rulers who bear a burden of responsibility so heavy that now and then they crack and commit suicide. (Kapitän Mors or Captain Future would never do this.) It started innocently enough with a flying saucer novel in 1954, *Los hombres de Venus* (The Venus People), but the Aznar family soon went on to bigger things as Miguel Angel Aznar, the scion of the Aznar family, establishes a dynasty on Venus in the third novel of the series, *La ciudad congelada* (The Frozen City, 1954). The family travels in time, returning to Earth in the twenty-seventh century. Earth is devastated by 'Gray Men' from Mars, a few thousand Spaniards flee out into space to create their own empire under the Aznars, and from then on they never look back. The Aznars live in a universe which is inimical to Man—the worlds they conquer sooner or later turn against them, strange beings do their best to kill them, and when there are no external enemies around, the Aznars do themselves in, one way or another. It is indeed Shakespearian tragedy, of a kind very seldom met in science fiction and never in space opera. I will not try to recapitulate this 35-volume epic—that would make a book of its own. I will only say that in many respects the Familia Aznar series is probably the best space opera series ever written. It has plenty of the faults of space opera but there is also something else—perhaps the realization that Man is a small being in an infinite universe, struggling against all odds to survive, failing again and again but always willing to try once more.

The term 'space opera' was originally coined by the American writer Wilson Tucker in the January 1941 issue of the fan magazine *Le Zombie* as a name for the

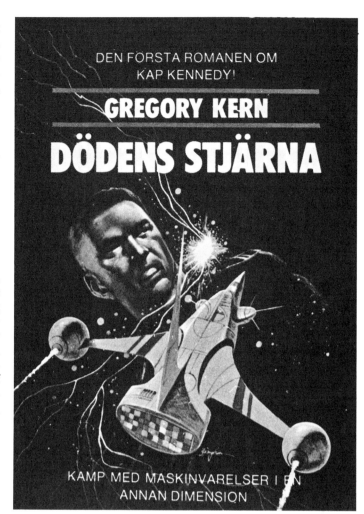

DEN FÖRSTA ROMANEN OM KAP KENNEDY!

GREGORY KERN

DÖDENS STJÄRNA

KAMP MED MASKINVARELSER I EN ANNAN DIMENSION

'hacky, grinding, stinking, outworn spaceship yarn'. Probably no space opera series so well deserves this definition as the greatest of them all, the German *Perry Rhodan*.

In terms of copies sold and money made, Perry Rhodan and its numerous offshots are easily the most successful science fiction stories in the world. According to the publisher, Ace Books, the series has so far had worldwide sales of more than 100 million copies. In Germany, where the Perry Rhodan magazine appears on a weekly basis, sales exceed 300,000 copies per issue. There are at the moment also editions in Japan, Holland, Belgium, Italy, Britain and France. This, however, is only half of it. Perry Rhodan is primarily a business object, selling all sorts of stuff to its youthful readers, from stamps, year-books, spaceship models and records, to posters, games and comics, all of it bearing the trade mark of Perry Rhodan, 'der Erbe des Universums'. There are also Perry Rhodan conventions, Perry Rhodan clubs and Perry Rhodan fan magazines. Even a Perry Rhodan film, with more of it to come. It is big business indeed, and the originators are now very rich men.

It all began in 1961, when the German science fiction writer Walter Ernsting and a few likeminded souls managed to persuade Moewig Verlag in Munich to publish a weekly pulp magazine series about Perry Rhodan, Peacelord of the Universe. A group of German writers, now including, among others, Karl-Herbert Scheer, Kurt Mahr and Hans Kneifel, coordinated first by Walter Ernsting and now by William Woltz, started churning out 68-page adventures, using every hack science fiction

Swedish and Japanese editions of Cape Kennedy stories; the 500th Perry Rhodan issue; and Mark Powers, a Rhodan imitator

cliché conceived. It began innocently enough, with Perry Rhodan as just an ordinary superman piloting the first spaceship to the Moon, but it soon picked up speed as good ol' Perry met the Secret Masters of the Universe, became immortal, and started chasing numerous alien monsters. The Solar Empire was soon founded, with Perry as dictator, and from then on things got bigger and better with every blood-dripping issue. The fans love it. It also appears that Perry Rhodan fans read very little science fiction except the Perry Rhodan stuff—naturally enough, since Walter Ernsting *et al* have managed to cram all hack science fiction into this single series. Perry is today the hero of hundreds of thousands of teenagers in a number of countries, and growing numbers of Perry Rhodan fan clubs and Perry Rhodan magazines give glowing tribute to their hero. In December 1975, Kurt Mahr finished the 767th Perry Rhodan adventure. It was just like the others.

One interesting offshoot from this series of cosmic junk is the American version of Perry's adventures, now more than 100 volumes and still going strong, with Perry Rhodan conventions and Perry Rhodan magazines appearing all the time. This edition is edited by the mercurial Forrest J. Ackerman in a breathtaking gosh-wow-wow-boy style which has probably won the series more loyal fans in the United States than the Perry Rhodan tales themselves would have done. An unconventional mixture of paperback and magazine (Forry Ackerman

**Above: Space opera heroes in the grand tradition, plotting their course through the universe, in 'Forbidden Planet'
Right: The British television series 'Space: 1999' shows that space opera still lives, even in its most impossible form**

calls it a 'magabook' or 'bookazine'), it manages to give the impression of pure, unadulterated joy in fannishness and it is in effect the world's largest fan magazine, enjoyed even by those who detest Perry Rhodan. Forrest J. Ackerman is privately a shy, somewhat retiring man and surely one of the most lovable people within the science fiction field, still a fan, still revelling in every minute of his job. (He was born in 1916 and has been an enthusiastic fan since the early 1930s.) When he is turned loose at a typewriter, Efjay the Terrible emerges with a prose that must be read to be believed and an enthusiasm that knows no bounds. If there is anything decent in this Perry Rhodan business, it must be Forry Ackerman and his wife, Wendayne. He manages to make even Perry Rhodan bearable as a paperback series. Wendayne translates it so well that it comes out much better in English than in the original German.

Perry Rhodan is the best known of the German space opera heroes, but he is by no means alone in defending German *lebensraum* against vile aliens. There is, or was, also *Rex Corda*, 'Retter der Erde', with 38 books appearing between 1966 and 1967; *Ren Dhark*, whose improbable adventures were chronicled in no less than 98 unmemorable volumes between 1966 and 1969, most of them written by Kurt Brand; *Mark Powers*, 'Der Held des Weltalls', with 48 books between 1963 and 1964; *Arn Borul*, with 65 volumes between 1972 and 1975; *Raumschiff Orion*, with 33 volumes between 1968 and

1969, and so on. The Germans love their space opera heroes and they have had more of them than any other country in the world.

Unwilling to leave the universe to these German heroes, America recently launched its own invincible space opera hero into space: Cap Kennedy and his loyal friends. They work for the Terran agancy FATE, saving the universe at least once a month. The series has now been discontinued in the United States, but is doing very well in other countries, including Germany, where Cap is known as Commander Scott, 'Agent der Erde', saving the universe on a bi-weekly basis. The author behind the pseudonym 'Gregory Kern' has been a closely guarded secret, and most Big Names within the science fiction field have been suggested. Since they now are being written by a group of German pulp writers that include Ronald Hahn, Horst Pukallus and Manfred Wegener, and the original author has left the scene after writing the first seventeen novels, I might as well unmask him. The original 'Gregory Kern' was the British science fiction writer E. C. Tubb, who has now gone on to do other things, among others to continue his *Earl of Dumarest* space opera novels which started with *The Winds of Gath*

(1967) and now runs to sixteen volumes telling of Mr Dumarest's attempts to get back to Mother Earth, fighting a group of alien cybernetic intellects, 'the Cyclan', all the way. Every volume in the series sees him fail once again, and Dumarest is not much closer to Earth than he was ten years ago. Lots of things happen all the time, though, which I suppose is all that really matters in space opera.

I hesitate to call A. Bertram Chandler a space opera writer, since this charming Australian, a former merchant navy officer and for the past thirty years a highly appreciated science fiction author, certainly uses the time-honoured tools of space opera, but not in a way that would fit Wilson Tucker's definition. Chandler has now and again been accused of writing 'sea stories thinly disguised as science fiction', and his 'Rim World' novels, featuring Commodore Grimes, do at times read like tales from the high seas. Being a marine officer, though, Chandler argues that the spacemen of the future, manning real spaceships, making long voyages, will have more in common with today's seamen than with today's airmen—or even, come to that, with today's astronauts. This he has proceeded to prove very convincingly in a number of short stories and novels, starting with *To Run the Rim* (1959), which takes place in the wastes of the rim of the galaxy where anything could happen and very frequently does. This could have been the setting for the usual sort of heroics among the stars, but Commodore Grimes and his men are quite convincing as human beings, very far removed from the incredible heroes of formula space opera, and while Chandler in these stories uses a space opera backdrop as it were, they remain good, solid and serious science fiction with as much Sense of Wonder as any wild space opera tale. Chandler uses all the tools of the traditional space opera, but he uses them with the skill of an artist and he stands head and shoulders above everyone else in this particular branch of science fiction. His realistic stories of the colonization of the Rim Worlds at the fringe of the galaxy are highly readable—space opera as it ought to be written but very, very seldom is.

These are merely a few Big Names in an ocean of valiant space opera heroes, but I think will serve to give an idea of what it is all about. For space opera is, when you get down to it, not a matter of futurism or credibility or literary quality or any of the traits that makes good science fiction good; it is Sense of Wonder in pure, undiluted form, the dreams of absolute, unlimited power as the basis, and gigantism and good versus evil as the main ingredients. It takes place in space and in the future, since this gives ample room for gigantism, but apart from that it has more in common with Wild West fiction than modern science fiction. It is not good literature by any standards, and it is certainly not good science fiction; and with the possible exceptions of Pascual Enguidanos Usach and E. E. Smith it has always been written by hacks who cared little about what they wrote, as long as they got paid for it. Still, these modern fairy tales are read and appreciated by huge numbers of avid readers. The American critic and fan Alva Rogers gives, in his book *A Requiem For Astounding* (1967), a loving tribute to the space opera of his lost youth which I think sums up both typical adventures and the reader attitude very nicely. Despite whatever irate critics—including me— may have to say about space opera, this is really what it is all about, and only a true space opera afficionado can understand it: *Who can ever forget the thrill of reading* The Legion of Space *by Jack Williamson for the first time? The first part of this classic began in the April issue and ran for six breathtaking instalments. The adventures of John Star, Giles Habibula, the mighty Hal Samdu, and Jay Kalam on the evil world of the Medusae, the planet Yarkland, as they fought to save the lovely Aladoree Anthat and the secret weapon, AKKA, which she alone held in her mind and which was the only salvation of Earth, were high adventure indeed with a Sense of Wonder in ample measure.*

THE HUMAN ANGLE

It has been said that science fiction is primarily a literature of ideas, and I am sure this is true. Somehow, however, I get the impression that these ideas are so grand in scope that they seldom touch the ground ordinary mortals walk upon, and this might be the one point on which the genre as such leaves itself open to serious criticism. The 'Sense of Wonder' rightly pointed out as a main ingredient in science fiction does alienate the genre from other, less spectacular aspects of human life and endeavour. There is a frightening truth somewhere in the American author Poul Anderson's tasteless remark in his introduction to the fourth Nebula anthology, of 1970, that '(Science fiction) remains more interested in the glamour and mystery and existence, the survival and triumph and tragedy of heroes and thinkers, than in the neuroses of some snivelling faggot.' Anderson was referring to American science fiction, but these tendencies can be found in other parts of the world as well, which surely must suggest that something is very wrong with the genre. It is not heroes that carry the world on to new and greater heights, it is and it has always been the malcontent, the alienated, the neurotic, the 'snivelling faggot' as it were, and this has indeed been recognized in much science fiction. Still, and particularly in a time and age when success is what counts and the devil take the loser, we might expect that sort of sentiment.

As I have pointed out elsewhere in this book, science fiction deals mainly with change, but by tradition this change has been one of mechanics, of practical politics, such as the cheap energy Utopia, one of revolutionary inventions or extraterrestrial invaders. Changes of sexual mores or the fundamental relationship between man and woman has been more lightly touched upon. Even when Utopian writers envisage a breaking up of the old family nucleus, women still know their place, men still rule, fight, explore. Even the great advocate of female liberation, H. G. Wells, the author of a number of important marriage novels, was a reactionary when it came to woman in his science fiction stories. The future was, and is, a male world with woman at best taking the place of a nice but stupid Dr Watson. The typical female in science fiction was equivalent to the beautiful and homely Gräuben in Jules Verne's *Voyage au centre de la terre* (Journey to the Centre of the Earth, 1864), who takes her leave of the intrepid explorers, saying that she would love to go with them, but that 'a poor little girl like me would only give you trouble'. In the Utopia described by Edward Bellamy in *Looking Backward* (1888), women are equal to men *in theory,* but the practice is somewhat different. They live in a self-contained universe within this Utopia, never allowed into the male world, a sort of *apartheid* where all the benefits of civilization are assured but where the responsibilities which alone would make them true and equal citizens of the welfare state are lacking. With science fiction, and particularly Utopias, faithfully mirroring the attitudes of the contemporary world, this is to be expected.

The women in science fiction are helpless creatures, the reward of the victorious hero, pieces of property to be abducted by villains or slimy monsters and recaptured at the end of the story. They are not really human beings, they are pieces of delicious meat owned by the hero, and woe to the villain who tries to steal it! The most obnoxious examples of this are probably the *Gor* books by the American writer John Norman, which are not only unparalleled examples of male chauvinism and unusual sex, but also bestsellers. In the world of Tarl Cabot, sword-toting hero upon the strange planet Gor, women are nothing but cattle, to be bought and sold and enjoyed at the discretion of the male owner. The Gor novels also abound with the usual sexual perversions like sadism,

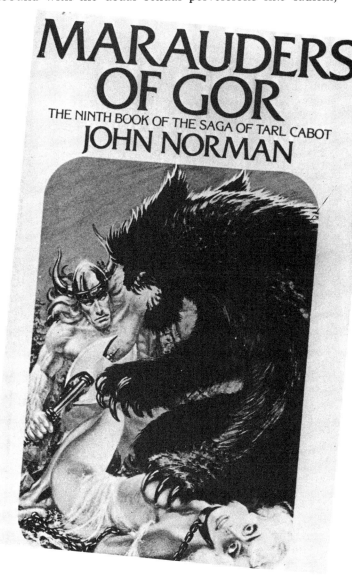

Above: Recent Gor novel, with the usual ingredients
Right: Symbolism in space fiction. Illustration by Virgil Finlay in 'Amazing Stories', September 1951

1/-
T. BRITAIN

AMAZING
STORIES

very lovely woman was a fragile toy

Contrasting graphic styles on covers

ФАНТАСТИКА-72

Above: Soviet SF anthology 'Fantastika—72'

Right: German edition of Stanislav Lem novel

Science
Fiction

Sex, serpents and snails used with gusto on magazine covers

masochism and bondage. John Norman, the pseudonym of a scholar, seems particularly interested in bondage, and devotes many pages to drooling descriptions of nubile young girls being bound and raped, bound and lashed, bound and degraded in a thousand imaginative ways. But, most of all, these sick novels revel in the idea of woman as slave, the helpless victim of a 'real' man's every whim. The men love it, and so do, in this world of fantasy, the women. For all women, Mr Norman assures us, really want to be whipped, raped and subjugated. Women are like that, he tells us. Examples could be taken from any of the Gor books, they are depressingly similar in their attitude towards women; not even patronizing, which would be bad enough, but downright hostile. The seventh volume of the chronicles of Gor, *Captive of Gor* (1972), describes the kinky adventures of Ms Elinor Brinton of New York City, 'beautiful, rich, spoiled, used to having her way with the men of Earth . . . hunted down and abducted by alien beings to find herself a captive of Gor, where men are absolute masters, and women their complete slaves', to quote the blurb. Among the many revealing glimpses of Mr Norman's attitude towards women I am picking one, where Ms Brinton, now a happy slave on Gor, ruminates on her proper station in life:

I enjoyed the smells of the camp, and its sounds. I watched two warriors practising with their swift, short blades on a square of sand. The ringing of the metal excited me and frightened me, the swiftness and cruelty of it. How brave men must be, I thought, to stand so to one another, so close,

in combat so near, face to face, wrist to wrist, eye to eye, short, vicious, sharpened ringing blade to short, vicious, sharpened ringing blade. I could not have done this. I would have cried out and fled. What could a woman be but the prize of such men? For a moment I wished myself back on Earth where there was little for a man to do which could not be done as well, or better, by a woman. But then, as I watched the warriors at their practice, something deep in me did not wish this. Something deep in me, primitive, helpless, and vulnerable, rejoiced that I stood not on Earth, but on Gor, where there were such men. Suddenly my legs felt very bare, and my arms. I was suddenly frightened. What if they should finish their sport, and turn to look upon me, and command me to serve them? Would I not, as a woman, have to give them immediate response? Could I have helped myself, kept myself from yielding immediately and completely to them? When such men command, what could a woman do?

John Norman has also written other masterpieces of kinky sex, including a novel, *Time Slave* (1975), in which a spoiled, liberated woman is sent back 50,000 years in time and a big hero repeatedly rapes her and kicks her around until she finally realizes she was born to be a slave.

This approach to women and sex is happily not typical of science fiction as such. A more common approach to women in science fiction has been, and continues to be, the one exemplified below by a scene from a pulp magazine novel, Edmond Hamilton's *The Comet Kings* (1942). It is a Captain Future adventure, and in this scene the noble Captain talks sweet love with his faithful woman Joan, who will soon be abducted by yet one more master villain:

'Why, Joan, what's the matter?'

'Oh, nothing—I'm just foolish', she muttered. 'But I can't

help being a little sorry to leave the comet.'

He did not understand. Joan looked up at him with deep emotion in her fine eyes.

'Out there, Curt, you belong to the whole System. I know you love me, but duty comes first—your obligation to use your scientific powers to help the System peoples.

'But if we'd been forced to remain on the comet world, cut off forever from the outside, nothing else would have come between us. It could have been a paradise for us. But it's lost now.'

Curt Newton bent and kissed her.

'Joan, don't feel that way. Someday when our work is done, we'll find our own paradise. I know a little asteroid that's waiting for us. It's just like a garden. Someday.'

A large part of the blame for this love-romance-home-and-children version of women in science fiction must be attributed to the fact that American science fiction was a creation of the pulp magazines. But science fiction, with its emphasis on mechanical solutions to everything and its preoccupation with galaxy-spanning ideas and themes, has never really condescended to bother itself with the individual lives of individual people. The characters in science fiction have habitually been stock ones, symbols representing different facets of the story. Occasionally sexual mores are the basis of a story, as for example one world described in Frederik Pohl and C. M. Kornbluth's novel *Search the Sky* (1954), where women rule and men have taken the roles usually assigned to women; but this is merely a version of the upside-down-world found at the Feast of Fools in Medieval times, a great big joke, so ridiculous that no one can really take it seriously. No one questions the fact that women are weak and helpless and impractical and unfit for anything but admiring the hero and occasionally being abducted by the villain. In a recent Swedish example of what we might

Above: Strange happenings in outer space—an amusing
short-short tale by French artist 'Moebius' and script writer
Philippe Druillet (1974)
Right: The French comic strip Barbarella first appeared in 'V',
1962. It soon degenerated into the usual flesh market

call the male chauvinist pig attitude, Dénis Lindbohm's
Eden utan Adam (Eden Without Adam, 1975), the hero
returns to Earth from several thousand years of deep-
freeze in orbit to find all men extinct and women proc-
reating via parthenogenesis. The women regard him as a
freak, a sort of human hymenopteron who always wants
to put that *thing* into them, planting eggs that will grow
into human beings. Very unpleasant. He soon teaches
them, however, and the women fight to be raped by him.
These women may act as though they didn't need men at
all, but don't let that fool you. Just knock them around a
little and they will soon find their place again, in the
kitchen and in the bed of the victorious hero. Again, what
we have here, is women as property. We all know that
women indeed *are* property in a large part of the world.
But this does not excuse science fiction, which we expect
to be more far-seeing and open-minded.

Instead, we all too often find the basic sex fright of
authors like John Norman popping up in various disguises—like the too clever and too manly robot expert
Susan Calvin in Isaac Asimov's celebrated robot stories,
who loves robots more than men and certainly must be a
little bit odd, probably an unwanted spinster who could
not find a man—and in more direct form in a short story

Hero and heroine await flying sex symbol

'Of course', the manager said. 'But you ain't no pervert, are you?'

'Certainly not!'

'You an outworlder?'

'Yes. How did you know?'

'The suit. Always tell by the suit.' The fat man closed his eyes and chanted, 'Step up, step up and kill a woman! Get rid of a load of repressions! Squeeze the trigger and feel the old anger ooze out of you! Better than a massage! Better than getting drunk! Step up, step up and kill a woman!'

Sheckley's story is a wry comment on the treatment of women and sexuality in science fiction. Sexuality has occasionally been treated in a mature and convincing way in European science fiction, as early as Hanns Heinz Ewer's already mentioned novel *Alraune* (1919), and Europe has even produced a number of purely pornographic science fiction novels. Generally, though, the genre as been playing it safe and sexuality as the main theme of a science fiction story did not appear in American magazine science fiction until Philip José Farmer made a break-through with his novel *The Lovers* (1952), the story of sexual relations between a human male and an extraterrestrial insect that had developed protective mimicry exactly like a woman. Farmer later wrote several other stories dealing with sexuality that are among the best ones on this theme, later collected in book form as *Strange Relations* (1960), while one of the leading gurus of American science fiction, the brilliant Robert Silverberg, has written a number of short stories and novels by the American author James Gunn, *The Misogynist* (1952), which argues that women are a different species preying upon man, murdering those who expose their horrible secret. Robert Sheckley has commented upon this many times, and one of the best examples is his short story *Pilgrimage to Earth* (1956), where an adolescent boy from a backward planet comes to Earth to taste the forbidden fruits of a decadent civilization, ending up in a shooting gallery where the most exquisite pleasures can be had for a price:

'Try your luck?'

Simon walked over and saw that, instead of the usual targets, there were four scantily dressed women at the end of the gallery, seated upon bullet-scored chairs. They had tiny bulls-eyes painted on their foreheads and above each breast.

'But do you fire real bullets?' Simon asked.

'Of course!' the manager said. 'There's a law against false advertising on Earth. Real bullets and real gals! Step up and knock one off!'

One of the women called out, 'Come on, sport! Bet you miss me!'

Another screamed, 'He couldn't hit the broad side of a spaceship!'

'Sure he can!' another shouted. 'Come on, sport!'

Simon rubbed his forehead and tried not to act surprised. After all, this was Earth, where anything was allowed as long as it was commercially feasible.

He asked, 'Are there galleries where you shoot men, too?'

A fate worse than death at the hands of a mad scientist

advocating the pleasures of group sex with or without the aid of electronic devices. Today, the leading exponents of sexuality in science fiction are certain French science fiction comic artists, particularly 'Moebius' and the script writer Philippe Druillet with some of the most unusual stories dealing with sex ever seen within the genre. Or what do you think about a story in which a gigantic space monster tries to rape a space ship but is scared away by the intrepid pilot who then to his horror finds that *he* got pregnant? (*Rut*, 1974).

Females in science fiction are passive victims of circumstances, alienated from the flow of events, only occasionally dragged into it when monster or villain come round and try to steal the hero's property. They are very fragile things, in need of a real man for strength and protection. But where would the man of science fiction turn? We certainly do find alienated men in the genre, outcasts of human civilization trying to find their niche in the world, all the time facing incredible hardships and ridicule.

In science fiction, these lonely outcasts are known as supermen, mutations or scientifically altered men with no natural place among ordinary human beings. Contrary to the women in science fiction, though, they are not content with the kitchen or the bed; they face up to the world and conquer it. Or they at least die trying to do it.

The greatest and strangest of all supermen of science fiction is, of course, *Le Surmâle* (The Supermale, 1902) by Alfred Jarry. The prototype of all subsequent supermen in the genre, the hero of this novel, André Marcueil, is a man with an unassuming appearance which reveals none of his superhuman powers. They are let loose when he is changed into an Indian, an incredible character with mythical physical and sexual powers.

One year after *Le Surmâle*, H. G. Wells used a different set of symbols in order to, as he put it, 'press home the theme that human beings are now faced with changes that require vast readjustments in the scale of their ideas.' This novel, *The Food of the Gods* (1903), tells about an alkaloid that causes living beings to grow six or seven times their usual size. Babies who have eaten it grow into forty-foot young men, with superior physical, moral and intellectual powers, constrasting sharply with the ordinary little men who try to destroy them. What the little men are really trying to destroy, of course, is progress and change, and their final victory over the colony of giant supermen is a bitter comment on Man's fear of change.

This is a far cry from Nietzsche's Superman, whom he hoped would soon appear in Europe, crush the Jews, give the masses proper discipline and form a ruling caste for the world to follow. More on a par with that particular superman are recent variations on the theme, starting with an unusual British example, known as 'the Winged Man', who appeared in a 30-part serial in 1913, written by E. Dudley Tempest. The Winged Man was much more like a super-villain than any of the subsequent pulp magazine supermen, a ruthless man with no compassion whatsoever for ordinary people. Waited upon by a truly sub-human creature, the faithful Ghat, he lived in splendid isolation in a hidden Yorkshire cave where all surfaces were covered with solid gold. Here, the Winged Man lurks, 'ready for any act of desperate evil that might suggest itself to him'. He is unmistakably evil, as we can learn from the following brief episode, which happens just after the faithful Ghat has saved his master's life:

Space woman of the classic type, her scanty bikini contrasting with the bulky male space wear. Illustration by Earle Bergey, 1945

With a cry of dismay, Ghat sprang to his master's side. The dwarf's body matched his repulsive face. Barely four feet in height, his crooked back formed a bow with his misshapen legs; his long, hairy arms reached almost to his ankles, and his enormous splay feet struck the ground at every step with a horrible flapping sound.

'Master, you are not dead? Speak to Ghat. Strike him! Anything to show you are not dead!' cried Ghat, wringing his hands as he bent, in a grotesque sorrow, over his dread master.

A swift blow across the dwarf's mouth answered his appeal.

'Cease, you whining dog! Think you the Human Bat can die—die?' snarled the Winged Man, struggling to a sitting position.

Ah, they don't make servants like that any more. Nor supermen.

Pulp magazine heroes were, of course, also supermen; Kapitän Mors, Perry Rhodan, Captain Future and Doc Savage are only a few examples of this breed of saviours of mankind. These, however, are only crude variations on a common crude theme with which we need not concern

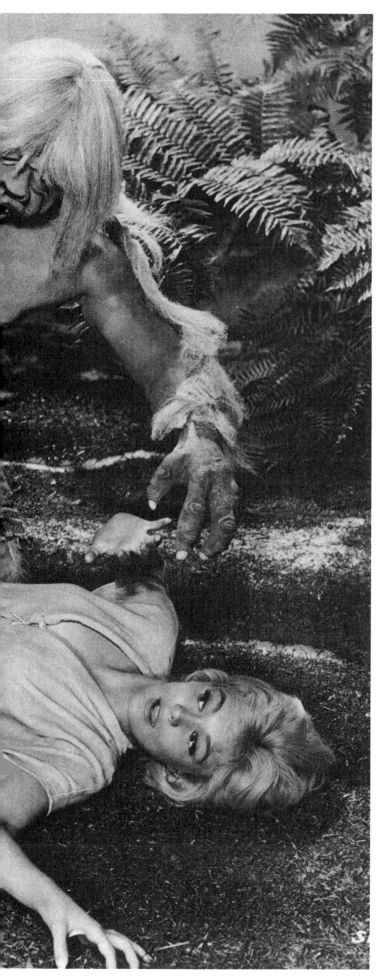

Left: Lecherous monster laying hands on nubile property. From 'The Time Machine' (1960)

Above: E. Dudley Tempest's 'The Winged Man', a forerunner of the US Batman, is shown murdering a couple more gently than usual (1913)

ourselves here. A more mature variation of the superman theme appeared with the German science fiction author Hans Dominik's now classic novel *Die Macht der Drei* (The Power of the Three, 1922), in which no less than three supermen, a Swede, a German and an Indian, use new energy principles to stave off an imminent world war. The incredible powers at their command prove to be too much for even supermen, though. It corrupts them, and they fail in their work. The Swede and the German die, and the Indian hides in a Tibetan monastery. A variation of this classic, Olaf Stapledon's *Odd John* (1935), tells of the trials of one mutation, very similar to the Indian in Dominik's novel, an intellectual superman who ultimately searches out others of his kind and then founds a colony on an uncharted Pacific island. (The supermen of Dominik's novel founded their colony near the North Pole.) They, too, are destroyed in the end, proving once again that Earth is not yet ready for supermen.

An earlier classic in the field, and the one that set the tone for most subsequent mutant novels, is the British architect and writer John Davys Beresford's novel *The Hampdenshire Wonder* (1911), the story of a seemingly idiot child who is actually an intellectual superman, as much above ordinary people as they are above Neanderthal man. He reads the *Encyclopaedia Britannica* at the age of four and is at this early age so much beyond other people, including his 'teacher', the local squire, that no one can communicate with him. It is a story about loneliness, of an outcast in a society which cannot understand him or even communicate with him, and the story up to the boy's final destruction by a hydrocephalous idiot (the only one over whom the boy has not control) is a moving one.

More positive in its outlook is an American classic in this particular sub-branch of science fiction, A. E. Van Vogt's *Slan* (1940), in which the mutant, young Jommy Cross, is hunted by the 'normal' humans who for centuries have waged a merciless war of extermination **against** his species, the Slans. Slans are supermen in all respects: they have superior intelligence and physical strength, they can read thoughts and react with superhuman speed to stimuli. After much cloak-and-dagger intrigue, typical of the pulp magazine world for which the novel was originally written, Jommy Cross finally ends up marrying a Slan princess, learning also that human leaders are Slans (!) and that the future belongs to these supermen.

Incidentally, young Jommy Cross appears to have had an American ancestor, Starr Cross, whose adventures were chronicled in a novel by H. E Chase, *A Double Life, or, Starr Cross* (1884). Starr Cross was gifted with the powers of mesmerism, mental possession and levitation, but used these for evil ends. Very naughty of him; so he did not get a true Slan princess.

A more recent superhuman story is Theodore Sturgeon's modern science fiction classic *More Than Human* (1954), describing the next step in man's evolution, from human being into a kind of superman that is not an individual but a group of people. Meshing minds and bodies, six outcasts become a united force unharnessed by the restraints of conscience.

Central to the superman idea is, of course, the outcast, loneliness, the feeling of standing apart from other human beings. After the original science fiction classics dealing with supermen, Alfred Jarry's *Le Surmâle* and Hans Dominik's *Die Macht der Drei,* virtually all science fiction stories dealing with supermen have dealt with *young* ones, young and angry and alienated supermen, misunderstood by a cruel and stupid world. Most adolescents at one time or another feel that they stand outside the world, that no one really understands them and that other people are stupid. Science fiction fans tend to form a high opinion of their own group of science fiction fan friends, strengthening the conviction that they are really a breed of select supermen, standing apart from the mundane world which does not read or understand books—particularly science fiction. Tests made by and on fans on many occasions, in many countries during the past thirty years or so, unanimously suggest that fans—in their own opinion, at least—are more intelligent than other people. No wonder superman tales have always been popular in science fiction. A. E. Van Vogt's *Slan* even started a Utopian community of sorts in 1943, when a group of American fans in Battle Creek, Michigan, lived together for nearly two years in the 'Slan Shack' community. Only fans were invited, and grandiose plans were drawn up for a 'Slan Center' consisting of an entire city block in Battle Creek, with its own grocery store, general store, common heating plant and electricity generating plant. Utopian societies have certainly been founded on flimsier premises than a common interest in science fiction and the belief in the Slanishness of oneself and one's friends, but the project never materialized and the original Slan Shack, an eight-roomed house sheltering a dozen or so fans, finally was abandoned as well.

An exception to the misunderstood adolescent superman of science fiction is in one of my own favourites, the Mule, in Isaac Asimov's celebrated *Foundation* trilogy (*Foundation, Foundation and Empire,* and *Second Foundation,* originally published as eight stories in the American magazine *Astounding* from May 1942 through November 1949). The Mule, an enigmatic mutation of superior intelligence and with the ability to play upon people's emotions, appears in *Foundation and Empire,* soon unifying the entire known galaxy into a new, strong empire, using complicated Byzantine intrigues the like of which have seldom been seen in science fiction, until he finally meets his end in *Second Foundation.* A frail human being without most of the hero traits usually found in literary supermen, he is an oddly convincing and tragic personality and complex person who in many respects is the real principal character of the trilogy, certainly the most interesting of all the cardboard characters inhabiting this classic. He is no hero, though, and no science fiction fan community was ever founded to honour him.

The superman is in many respects the Utopian ideal of science fiction on a more personal level, coupled with the inevitable feeling of loneliness felt by many adolescents who prefer to read books instead of running round and hitting the other kids on the head with a baseball bat. The underlying dream of power is here, as is the feeling

Left: Modern superman with sinus trouble—Spiderman, of 'Marvel' comics fame

Above: In this 1803 Swedish print, old hags are bundled into the windmill to emerge as pretty young girls

that one really ought to have the chance to change the whole world into something more glorious, or at least something more interesting. The fact that A. E. Vogt's *Slan*, by far the simplest of all the superman stories, is also the most popular in science fiction, never out of print since it first appeared, tells, I think, a lot about the psychological mechanisms behind the lure of this science fiction theme.

Pursuing the age-old question of *whence and whither?*, science fiction offers immortality as one spin-off from supermanship. But whereas immortality is viewed as a somewhat mixed blessing in, for example, a classic like Charles Maturin's novel *Melmoth the Wanderer* (1820) or Eugène Sue's *Le juif errant* (1844), modern science fiction is inclined to regard immortality not as a curse, but as something worth fighting for, the reward for successful heroics. Successful space opera heroes like Perry Rhodan are of course immortal, if for no other reason than to allow them time for all their heroic deeds. Robert Herrock, the improbable hero of A. E. Van Vogt's novel *The Weapon Makers* (1943), is immortal, as is the double-brained hero Gilbert Gosseyn of Van Vogt's strange novels *The World of Null-A* (1945) and *The*

Pawns of Null-A (1948). But Mr Gosseyn attains immortality by moving on to a new body now and then in the best Jarry or Rigaut tradition. It is all fun and games, like the classic immortals of blood-and-thunder science fiction such as Rider Haggard's *She* (1887), in which the chief villian, the high princess Ayesha, is mighty old and supposedly never will die. Immortality has also been used occasionally as a gimmick in science fiction, as in Fredric Brown's excellent short story *Letter to a Phoenix* (1949), the story of a man who is not really immortal, only extremely long-lived, who has lived since the time of Atlantis and tells about the cyclic development of Man's civilization in a way somewhat reminiscent of Jules Verne's *L'éternal Adam* (1905). Or, why not, the eternal soldier, Mr Blacke, in Harry Harrison's hilarious parody on space opera, *Bill, the Galactic Hero* (1965), who has been around at least since the age of the dinosaurs, making a living as a professional soldier since the army always has been and always will be the safest place. Civilians die in wars, but the soldiers live on.

I actually know very few works of science fiction in which this theme is handled in a serious way, as one would handle a mile-long space ship or a galactic empire or some other of science fiction's stock in trade. One excellent example, however, is Aldous Huxley's novel *After Many a Summer* (1938), dealing with an eccentric multi-millionaire in California, searching for an old remedy for old age, in effect a drug guaranteeing immortality or something very close to that. It turns out that there is such a cure—but while it makes you forever young, it also transforms you into a gorilla-like beast. Similar doubts were voiced by Karel Capek in his play *Vek Makropulos* (The Makropulos Secret, 1922), in which eternal life makes man cynical, cold and dehumanized. (This play was four years later made into an opera by Leos Janacek.)

The American author Robert A. Heinlein appears to have become obsessed by the thought of fooling death and has written a remarkable wordage on this theme, from the well-known novel *Methuselah's Children* (1941), in which a race of extremely long-lived humans are hunted on Earth by their short-lived brethren, to the recent novels *I Will Fear No Evil* (1970) and *Time Enough for Love* (1973), long, rambling books trying to exorcise death and devising new methods of attaining immortality.

The most magnificent of all science fiction stories dealing with the age-old but in this particular genre astoundingly neglected dream, however, is probably Arthur C. Clarke's novel *Childhood's End* (1953), an almost metaphysical novel in which the hard surfaces of technology are softened by mysticism. What we have here is nothing less than the racial metamorphosis of mankind into the 'Overmind', something that probably could be called a god. It certainly can do most of the things a self-respecting god is supposed to do. Like Huxley and Capek, Clarke offers immortality only at the expense of humanity, but whereas Huxley and Capek offers it with a scornful smile, Clarke regards it with the eyes of a mysticist, as an immortality beyond the understanding of man, mankind's true destiny as it were. Thus we gain immortality, and somehow it sounds much more plausible, both as the final comment on the dream of superman, man's immortality and man's faith, than perhaps anything else written on the subject in science fiction.

August

Science and Invention

25 cen

FORMERLY
ELECTRICAL EXPERIMENTER

"THE MAN FROM THE ATOM"
See Page 329

SCIENTIFIC FICTION NUMBER

ADVENTURES IN THE PULP JUNGLE

The modern history of magazine science fiction began in April 1926, in New York when a Luxembourg-born immigrant launched a science fiction magazine filled with short stories by French, German and British writers and visually dominated by the artwork of an Austrian-born artist. The magazine was *Amazing Stories,* the publisher was Hugo Gernsback and the artist was Frank R. Paul.

Hugo Gernsback (1884–1967) emigrated from his native Luxembourg in 1904 for the greener pastures of the United States and soon proved himself an excellent

Left: The science fiction issue of Gernsback's magazine 'Science and Invention', August 1923
Above: Hugo Gernsback

businessman, totally devoted to the idea of science and technology as the saviour of mankind. Originally working with radio, he launched his first popular science magazine, *Modern Electrics,* in 1908, a magazine which did a more lasting service to radio amateurs in America than his science fiction magazines would do to science fiction. *Modern Electrics* was later changed into *Electrical Experimenter,* which livened up the strictly scientific content with occasional science fiction stories, and then into *Science and Invention,* which regularly published science fiction—just as many other popular science magazines did at this time. By the end of the 1920s he owned a magazine empire with publications such as *Radio News, Your Body* (which in typical Utopian tradition offered Science as a means to cure mankind of all its physical, sexual and psychological problems), *Tid Bits* and *Cooko Nuts.* It was inevitable that he would sooner or later try his hand at a science fiction magazine; this was the time of the specialized pulp magazines, and Hugo Gernsback must have heard about the successes of the science fiction issue of the British *Pears' Annual* in 1919 and the *Phantastik der Technik* issue of the German *Der Orchideengarten* in 1920. So, in 1923, Gernsback emulated these precursors with a science fiction issue of *Science and Invention,* and the following year tried to launch a science fiction magazine, called *Scientifiction.* It did not work out, but he persisted and finally started *Amazing Stories* in 1926.

Amazing Stories was by no means the first science fiction magazine, and far from the best published so far. European science fiction magazines like *Stella, Hugin* and *Der Orchideengarten* had been catering for science fiction readers since the early 1880s, and a number of magazines like the British *Pearson's Magazine,* the French *La science et la vie, Journal des voyages* and *Travers le Monde,* and the Russian *Priroda i lyudi,* were sometimes indistinguishable from science fiction magazines. Even the United States had a few magazines catering for science fiction readers, notably *Argosy* and *Weird Tales.*

Gernsback was preceded in North Europe by two men with personalities even stranger than his, who launched modern science fiction magazines before he did, and did it better, but who for various reasons did not persist and ultimately succeed like Gernsback did. The Swedish engineer, author, and publisher Otto Witt (1875–1923) was in many respects a Gernsback before Gernsback, a furiously chauvinistic man, a believer in science and technology as the saviour of mankind, a Utopian at heart who for many years tried—unsuccessfully—to reform the

world through science fiction. The author of numerous novels and non-fiction books, he launched the science fiction magazine *Hugin* in 1916 and filled 86 issues of this curious magazine with his own writings—articles, short stories, reviews, even novels—glorifying the science of the future and quite a number of unusual inventions of his own creation. Illness forced him to cease publication of the magazine early in 1920. Had Otto Witt been less a preacher of the wonders of the future and more a businessman, things might have turned out differently; as it was, *Hugin* sank without a trace.

The Austrian writer Karl Hans Strobl (1877–1946) was an even odder man, even more violently chauvinistic than Witt, one of the most important of the fantasy writers of the fantasy renaissance taking place in Germany from about 1900 until 1930. He edited the Austrian-German magazine *Der Orchideengarten* during its three years of existence, 1919–21, making it into a leading science fiction and fantasy magazine that published practically all the leading European writers in the genre. A total of 54 issues of this magazine were published before it folded. Strobl then became an avid Nazi, and during World War II was the local Viennese head of the infamous 'Reichsschrifttumskammer'. During its brief life, *Der Orchideengarten* was a good and intelligent science fiction magazine, but this one, too, sank without much trace. *Hugin* and *Der Orchideengarten* failed, died and were forgotten. *Amazing Stories* lived on.

There were many reasons for this, one of course being that Hugo Gernsback appeared with the right product at the right time, offering a simplified version of the future to an audience ignorant about science, politics and sociology, and thus worried about the rapidly changing world in which it was caught. Using the pulp magazine formula of cops and robbers in a slightly new overcoat, and reprinting those European works which best fitted into this formula, he presented American readers with the sort of science fiction that Jules Verne had written fifty years, and H. G. Wells thirty years, earlier. It was old hat in Europe, but American magazine readers had never seen anything like it before. Gernsback then started moulding local authors into the sort of writers he wanted—Murray Leinster, Ray Cummings, Otis Adelbert Kline, Francis Flagg and others, who soon learned to write exactly the pulp magazine fairy tales exhorting the wonders of science that Gernsback felt the public needed and secretly wanted. 'By "scientifiction",' Gernsback wrote in the first editorial for *Amazing Stories*, 'I mean the Jules Verne, H. G. Wells, and Edgar Allan Poe type of story—a charming romance intermingled with scientific fact and prophetic vision.'

Nothing wrong with that, but the man destined to carry out Gernsback's wishes was Dr T. O'Connor Sloane, a scholar seventy-five years old who was an inventor, science writer and Thomas Alva Edison's son-in-law. Excellent grades as far as Gernsback was concerned, but a downright disaster for any publication with any sort of literary, intellectual or sociological ambitions. Luckily (for Gernsback), *Amazing* had no such ambitions. It was an out-and-out pulp magazine of the sort which was very popular in the United States at this time, a Kapitän Mors science fiction adventure magazine in a slightly modified version, minus the slight political undertones. Gernsback's magazine filled an empty niche in magazine publishing, and it was a success.

**Left: Typical 'Amazing' cover of Gernsback era, July 1926
Above: Cover of short-lived but famous Austro-German magazine 'Der Orchideengarten' (1919); and the emblem of The Science Fiction League, founded by Hugo Gernsback**

Andra årgången.   Nr 11. Den 15 juni 1917.

HUGIN

MOTTO:
»Giv åt släktet gosselynne,
Hoppfull håg och fantasi.»
Viktor Rydberg

TIDSKRIFT FÖR NATURVETANDE I ROANDE FORM

HUGIN har satt som sitt mål, att göra vårt vetande om de oss dagligen omgivande krafterna och företeelserna så *lättfattligt, intressant och roande* som möjligt. Den använder bl. a.:

den naturvetenskapliga romanens,
det tekniska kåseriets,
den idéväckande humoreskens,
äventyrsberättelsens och
den tekniska sagans

former för att beskriva alla vardagslivets företeelser och krafter.

HUGIN är således *populärvetenskaplig* i detta ords allra bästa betydelse.

HUGIN utkommer 2 gånger i månaden i format lika med detta och upp till 48 sidor pr nummer.

Prenumerationspris: 5 kr. pr år, för 1 kvartal kr. 1: 50.
Lösnummerpris: 30 öre (å järnvägar 40 öre).
Lösnummerdistributör: Svenska Pressbyrån.

Redaktör och utgivare: **Otto Witt.**

Above: The first true SF magazine in the world
Right: Popular science magazines were so like SF
Far right: Otto Witt

What Hugo Gernsback did—and this was his great accomplishment, the one that could have made science fiction into an important literary tool long before it actually happened—was to create the specialized science fiction magazine into a culture and at a time which was eminently receptive to it. His predecessors had failed miserably, despite the fact that science fiction ever since the 1880s had proved to be the most popular parts of British, French and American popular magazines. Europe, torn apart by wars and depression, was not convinced that science and technology would create Utopia. The United States in 1926 was a booming country, confident in itself and its future, a leading industrial nation, and Hugo Gernsback's vision of the future, together with the lure of the future-war story, the abducted heroine, the intrepid hero and the loathsome villain, proved irresistible. By concentrating on the adventure and the popular science side of science fiction, ignoring all those qualities that had made science fiction respected in Europe, he created a new type of pulp magazine as it were, with obvious mass appeal. He made science fiction popular, which certainly was good, but the sort of science fiction he made popular was one that had been popular in Europe fifty years earlier. All over Europe, genuinely modern science fiction was published in magazines and book form, but Gernsback and his seventy-five-year-old editor never noticed it.

Amazing Stories and the dozens of other science fiction magazines that soon appeared to cash in on this virginal market—*Astounding Stories, Thrilling Wonder Stories, Air Wonder Stories etc.*—reached those who could not afford to read books or who just never ventured into book stores or libraries; the garish four-colour covers promised unusual thrills, and the contents were not more complicated than most people could understand. This was in contrast to science fiction in book form, particularly in Europe, which was becoming more and more highbrow, as it were, demanding more of its readers than they apparently were willing to give. All that Gernsback demanded of his readers was a dime or two. This was frowned upon by intellectuals, of course, and with their unwitting help Gernsback proceeded to turn mass market science fiction into a self-contained universe, blew up all bridges connecting it with the outer world, and created the science fiction ghetto.

This led to one good thing, though, even if that was an unexpected bonus and one that he never had planned on. In the June 1926 issue of *Amazing Stories*, Gernsback commented in his editorial on a surprising phenomenon of science fiction:

One of the great surprises since we started publishing Amazing Stories *is the tremendous amount of mail we receive from—shall we call them 'Scientifiction Fans?'—who seem to be pretty well oriented in this sort of literature. From the suggestions for reprints that are coming in these 'fans' seem to have a hobby of their own of hunting up scientifiction stories, not only in English, but in many other languages.*

What Gernsback had stumbled upon was the fact that readers of science fiction are generally not only interested enough to hunt up their favourite literature, but also care enough for it to write and comment upon it. Gernsback was not the first one to notice this, but he was the first to treat his readers decently. He started a reader's department, called 'Discussions', which proved to be of immense value for the rapid development of American science fiction when other science fiction magazines caught on and introduced their own readers' departments. From these pages of letters, arguments and discussions, emerged science fiction clubs and ultimately what is now known as a sort of semi-organized movement of science fiction fans, the 'fandom', something virtually unknown in Europe at that time. Fans even started to publish their own little mimeographed or printed magazines, fan magazines, or 'fanzines' for short. From this fandom and these fanzines, in their turn, came a generation of science fiction fans who ultimately took over the field in the United States, as editors, authors, illustrators and publishers of science fiction. This was Hugo Gernsback's main contribution to the field of science fiction, the successful feedback system, creating in time science fiction of high quality, when former fans like Donald A. Wollheim, Isaac Asimov, Robert A. Heinlein, Frederik Pohl, Forrest J. Ackerman and John W. Campbell put the stamp of their own personalities on the genre. Gernsback was for many years the grand-daddy of American science fiction, even picking a young science fiction fan, Charles Hornig, to edit a new Gernsback science fiction magazine, *Wonder Stories,* in 1933. Gernsback also founded the first national science fiction fan organization in the United States, The Science Fiction League, 1934. Two years later the New York branch of a science-fiction-slanted organization called International Scientific Association (ISA) started planning for a national gathering of science fiction fans. This convention, instigated by Donald A. Wollheim, took place in Philadelphia in October 1936. Three years later, a local science fiction club in New York, called New Fandom, held what was jokingly referred to as the First World Science Fiction Convention by the handful of those who attended, and this particular in-joke is still going on with new 'World' conventions every year. (In the United States, everything is the 'World' this or that or the other, but it does not really mean anything.) So far no true 'World' science fiction convention has ever been held anywhere, even though the big 1970 convention in Heidelberg, Germany, was considered to be a fairly international one. (The Third European Science Fiction Convention in Poznan, Poland, in 1976, had official delegates from twenty-three countries, which did not make it a 'World' one either.)

Hugo Gernsback was obviously an important and pivotal person within the science fiction field, and his pulp science fiction formula worked extremely well in the late 1920s and the early 1930s. There were limits to his genius, however, as shown when he attempted a comeback in the science fiction magazine field with *Science Fiction Plus* in 1953. A slick, expensively produced magazine, it showed all too well that Gernsback still lived in the 1920s and that he was trying to publish the old *Amazing Stories* once again in a world and a time that had changed enormously since 1926. Frank R. Paul did illustrations for his new magazine; a protégé of Gernsback, Sam Moskowitz, edited it; and the magazine looked like a remnant from an earlier age. *Science Fiction*

Plus lasted for seven issues and died miserably, mourned by no one except Gernsback and his friends.

Hugo Gernsback has been hailed as 'the father of science fiction'. He was obviously not. He was the father of American pulp magazine science fiction, with all that implies for good and bad, and the father of science fiction fandom. This is surely good enough and justifies his fame in North America as a modern pioneer. But his contribution to the genre was and is not one of contents but of package. He danced to the tune of the turn-of-the-century dime novels and popular magazines, with the added beat of modern marketing practices. Today the popularity of space opera television series like *Star Trek* and *Space: 1999* sing his praise and prove beyond doubt that his influence is not dead, that it is merely the package which has changed somewhat, that, growing sophistication of books and magazines notwithstanding, there is still room in other media for those young at heart.

Returning to the 1930s, which saw the Gernsback science fiction empire crash and other talents picking up the pieces, we find that the specialized science fiction magazines and science fiction fandom was still strictly an American affair, even though fan groups and fanzines now started to appear in Britain. A drastic change came with World War II, which, as one of its lesser results, brought about the American predominance in science fiction which Europe only during the last decade has managed to get away from. France got its first modern science fiction magazine, *Conquêtes*, in 1939, followed in rapid succession by two countries who were not directly involved in the war: Argentine and Sweden. The Argentine *Narraciones Terrorificas* was started in 1939, the Swedish *Jules Verne-Magasinet* in 1940, both importing American pulp science fiction wholesale to their respective countries. Pulp magazines were exported everywhere as ballast on ships to countries where, for obvious reasons, no science fiction was written or published during these years. American writers and publishers produced enormous amounts of science fiction, and when science fiction magazines began to appear in Europe after the war—the Belgian *Anticipations* in 1945, the British *New Worlds* in 1946, the Dutch *Fantasie en Wetenschap* in 1948—American science fiction held a veritable stranglehold on European science fiction. When what we might call the 'second wave' of European science fiction magazines appeared in early 1950s, the Italian *Scienza Fantastica* and *Urania* in 1952, the Norwegian *Tempo-Magasinet* in 1953, the Swedish *Häpna* in 1954, the German *Utopia-Magazin* in 1955, they were forced by cirumstances and the availability of American science fiction to devoting themselves almost exclusively to material written in the United States. This was also the case with science fiction magazines in other parts of the world—the Australian *Thrills Incorporated* started in 1950, the Argentine *Mas Alla* started in 1953, the Mexican *Enigmas* and the Japanese *Seiun* started in 1955. all of them filled with mostly American material.

All these countries had a science fiction tradition quite different from that of the United States, mostly one of novels, and there were of course no authors or editors brought up within a local science fiction fandom or with local science fiction magazines. American magazine publishers sold their wares aggressively throughout the world, thereby forcibly bringing science fiction in other

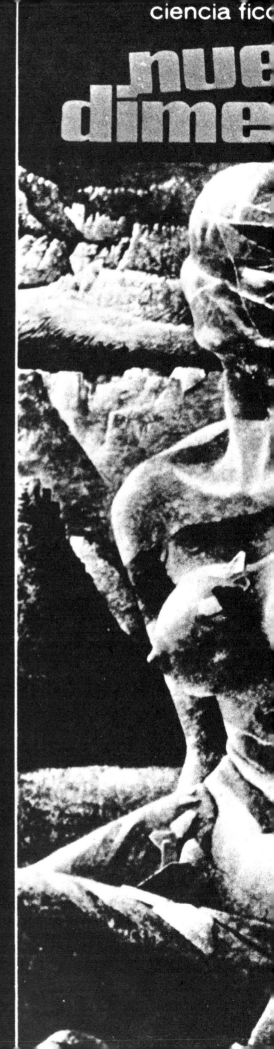

ciencia fic

nue
dime

fantasia

Udenfor Rummet

Far left: The Soviet author Anatoliy Dneprov
Left and above: Spanish ('Nueva dimensión') and Norwegian
('Planet-Magasinet') SF magazines

countries into the world of magazine science fiction. Eastern Europe resisted, naturally, with the result that it was saved from crude pulp science fiction, but also from the excellent science fiction now being exported, particularly through foreign editions of *The Magazine of Fantasy and Science Fiction, Galaxy* and other American magazines. America revived European science fiction, for good or bad, but Eastern European science fiction refused to be revived, with the result that it is only now making its voice heard in the rest of the world—much thanks to the aggressive help of the Soviet Copyright Bureau, VAAP. Romania had no science fiction magazine until the excellent bi-weekly *Colectia Povestiri Stiintifico-Fantastice,* edited by Adrian Rogoz, appeared in the late 1950s; the first Yugoslavian science fiction magazine, *Kosmoplov,* appeared as late as in 1969, the Hungarian magazine *Galaktika,* edited by the eminent science fiction scholar Péter Kuczka and one of the two or three best science fiction magazines in the world today, came in 1972. No science fiction magazines, at all exist in the Soviet Union as I write this; in their place are two excellent anthology series, *Fantastika,* and *Almanakh nauchnoy fantastiki,* that perhaps best can be compared to anthology series like the American *Clarion,* the Yugoslavian *Andromeda* or the German *Polaris.* The closest thing to a Soviet science fiction magazine is *Iskatel* (Explorer) which is sometimes filled with up to fifty per cent science fiction. It is oriented towards teena-

Romanian, Mexican and US magazines
Far right: Ivan Yefremov, author of 'Andromeda'

gers, though is mostly on the level of *Flash Gordon* and *Star Trek*, and is not very good. Pre-revolutionary Russia had more than its share of pulp adventure magazines, just as bad or worse than their British and American counterparts, very much like *Argosy*. The prominent St Petersburg publisher P. P. Soikin published enormous amounts of science fiction, including an 88-volume edition of Jules Verne's novels and a very popular adventure magazine, *Mir priklyucheniy*, which presented science fiction by H. G. Wells, Arthur Conan Doyle, Max Pemberton and others, plus Russian science fiction authors—who to a large degree took English-sounding pen-names because obviously only the British could write science fiction.

That, however, was during the pre-revolutionary, *laissez-faire* age of Russia. One can argue that Soviet science fiction fans do not really need specialized science fiction magazines, since science fiction is regularly published in big weeklies like *Yunost* (with a circulation of more than 2,500,000 copies), *Sveta*, *Znaniye-sila*, *Tekhnika-molodezhi*, *Nauka i zhizn* or *Aurora*. With a hard cover book costing less in the Soviet Union than a science fiction magazine in the West, science fiction fans there do not appear to envy their Western counterparts. They keep up with what is happening outside their own country, too. A recent issue of the Soviet literary magazine *Literaturnoye obozreniye* (No 9, 1976) devotes seven large-sized pages in fine print to reviews of current American science fiction.

194

Above: The Romanian writer Adrian Rogoz
Right: Yugoslav, Italian and British magazines

The world of science fiction magazines is very much a reflection of the science fiction ghetto, and in Eastern Europe science fiction never needed to lock itself in the ghetto. Moreover, it had no Gernsback to turn the key. The genre is respected, all national writers' associations have very active science fiction departments (the one in Hungary is publishing *Galaktika* and now has plans of launching yet another science fiction magazine). Small science fiction magazines, mimeographed fanzines, do exist, but do not play the important part of such publications in the West, although organized science fiction fandom can be found everywhere in Eastern Europe, including Albania. The *Klub Prognostica i fantastika* in Sofia, Bulgaria, in particular, has done an excellent job lately in the way of fanzines.

Today, magazines appears to have played out most of their role in science fiction, even in the United States. Outside that country, magazines have not been that important. In 1953, the peak year for science fiction magazines, thirty-three science fiction and fantasy magazines were published in America. In Britain eight were published, in Italy four, in France three, in Argentine two, in Australia, Mexico, Holland and Norway one each. That was all. Today—if I might be allowed some more statistics—the trend is more than ever away from magazines and towards books. In 1975, the last year for which I have reliable statistics, ten science fiction and fantasy magazines were published in the United States, with a total of 89 issues. During that same year 890 books were published, or ten for each magazine issue. Comparing this with my native Sweden (whose population is about four per cent that of the United States), we find a total of one science fiction magazine published,

196

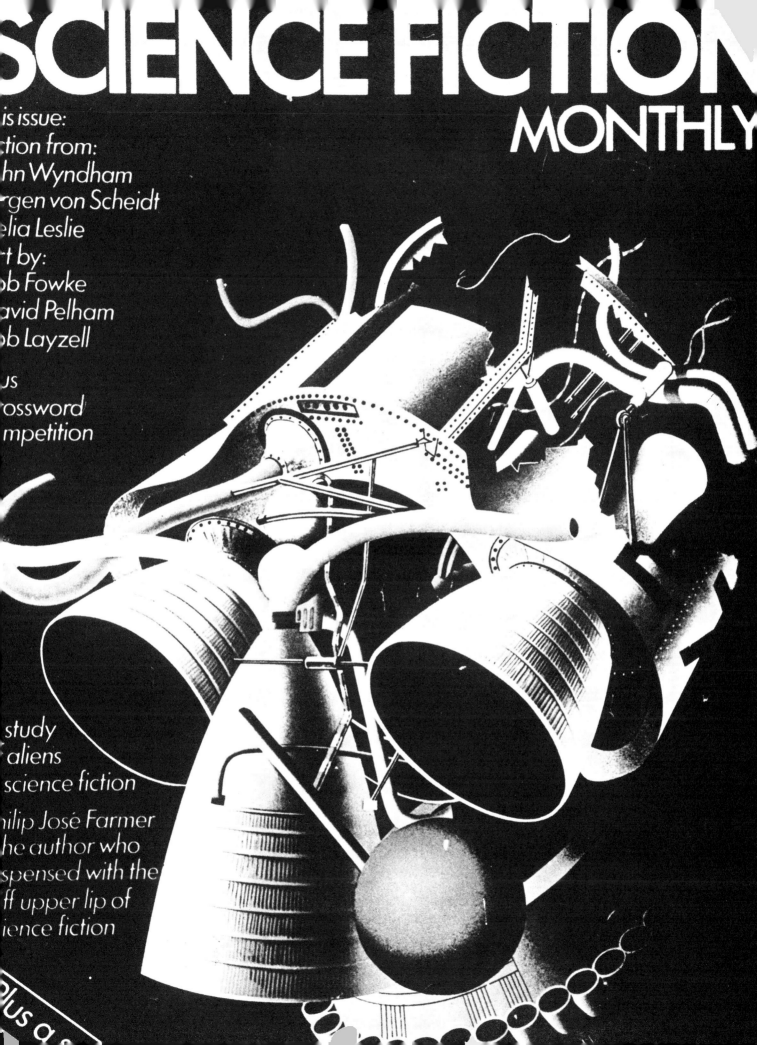

SCIENCE FICTION
MONTHLY

is issue:

ction from:

hn Wyndham

rgen von Scheidt

elia Leslie

t by:

b Fowke

avid Pelham

b Layzell

us

ossword

mpetition

study

aliens

science fiction

hilip José Farmer

he author who

spensed with the

ff upper lip of

ience fiction

lus a s

with four issues, while 118 books were published, or almost 30 books per magazine issue.

Behind the science fiction magazines of today stand quite a number of amateur and semi-professional publications catering for a variety of interests within the science fiction field. There are fanzines almost indistinguishable in presentation and quality from professional magazines (the German *Science Fiction Times* and the American *Algol* are outstanding examples of this); there are fanzines filled with nothing but letters, or reviews of current books, or editiorial monologues; and there are fanzines devoted to giving news and information about the science fiction field. I found the figures on book and magazine publishing in the United States for 1975 in the best of these news fanzines, *Locus*, which for a number of years has provided people within the science fiction field with all sorts of useful information. One of the most ambitious undertakings in recent years has indeed taken the form of a sort of fanzine, the splendidly produced, mimeographed series *Ides et autres,* published in Belgium under the general editorship of Bernard Goorden. So far 15 volumes have been published, presenting short stories from and essays about the science fiction scene of Latin America, Spain, China, the Soviet Union, Italy, Germany etc, plus scholarly essays on themes in science fiction. The Hungarian fanzine *SF Tajekoztato* (SF Bulletin) is in many respects better than many professional science fiction magazines in the West; and many fanzines, like the French *Spirale*, have become professional magazines of very high quality. There are also, as I have mentioned earlier, professional publications, like the American edition of *Perry Rhodan,* that really are fanzines, catering for none but the enthusiastic fans.

These specialized science fiction publications have probably done their share in bringing down the number of magazines to the point where only the best survive. The American magazine, *The Magazine of Fantasy and Science Fiction,* is one of the three best in the world (the other two being the Spanish *Nueva Dimension,* undoubtedly the leader in content, presentation and layout ever published, and the Hungarian *Galaktika*). The recipient of a number of well-earned awards for excellence in the field, it has remained since 1949 a leading magazine with high literary standards which I am sure will survive where others will succumb to the rising tide of annual anthologies.

The trend away from magazines in the science fiction field is one that can be seen everywhere. The British magazine *New Worlds,* whose genial and competent editor John Carnell brought up a generation of outstanding science fiction authors including Brian W. Aldiss and John Brunner, fell upon bad times in 1964 and now appears as a sort of paperback anthology, its place as a forum for new short stories in Britain being taken over by the *New Writings in SF* anthology series launched by John Carnell and since his death in 1972 edited by Kenneth Bulmer. The Swedish *Jules Verne-Magasinet,* still going strong after thirty-seven years of publication, is now published as a sort of bi-monthly quality paperback anthology series. In the United States, the last of the strong-willed magazine greats, *Astounding/Analog*

Far left: Hungarian magazine, 'SF Tajekoztato'
Left: Leading Soviet writers and editors Aleksandr Kazantsev and Bella Kluyeva

blick
IN DIE ZUKUNFT

SCIENCE FICTION CLUB EUROPA · SCIENCE FICTION CLUB DEUTSCHLAND e. V.

German and US magazines

magazine's editor John W. Campbell is dead, and other shapers of modern science fiction are concentrating on anthologies. Donald A. Wollheim, for many years a leading magazine editor and the editor of the first true anthology of science fiction short stories, *The Pocket Book of Science Fiction* (1943), is now owner and editor of the only American publishing company entirely devoted to science fiction, DAW Books. In Europe, the powerful voices of science fiction, those who find new writers, help them find their style and publish them, are not magazine editors but editors of book series—Gérard Klein and Jacques Sadoul in France, Danny de Laet in Belgium, Jacques van Herp in Holland, Ion Hobana in Romania, Péter Kuczka in Hungary, Czeslaw Chruszczewsky in Poland, Herbert Franke and Franz Rottensteiner in Germany, Jon Bing and Tor Age Bringsvaerd in Norway, Zoran Zivkovic in Yugoslavia, Bella Kluyeva in the Soviet Union, Ivo Zelezny in Czechoslovakia, Sebastian Martinéz in Spain, Gianni Montanari and Giorgio Monicelli in Italy—these and many more are shaping European science fiction today, and they are doing it not through the science fiction magazines, but through book series.

I am not trying to belittle the importance of the authors, but between the author and his audience always stands the editor who decides what is fit to print and who finds and encourages the new talents. This can lead to situations like the one in the late 1920s, when Hugo Gernsback and other American magazine editors laid down their version of the 'theory of limits' for their authors, who either had to go along with them or starve.

In the Soviet Union, Stalin and his Commissars did the same for Soviet science fiction writers. Both did science fiction great damage in their respective countries; but in the United States there soon appeared quite a number of editors, each preaching his own theory of limits, which at least enabled the writer to find the editor most receptive to his works. That did not happen in the Soviet Union until the middle 1950s, when the Stalin Cult had disappeared.

When Hugo Gernsback launched *Amazing Stories* in 1926, he brought out science fiction from the book stores and the libraries to the streets, to the sellers of popular magazines. Since he was not an experimenter, he also brought down the quality of the genre to the lowest common denominator of other magazines. The quality of science fiction has gone up since then, and away from the magazine racks, and I find without much surprise that science fiction is now back where it started, in the book stores and the libraries, cleansed and purified, perhaps even ennobled, by its time among the slave-gangs of pulp fiction.

As a European, I find myself having a peculiar love-hate relationship with the American science fiction scene, particularly the side of it represented by its magazines. I was born in 1941, and like many other Europeans of my generation I found science fiction first through the writings of Jules Verne and Hans Dominik, and then through American science fiction magazines. It took me many years to realize that there actually was a European heritage of this literature, that the genre actually had originated in Europe—and, in a sense, I felt that America had stolen this heritage, transforming it and vulgarizing it and changing it beyond recognition. A

201

generation of European science fiction readers are now re-discovering their own background, and it is a quite painful process. We find hundreds of eminent science fiction works hidden behind insurmountable language barriers, hidden behind all those British and American works which during the years have been all too easily available, to such a degree that everything else has disappeared from view. What is worse, we find that we are now so used to the particular American way of writing science fiction that some of our own heritage seems strange and even alien to us. Like a child revolting against its parents, this is bound to result in unjustified down-playing of the merits of American science fiction, while some European works might find themselves unjustly praised, solely because they are European. This, I think, is the case with the Polish author Stanislaw Lem, who has mastered the technique of writing science fiction in the American style so well that many critics automatically assume he must be better than American writers in the field.

This book is not an impartial one; no book of this kind is or can be. But European science fiction readers have too many times seen books purporting to tell the true history of science fiction, ending up telling nothing but the true history of English-language science fiction. This, if you will, is the inevitable backlash. There is a world outside Britain and the USA; it cannot be ignored any longer. As a European, I am tired of seeing references to 'World Science Fiction Conventions' that never were and never will be anything but local American ones. I am tired of reading about the magazine *Amazing Stories* as 'the first science fiction magazine in the world' and its founder as 'the father of science fiction', when I know this is simply not true. I am tired of seeing, year after year, the 'Award for the best science fiction novel in the world' being restricted to novels published in the United States, when I know that the majority of new science fiction books are published not there but in Europe. I am tired of checking lists of books in science fiction series in the Argentine, or Japan, or Germany, and finding the same tired old American authors popping up again and again. I am tired of seeing self-proclaimed American and British scholars of science fiction revealing their complete ignorance about everything outside their own countries, confidently acting as if there did not exist a world outside their own. I am tired of Europeans, Asians and Latin Americans actually believing this. I am sick and tired of seeing European countries importing science fiction junk, when our own junk is bad enough.

I know that many of the best science fiction authors are British and American. But they are not the only good ones, however unlikely that might seem to readers reared on a fare consisting of science fiction in magazine form. The magazines are only one part of the genre, the adolescent stage, if you will, and that one is now over. With the magazines now playing a less important part in science

Above: The Swedish SF magazine 'Häpna!', in its heyday
Right: What much of this book has been about

fiction, I am confident that we will see a more mature literature emerge, one that combines the best of American, British, European, Australasian, Asian and Latin American into a new and exciting whole. British and American science fiction magazines have done the genre much good; without them I am not sure we would have much science fiction anywhere today. Still, I am happy to see them go.

I was one of those science fiction fans brought up on pulp magazines. I still love that particular smell of old, cheap paper slowly disintegrating into dust. I love the lurid Paul, Bergey, Schomburg and Wesso covers, depicting every stupid hack situation you ever could think of. I have yards of these magazines lining the walls of my study, and the all-pervading smell (my wife says stench) of these goodies makes me greet each new working day with renewed enthusiasm. They were a part of my youth, my formative years, the things that fired my imagination once and prepared me for more subtle science fiction. But this is all emotion. I know they are mostly bad, that the writings are crude and the famous artists of the 'golden' era less than acceptable by any standards other than those dictated by nostalgia. Let's face it: they were no good. They did much bad for science fiction, and much good, but their time is over. Science fiction remains, warts and all, and our place is not in the 1930s, 1940s or 1950s, but here and now. Science fiction is changing, as it should do, and the heroes of yesterday are the villains of today. Science fiction magazines brought us part of the way, and they did their job well. Now is the time for other ways.

TALES OF WONDER

Nº 3

1/-

THE HORROR
IN THE
TELESCOPE
BY
EDMOND HAMILTON

BIBLIOGRAPHY

Some recent works about science fiction

ALDISS, BRIAN W., *Billion Year Spree*. London: Weidenfeld & Nicolson 1973

BRITIKOV, A. F., *Russkiy sovietskiy nauchno-fantastityeskiy roman*. Leningrad 1970

CARNEIRO, ANDRE, *Introducão ao estudo da science fiction*. Sao Paolo: Comissão de Literatura 1968

CLARESON, THOMAS, *The Emergence of American Science Fiction: 1880–1915*. Ann Arbor: University Microfilms 1956

GALLAGHER, LIGEIA, *More's Utopia and its Critics*. Chicago: Scott, Foresman and Company, 1964.

GUNN, JAMES, *Alternate Worlds*. Englewood Cliffs: Prentice-Hall 1976

HAINING, PETER, *The Penny Dreadful*. London: Gollancz 1975

KACZMARKA, JERZEGO, & KLEDZIKA, BRONISLAWA (Editors), *Materialy z miedzynarodowego spotkania pisarzy-tworcow literatury fantastyczno-naukowej*. Poznan: Wydawmictwo Poznanskie 1974

KYLE, DAVID, *A Pictorial History of Science Fiction*. London: Hamlyn 1976

LEM, STANISLAW, *Fantastyka i futurologia*. Kraków: Wydawnictwo Literackie, 1973

LYAPUNOV, BORIS, *V mire fantastiki*. Moscow: Istadelzhstvo Kniga 1975.

LUNDWALL, SAM J., *Science Fiction: What It's All About*. N.Y.: Ace Books, 1971

NAGL, MANFRED, *Science Fiction in Deutschland*. Tübingen: 1972

NORDHOFF, CHARLES: *The Communistic Societies of the United States*. N.Y.: Schocken 1971

PARNOV, YEREMEY, *Fantastika v vek NTR*. Moscow 1974

QVARNSTROM, GUNNAR, *Dikten och den nya vetenskapen*. Lund: Gleerup 1961

ROTTENSTEINER, FRANZ, *The Science Fiction Book*. London: Thames and Hudson 1975

SADOUL, JACQUES, *Hier, l'an 2000*. Paris: Denoel 1973

SADOUL, JACQUES, *Histoire de la science fiction moderne*. Paris: Albin Michel 1973

SANZ, JOSÉ (Editor), *FC Simpósio*. Rio de Janeiro: Instituto Nacional do Cinema 1969

SCKERL, ADOLF, *Wissenschaftlich-phantastiche Literatur*. Berlin: Kulturbund der DDR 1976

TUCK, DONALD H., *The Encyclopedia of Science Fiction and Fantasy*. Chicago: Advent 1974

VERSINS, PIERRE, *Encyclopédie de l'utopie et de la science fiction*. Lausanne: L'age d'homme 1972

WOLLHEIM, DONALD A., *The Universe Makers. Science Fiction Today*. N.Y.: Harper & Row 1971

INDEX

206